RADICAL
TRADITIONS

THEOLOGY IN A POSTCRITICAL KEY

SERIES EDITORS

Stanley M. Hauerwas, Duke University,
and Peter Ochs, University of Virginia

RADICAL TRADITIONS cuts new lines of inquiry across a confused array of debates concerning the place of theology in modernity and, more generally, the status and role of scriptural faith in contemporary life. Charged with a rejuvenated confidence, spawned in part by the rediscovery of reason as inescapably tradition constituted, a new generation of theologians and religious scholars is returning to scriptural traditions with the hope of retrieving resources long ignored, depreciated, and in many cases ideologically suppressed by modern habits of thought. RADICAL TRADITIONS assembles a promising matrix of strategies, disciplines, and lines of thought that invites Jewish, Christian, and Islamic theologians back to the word, recovering and articulating modes of scriptural reasoning as that which always underlies modernist reasoning and therefore has the capacity — and authority — to correct it.

Far from despairing over modernity's failings, postcritical theologies rediscover resources for renewal and self-correction within the disciplines of academic study themselves. Postcritical theologies open up the possibility of participating once again in the living relationship that binds together God, text, and community of interpretation. RADICAL TRADITIONS thus advocates a "return to the text," which means a commitment to displaying the richness and wisdom of traditions that are at once text based, hermeneutical, and oriented to communal practice.

Books in this series offer the opportunity to speak openly with practitioners of other faiths or even with those who profess no (or limited) faith, both academics and nonacademics, about the ways religious traditions address pivotal issues of the day. Unfettered by foundationalist preoccupations, these books represent a call for new paradigms of reason — a thinking and rationality that are more responsive than originative. By embracing a postcritical posture, they are able to speak unapologetically out of scriptural traditions manifest in the practices of believing communities (Jewish, Christian, and others); articulate those practices through disciplines of philosophic, textual, and cultural criticism; and engage intellectual, social, and political practices that for too long have been insulated from theological evaluation. RADICAL TRADITIONS is radical not only in its confidence in non-apologetic theological speech but also in how the practice of such speech challenges the current social and political arrangements of modernity.

RADICAL TRADITIONS

Talking with Christians

MUSINGS OF A JEWISH THEOLOGIAN

David Novak

WILLIAM B. EERDMANS PUBLISHING COMPANY
GRAND RAPIDS, MICHIGAN / CAMBRIDGE, U.K.

© 2005 Wm. B. Eerdmans Publishing Co.

Wm. B. Eerdmans Publishing Co.
255 Jefferson Ave. S.E., Grand Rapids, Michigan 49503 /
P.O. Box 163, Cambridge CB3 9PU U.K.

Printed in the United States of America

10 09 08 07 06 05   7 6 5 4 3 2 1

ISBN 0-8028-2842-6

www.eerdmans.com

Hear the truth from whoever has uttered it.

— Maimonides,
The Eight Chapters: Introduction

Contents

Preface

This book is a collection of essays of mine written over the past twenty-five years or so. Almost all of these essays have been previously published. Some minor changes in the text have been made from time to time for the sake of greater clarity in this new book, but the arguments have remained the same. All of these essays deal in one way or another with Christianity, and all of them are written from a Jewish perspective.

The title and subtitle of the book tell the reader about the overall context of all of these essays, and about the fundamental concern of the author that runs through all of them.

Although almost all of the essays are based on lectures given *to* largely Christian audiences, they actually began in conversations *with* serious Christians, especially *with* some important Christian theologians. During the years the ideas discussed in these essays were being thought and then written, I have been privileged to have been in personal touch with a variety of Christian theologians such as Markus Barth (my teacher of New Testament at the University of Chicago), Germain Grisez (my *Doktorvater* at Georgetown University), Louis Dupré (my teacher of philosophy at Georgetown before his departure for Yale), George Lindbeck, Robert Jenson, Stanley Hauerwas, Eugene F. Rogers Jr., Kendall Soulen, Avery Cardinal Dulles, S.J., Francis Cardinal George, O.M.I., Edward Oakes, S.J., John Pawlikowski, O.S.M., Kathleen Coveny, Robert Tuttle, John Witte, Bruce Marshall, and others. Special mention is due Father Richard John Neuhaus (with whom I have been so involved in the work of the Institute on Religion and Public Life for more than fifteen years) and Robert Louis Wilken (my unforgettable colleague for seven and a half years at the University of Virginia). As for the great Christian theologians from whose works I have learned so much, the reader will note the influence of Augustine, Anselm, Thomas Aquinas, John Calvin, Karl Barth (whom I once met, quite briefly), and Paul Tillich (whose lectures at the University of Chicago I would often attend in the late 1950s). To all of the above I dedicate this book in the interest of continuing the dialogue between Jews and Christians — whether direct or indirect — that is of such great theological significance for both communities. I am grateful for having been able to participate in that dialogue all these years.

But why have I been so interested in talking *with* Christians, even though as a Jewish theologian my first theological interlocutors are always my fellow Jews? Some of these reasons have already been presented in my previous book dealing with Christianity, *Jewish-Christian Dialogue: A Jewish Justification,* published by Oxford University Press in 1989. That book intended to show how the Jewish tradition enables a Jewish thinker to treat Christianity with respect, and how that respect can be realized with full theological integrity on the part of a Jewish thinker. But this book tries to show how that respectful engagement can be conducted on some more specific theological points. Nevertheless, these points of true commonality must be carefully selected. That is why there are no discussions here of the Incarnation, the Trinity, or Christian ecclesiology. Such topics are not the business of a Jewish theologian to discuss critically. He or she need only recognize their importance for his or her Christian interlocutors and silently respect that importance, at least in public.

The subtitle of this book, *Musings of a Jewish Theologian,* indicates that I am engaged in the enterprise of Jewish theology, whose concern is the theoretical meaning of the practice of Judaism. That engagement can be cogently conducted only by someone committed to and involved in keeping the commandments *(mitsvot)* of the Torah, in what has come to be called "Judaism." My conversations with Christians that are the leitmotif of this book are an important part of my own theological project. Why? There are several reasons.

One, for Jews like myself who live in a multicultural society like that in North America, Christians of late have become the persons most likely to understand us Jews when we need to make our communal claims of recognition on that larger society. That this has been my experience and the experience of some other Jewish scholars still strikes many of our fellow Jews as odd, no doubt due to the fact that until recently most Jews experienced at best indifference and at worst hostility from Christians, especially when it came to matters of theology. There are historical reasons for this change in Christian attitudes, but there is a theological reason that some Christians and some Jews have rediscovered of late. That is, Christianity speaks a language that is largely Jewish, a language most of whose vocabulary and grammar come from the same sources that living Judaism draws upon — namely, the Hebrew Bible and the Judaism of the late Second Temple period.

Nevertheless, despite this strictly theological commonality, my theological engagement of Christianity has consciously employed a philosophical idiom more often than not. Since a philosophical idiom has also been employed by Christian theologians, especially when speaking of non-Christians, philosophical speech has great dialogical potential. Living in the same secular world in remarkably similiar ways, it is inevitable that philosophy, being the most intelligent use of the language of that world, will provide a medium for wordly Jews and Christians to converse with each other. Philosophy provides a way of speaking with each other as equals on neutral ground, unlike our more strictly theological languages where one side inevitably makes the rules for the other side to follow.

As a use of language, philosophy is not univocal. It has a variety of voices. Thus the reader will note that the philosophical voice I employ most often (and it is hoped most consistently) is that of Kant. But let the reader also be aware that my use of Kant is my use of his methodology, not my acceptance of his philosophical premises, let alone my acceptance of his philosophical conclusions. My quasi-Kantianism is epistemological, not ontological, and certainly not the autonomous voice of Kantian ethics. So, the Christian theologians with whom I converse need not be Kantians (as I am not) any more than they need be Jews (as I am). Furthermore, by employing only a certain philosophical methodology, I try to avoid the type of earlier modern theology done by both Jews and Christians that consistently tried to justify their respective theological premises and conclusions by an appeal to the premises and even the conclusions of some secular philosopher or other. That frequently led to the type of polemics where Jews and Christians attempted to argue who are the better Kantians or the better Hegelians, to name the two most prominent early modern options. By a more critical use of philosophy, even when we have our inevitable preferences, both Jewish and Christian theologians are better able to speak to each other *in* the secular world precisely because we now know better that we are not *of* that world. All this better enables us to speak *to* each other *with* each other rather than *against* each other — either as we spoke against each other theologically during the Middle Ages, or as we spoke against each other philosophically during much of modernity *to* someone else who functioned as a non-Jewish or non-Christian *tertium quid.* Our mutual task is to survive in that secular world without any hope of conquest or fear of surrender. I am convinced — theologically, historically, and philosophically — that we cannot do that alone, at least intellectually.

In conclusion, I thank Stanley Hauerwas and Peter Ochs for including this book in their Radical Traditions series at Eerdmans, and to all those at Eerdmans who shepherded this book through the whole production process. Last, and by no means least, I thank my University of Toronto doctoral student and research assistant, Matthew LaGrone, for his exceptional skill in copyediting and preparing the indices to this book.

Toronto, Ontario
Marcheshvan 5765
November 2004

What to Seek and What to Avoid
in Jewish-Christian Dialogue

Then shall all those who fear the Lord speak, each to his neighbor, and the Lord shall listen and hear. It shall be written in a book of remembrance before Him, for those who fear the Lord and contemplate His name.

MALACHI 3:16

In this text, the prophet speaks of a time when the worshipers of God will communicate in a new way. From an earlier verse, it is clear that the worship of God, which is the basis of this new conversation, is not confined to the Jews: "For from the rising to the setting of the sun My name is great among the nations" (Mal. 1:11). Since Jews and Christians have the most to say to each other about God and his ways with humankind, perhaps the prophet is pointing toward the new conversation that is now taking place between serious Jews and serious Christians.

The new conversation between Jews and Christians may avoid the anger and suspicion that have characterized most of our past conversations. Due to this new sense of trust between us, deeper understanding each of the other is slowly emerging. Now it is important to reflect on why this new conversation has been so hopeful and why it has led to such new understanding, not only a new Christian understanding of Jews and Judaism

This essay previously appeared in *Christianity in Jewish Terms,* ed. Tikva Frymer-Kensky, Peter Ochs, David Novak, Michael Signer, and David Sandmel (Boulder, Colo.: Westview Press, 2000), pp. 1-6.

and a new Jewish understanding of Christians and Christianity, but perhaps even a new Christian understanding of Christianity and a new Jewish understanding of Judaism. As such, this new conversation, called by many "the dialogue," has already had profound ramifications both externally and internally.

We are now at a stage in the dialogue where we have enough experience of what has already happened between us to reflect on the conditions that have made it possible. These are methodological issues, but they have practical import since our successful continuation of the dialogue, even its improvement, requires that we know how it has been sustained as something much more than a historical accident.

What to Seek

Underlying the dialogue are two positive preconditions. First, each side must be willing to see the other side in the best possible light from within its own tradition. Second, that vision must not lead to any distortion of what each tradition, itself separately, teaches as the truth.[1] True dialogue requires the adherents of each tradition to find justification for the other tradition from within his or her own tradition. One cannot use understanding of the other as any kind of escape from full commitment to the authority of Judaism for Jews or of Christianity for Christians.

What to Avoid

Participants in Jewish-Christian dialogue must be careful to avoid five negative conditions, all of which are dangerous theological stumbling blocks: disputation, proselytization, syncretism, relativism, and triumphalism. The very recognition of these dangers makes a valuable contribution to the dialogue. By carefully separating the dialogue from these five dangers, we infer the positive from the negative, which has long been a feature of rabbinic thinking.[2] From what ought not be done we can learn what ought to be done.

---

1. See David Novak, *Jewish-Christian Dialogue: A Jewish Justification* (New York: Oxford University Press, 1989), pp. 14ff.
2. See *Babylonian Talmud* (hereafter "B."): Nedarim 11a and parallels.

Avoiding Disputation

Dialogue takes the form of a disputation when the adherents of each tradition assume that everything the other tradition asserts is denied by their own tradition. This is what occurred in those public debates in the Middle Ages, when Jews and Christians faced each other as adversaries, even as enemies. In this type of hostile atmosphere, the goal is for there to be a winner and a loser. The memory of these disputations, which were always instigated by the Christian rulers who had political power over the Jews, has made many Jews wary of the new dialogue with Christians. There are still many Jews who believe that if Christianity asserts something, Judaism therefore denies it. Indeed, for some Jews, Judaism means nothing more than not being Christian.

Jews must understand that there are many commonalities between Judaism and Christianity and that to deny them is as much a distortion of Judaism as it is a distortion of Christianity. Jews need to understand that those Christians who have entered the dialogue with Jews in good faith do not seek the defeat of Judaism. Jews entering the dialogue must also not seek the defeat of Christianity, even in situations where we now might have political or emotional power over Christians.

Avoiding Proselytization

The dialogue takes the form of proselytization when the adherents of one tradition seek to persuade the adherents of the other tradition that they truly have what the others have been seeking all along. Proselytization is rooted in the hope that the others will become converted to one's own faith by their contact with members of one's own tradition. Proselytization has been a greater danger for Jews than for Christians because Christianity can claim that it includes all of Judaism and then carries it beyond the level now maintained by the Jewish people. Judaism cannot make a similar claim any more than parents can claim to have succeeded their children. Even if Christians generally hope that all humankind will come to the Church, they should not use dialogue with Jews as a specific occasion for realizing that hope. The dialogue must respectfully recognize that the differences between Jews and Christians here and now are of greater importance than the commonalities that the dialogue acknowledges and develops. The dialogue must be justified as an end in and of itself and not used as a means for some other agenda.[3]

Avoiding Syncretism

Syncretism is the attempt to construct a new religious reality out of elements of Judaism and Christianity. But no religious tradition, least of all Judaism or Christianity, could accept the replacement of its ultimate claims by a new religion.[4] Indeed, both Judaism and Christianity would have to see the construction of such a new religious reality as a form of idolatry. In Judaism and Christianity, it is God who reveals to the covenanted community *how* God is to be worshiped and not just *that* God is to be worshiped. In fact, according to some Jewish and Christian teaching, that no other god is to be worshiped is something humans can know even before any specific revelation.[5] Idolatry is the worship of "a strange god" *(el zar)*.[6] The wrong worship of the right God is called "strange service" *(avodah zarah)*, which means the worship of God by humanly constructed rather than by divinely revealed means.[7] Judaism and Christianity are grounded in revelation. Syncretism denies the ultimate character of either Jewish revelation or Christian revelation by substituting something else for both of them. It can thus turn an authentic religious dialogue into an ideological monologue. The integrity of this dialogue cannot stand syncretism in any form.

3. A good model for this is the concept of "mediation" *(pesharah)* in Jewish civil law. *Pesharah* is advocated (see B. Sanhedrin 6b-7a) when the full exercise of an individual claim in a property dispute would result in one side becoming the winner and the other the loser, thus resulting in a further rupture of the peace of the community in which both parties participate. To avoid this result, each party is to be persuaded (but not forced) to bracket his or her full claim with all its dissonance in favor of a partial claim in order to not further impede what the two parties have and should have in common.

4. See David Novak, *The Election of Israel: The Idea of the Chosen People* (Cambridge: Cambridge University Press, 1995), pp. 40ff.

5. See Maimonides, *Guide of the Perplexed*, 2.33, on Exod. 20:3; also, Rom. 1:18-23.

6. Ps. 81:10.

7. See Lev. 10:1; R. Judah Halevi, *Kuzari*, 1.97; also, M. Halbertal and A. Margalit, *Idolatry*, trans. N. Goldblum (Cambridge, Mass.: Harvard University Press, 1992), pp. 186ff.

Avoiding Relativism

In the atmosphere of modern secularism, which we can also call "relativism," in which most Jews and Christians now live, religion is taken to be a matter of private preference at best. Relativism is especially dangerous to the dialogue because it denies that some things are true all the time everywhere for everyone. But Judaism and Christianity make such claims. Indeed, these claims, like "God elects Israel" or "God is incarnate in Jesus," are what Judaism and Christianity are all about. In fact, Judaism requires Jews to die as martyrs rather than exchange Judaism for anything else, even something as similar to Judaism as Christianity.[8] Christianity makes a similar claim on Christians. Martyrs are willing to die for what they believe to be the highest truth one could possibly know in this world, because without a commitment to the existence of truth, one cannot affirm the truth of God. Martyrdom is therefore the ultimate expression of belief and represents the personal affirmation of public, universal, and perpetual truth. But with relativism, which sees all beliefs as simply private preferences, the martyr is the biggest fool.

The willingness of Christians to accept Jewish converts and the willingness of Jews to accept Christian converts shows that both religions reject relativism. Even though Jewish-Christian dialogue must not be an occasion for the conversion of either side, Jews and Christians recognize that conversion is always a possibility within the larger covenantal realities in which Jews and Christians participate. Jews know very well that Christianity is open to converts. But Christians must understand that even though Jews have not engaged in the type of active proselytizing that many Christians have engaged in, we have always accepted converts.[9] Indeed, most of those converts have been former Christians. Religious conversion is an impossibility for a relativist, since for the relativist there is no essential, intelligible difference between one religion and another.

There are good political and moral reasons why Jews have not engaged in proselytization. Politically, proselytization has frequently been dangerous for Jews. In the past, Christian societies even outlawed it, and it also involves the danger that too many persons of questionable commitment to the full authority of Jewish law might dilute the religious integrity of

8. See R. Abraham Gumbiner, *Magen Avraham* on *Shulhan Arukh*: Orah Hayyim, 128.37 based on B. Sanhedrin 74a on Lev. 22:32.

9. See Novak, *The Election of Israel,* pp. 177ff.

the Jewish community.[10] Morally, since Jews have been the objects of so much proselytization on the part of Christians, something we have deeply resented, most of us have been loath to do the same thing to others, especially since proselytization inevitably involves the denigration of the religion of the person being proselytized. Yet, despite these serious reservations, Jewish tradition has never actually ruled proselytization out.[11]

The reason that proselytization and conversion remain issues for both Jews and Christians is that truth is not relative, and thus the ultimate truth claims of Judaism and Christianity are not only different but mutually exclusive. The highest form of worship of the Lord God of Israel is *either* by the Torah and the tradition of the Jewish people *or* by Christ and the tradition of the Church. That the choice is framed in just this way is the result of the historical origins of Judaism and Christianity: both traditions originate in the history of Israel presented in the Hebrew Bible. Accordingly, our differences are over the same God who first appeared in that same history. One cannot live as a Jew and as a Christian simultaneously. One could well say that the greatest temptation for a Jew is Christianity and that the greatest temptation for a Christian is Judaism. That this is so explains why Jews and Christians have so much to talk about and, also, why the stakes in the Jewish-Christian relationship are so high.

Avoiding Triumphalism

Triumphalism is the insistence that not only the highest truth but the final truth has already been given to my community alone. Triumphalism poisons the dialogue before it begins. Jews are triumphalists when we assume that Christianity is nothing more than a deviant form of Judaism; Christians are triumphalists when they assume that Judaism is but a precursor to Christianity. Triumphalists believe that there is no commonality to discover between the two religions, and that therefore there is nothing to learn from dialogue. This claim, however, is historically false. It is also dangerous, as it prevents us from building areas of peace between us.

Jewish and Christian anticipations of the end of days contradict the triumphalists' assumption that our differences are final. For Jews, there

10. See B. Kiddushin 70b, and Rashi, s.v. *kashin gerim.*

11. See, e.g., *Pesiqta Rabbati*, chap. 35 on Zech. 2:15, ed. Friedmann, p. 161a, and chap. 40 on Lev. 23:24, p. 167b; *Tanhuma:* Tsav on Lev. 8:1, ed. Buber, p. 9b; Maimonides, *Teshuvot ha-Rambam*, 1, no. 149, ed. Y. Y. Blau (Jerusalem: Meqitsei Nirdamim, 1960), pp. 284ff. Cf. B. Yevamot 109a and *Tosafot*, s.v. "ra'ah."

is a time called "the Days of the Messiah"; for Christians it is called "the Second Coming."[12] In anticipation of this time, when human history will come to an end and the kingdom of God will be established on earth, Jews and Christians look forward to an everlasting divine redemption of Israel, of all humankind, indeed of the whole universe.[13] The end of days will be a time when, unlike the present, "the kingdom will be the Lord's" (Obad. 1:21). What, however, of those Jews who assert that it is precisely at the end of days that the triumph of Judaism will be manifest, and what of those Christians who assert that at the Second Coming Christianity will triumph? We must answer that the final judgment of all human history is not yet in. "No eye has seen but yours, O God, what will be done for those who wait for you" (Isa. 64:3).[14] The world-yet-to-come *(olam ha-ba),* this coming-future *(l'atid la-vo),* is mysterious; it lies on the other side of our present horizon. Therefore Jews and Christians cannot see their past traditions or their present efforts and differences as the last word. The different claims of Judaism and Christianity are only tentative. Surely what God will do at the end of history will be radical enough to surprise everyone — Jews, Christians, and all others who wait for that time here and now.

12. See C. H. Dodd, *The Apostolic Preaching* (New York: Harper & Bros., 1960), pp. 93ff.
13. See Isa. 66:22.
14. See B. Berakhot 34b; 1 Cor. 2:9.

From Supersessionism to Parallelism
in Jewish-Christian Dialogue

The Renunciation of Supersessionism

There is now a definite group of Christian and Jewish theologians who
have been long engaged in a general theological enterprise, sometimes
separately, sometimes together, where an important object of concern for
the Christians has been Jews/Judaism and an important object of concern
for the Jews has been Christians/Christianity. Some of us are still in the
process of continuing our respective work in formulating Christian theologies of Judaism and Jewish theologies of Christianity. More specifically, a
common conclusion that has already emerged from our long engagement
is that we all, in a variety of ways, have renounced supersessionism.[1] I
think all of us would agree that if one holds that God has exchanged the
Jewish people for the Church, thus canceling the election of Abraham and
his progeny, there is no incentive whatsoever for Jews to formulate a positive theology of Christianity. Moreover, whatever Christian theology of Judaism there could be would have to be essentially negative, namely, having
eliminated Judaism from present engagement by seeing it as *already* superseded by the Church once and for all.

Now it is obvious how Christians can be supersessionists and why the
renunciation of supersessionism requires great theological skill. But how

---

1. For the most thorough and theologically suggestive Christian treatment of this question, see R. Kendall Soulen, *The God of Israel and Christian Theology* (Minneapolis: Fortress
Press, 1996).

This essay previously appeared in *Jews and Christians: People of God*, ed. Carl E. Braaten and
Robert W. Jenson (Grand Rapids: Eerdmans, 2003), pp. 95-113.

could Jews possibly be supersessionists — unless, of course, they are suicidal? No, we Jews cannot be Jewish supersessionists with any integrity,
but many Jews can and certainly have been what I would call "counter-
supersessionists." Jewish counter-supersessionists are those who listen to
the argument of many Christians about the Church having superseded
the Jewish people as God's elect and then turn it on its head, thus seeing
Judaism as the Christian antithesis. Indeed, on a more popular level, there
are Jews who think that all they need to know and affirm of Judaism is
that it is *not* Christian, which means they need know nothing of Judaism
and next to nothing of Christianity. Moreover, the Christianity they set
themselves against is usually bad Christian theology.

When practiced by learned Jews, however, Jewish counter-supersessionism can be as plausible as Christian supersessionism. Working out
of a committed and knowledgeable background from within the Jewish
tradition, these Jewish theologians do not constitute Judaism to be the
antithesis of Christianity. Rather, they constitute Christianity to be the
antithesis of Judaism. So, whereas Christian supersessionists assert that
God has rejected the Jews and replaced them with the Church, Jewish
counter-supersessionists assert that Christians are a group of gentiles
who erroneously — even arrogantly — think they are now God's people exclusively, having been first led to this position by a group of renegade Jews
who removed themselves from Judaism. And the ultimate coup de grâce
of the Jewish counter-supersessionists is to assert that Christians do not
worship the Lord God of Israel as do the Jews but, rather, another god altogether. Thus the longest and perhaps deepest Jewish debate over Christianity, one that began when the Church became a decidedly non-Jewish
community and that has by no means ended, has been the question of
whether the Christians do or do not worship *our* God. If they do not, then
they are idolaters ipso facto.[2]

The logic of this Jewish rejection of Christianity runs parallel to the
logic of Christian supersessionism. Thus, when the trajectory of Christian
supersessionism runs its full course, it usually results in the following
conclusion: Since Jews reject God as triune, and since God is essentially
triune, therefore the Jews cannot be worshiping the same God as do the
Christians because of this rejection. Accordingly, Jews must be worshiping
another god. That means Jews are no different than pagans — even worse
since they cannot plead ignorance of the gospel. When the logic of the

---

2. See David Novak, *Jewish-Christian Dialogue: A Jewish Justification* (New York: Oxford
University Press, 1989), pp. 36-56.

Jewish rejection of Christianity runs its full course, it usually results in the following conclusion: Since Christians reject God as the One who elects — past, present, and future — the Jewish people forever, and since God cannot be conceived other than as the God of Abraham, Isaac, and Jacob, therefore Christians cannot be worshiping the same God as do the Jews because of this rejection. Accordingly, Christians must be worshiping another god. That means that Christians are no different than pagans — even worse since they began as renegade Jews.

That, then, is the logic of supersessionism, whether it be manifest in Christian rejections of Judaism or in Jewish rejections of Christianity. Clearly, the renunciation of supersessionism as either thesis or antithesis is the necessary precondition both for a more positive Christian theology of Judaism and for a more positive Jewish theology of Christianity. Since Christianity began in the Jewish people, it would seem that the Christian reaction to Judaism precedes the Jewish reaction to Christianity. Christians, being the newer community, had to have made their assertions to the Jews before Jews could have responded thereto. But once Christians renounce supersessionist claims against the Jewish people — namely, when they acknowledge that *their* God's covenant with the Jewish people is perpetual — then Jews cannot very well say anymore that Christians have denied what cannot be denied of God, namely, that God elects Israel, who is, minimally for Christians, the Jewish people.

This does not mean, of course, that the rival assertions of Judaism and Christianity will be overcome by renouncing supersessionism and its Jewish counterpart; indeed, these rival assertions must remain with us until the end, when God will overcome all human rivalries. But it does mean that the Jewish-Christian relationship and its attendant discourse need no longer be primarily adversarial. For almost all Jews, the confrontation with non-supersessionist Christianity has required us to rethink the whole way we talk theology to Christians — that is, those of us who want to talk theology to Christians. Indeed, the fact that the renunciation of supersessionism has been carried on by Christian theologians committed to the truth of Christianity, over and above Christian diplomats interested in better political relations with Jews, means that our Jewish rethinking must be carried on with correlative theological *gravitas*. Since supersessionism has been a leitmotif of Christian theology from patristic times to this day, the renunciation of supersessionism by Christian theologians has required not only great theological ingenuity but moral courage as well. And this effort of mind and will has already brought forth fruit. The most important result heretofore of the renunciation of supersessionism, both as thesis and antithesis, is that some of us Jews can now talk theology not only *to* Christians — which has usually meant *against* Christians — but *with* Christians as well. And, I might add, we Jews who have also been involved in this post-supersessionist effort have had to argue against anti-Christian strains in Jewish theology and deal with the great suspicion of Christians and Christianity on the part of many of our fellow Jews.

The Mutual Theological Need

If the renunciation of supersessionism now enables Jews and Christians to talk theology with one another, then we should understand *why* we need to talk theology with one another.

For Christians, the answer, paraphrasing Karl Barth, goes something like this: The promises God made through Jesus presuppose that God has already been keeping his promises to Israel. Indeed, for Christians, Jesus was sent to fulfill God's ultimate promise to Israel of redemption and then to extend it to the world. Nevertheless, God's initial promise to Israel is that she will not die but live, and live with duration as a covenanted people. The promises made through Jesus, which the Church accepts as normative, cannot be believed, therefore, if the Jewish people, who have a perpetual claim to be called *Israel,* are no longer present in the world.[3] The election of Israel as the Jewish people would only be terminable if one held with supersessionists as diverse as Baruch Spinoza and Friedrich Schleiermacher that the Jews elected God rather than that God elects the Jews.[4] Jewish election of God is contingent on the good behavior of the Jews; God's election of the Jews, however, means that the bad behavior of

3. For Barth's profoundly theological rejection of supersessionism, see Katherine Sonderegger, *That Jesus Christ Was Born a Jew: Karl Barth's "Doctrine of Israel"* (University Park, Pa.: Pennsylvania State University Press, 1992), pp. 131-33.

4. See David Novak, *The Election of Israel: The Idea of the Chosen People* (Cambridge: Cambridge University Press, 1995), pp. 22-49. For Schleiermacher's total dismissal of Judaism from Christian theological interest, see *On Religion,* trans. T. N. Tice (Richmond, Va.: John Knox Press, 1969), pp. 305-8. The essence of his extreme supersessionism is found in the following statement: "The truth rather is that the relations of Christianity to Judaism and Heathenism are the same, inasmuch as the transition from either of these to Christianity is a transition to another religion . . . we can no more recognize an identity between Christianity and Abrahamitic Judaism. . . . And neither can it be said that that purer original Judaism carried within itself the germ of Christianity" (*The Christian Faith,* trans. H. R. Mackintosh and J. S. Stewart [Edinburgh: T&T Clark, 1928], pp. 60-61).

the Jews can only impede the covenant, not lose it. To paraphrase a striking passage in the Talmud: God and the Jews are stuck with one another.
God is stuck with the Jews because he made an unconditional promise to
them that cannot be annulled without God becoming incredible.[5] And
the Jews are stuck with God because God is committed never to give up on
them.[6] Whenever the Jews reject God's covenant with them, God keeps offering it to us again and again.

Were the Jews no longer present in the world as a covenanted people,
then one would have to conclude that God broke his promise to them.
But, if God broke his original promise to Israel, which is precisely the hidden premise of supersessionism, then how could the Church — as the
branch grafted onto the tree — possibly believe God's ultimate promise to
her?[7] Only a Marcionite — who is the *reductio ad absurdum* of supersessionism — could posit that God's promise to the Church comes *ex nihilo* and
thus presupposes nothing before it. Only such a Gnosticism could be so
ahistorical, being a Gnosticism that ignores *Heilsgeschichte,* the history of
salvation. As the contemporary Protestant theologian Scott Bader-Saye
astutely points out, "The problem with becoming a replacement people is
that one has no assurance one will not meet the same fate as those who
went before."[8] The Achilles' heel of the philosophy of religion of Hegel,
who could be considered the greatest logician of supersessionism, is the
historical presence and energy of Islam, let alone the refusal of Judaism to
be deconstructed by Christianity or Islam.[9]

This recognition by Christians of their need for the Jews requires more
than just pointing to the fact of Jewish national survival. It requires that
Christians who have renounced supersessionism actually talk with Jews in
order to learn not only *that* the Jews have survived but also *how* the Jews
have survived, indeed how we have thrived both physically and spiritually,
which are two sides of the same coin. And at this point in history, it means
learning how we have survived and thrived in spite of the Holocaust (and
not because of it). In the present state of the world, especially, Christian
spiritual survival in some societies, and even Christian physical survival in
other societies, is just as precarious as Jewish survival has always been.

5. *Babylonian Talmud* (hereafter "B."): Berakhot 32a re Exod. 32:13.

6. B. Sanhedrin 44a re Josh. 7:11. See Novak, *The Election of Israel,* pp. 189-99.

7. See Rom. 11:17-21.

8. Bader-Saye, *Church and Israel after Christendom* (Boulder, Colo.: Westview Press, 1999),
p. 96.

9. See *Lectures on the Philosophy of Religion,* trans. R. F. Brown, P. C. Hodgson, and J. M.
Stewart (Berkeley: University of California Press, 1988), pp. 371-74.

Learning how God has not abandoned us to oblivion can greatly help you appreciate how God has not abandoned you to oblivion either. Learning what God has done for us in the past enables us to have faith in what God is yet to do for us in the future. By doing that for you, we Jews can fulfill God's assurance to Abraham that he and his progeny will "be a blessing" *(berakhah)* for the other peoples of the world (Gen. 12:3).[10] For Christians, to be able truly to learn from the Jews on this level surely requires that they formulate for themselves a Christian theology of Judaism. Having living Jews to talk with will prevent any such Christian theology of Judaism from becoming solipsistic, that is, a mere projection of what Christians would like Jews to be rather than what we truly are. As the contemporary Protestant theologian Clark Williamson puts it, "Jews, too, might serve the church critically by reminding it of what it is all too prone to forget, that it is called and claimed by the God of Israel."[11]

But why do we Jews need to talk theology with you Christians? Let us answer this question by inferring from the negative to the positive. Some Jews think that Jews do not need to talk theology with ourselves let alone with anyone else because Judaism has no theology. The most extreme advocates of this position are those Jewish secularists who think that Judaism has no *theo-logy,* no "God-talk," because Judaism has no God. I will leave it to these secularists to demonstrate how their position can be called "Judaism" with any true coherence. But there are religious Jews who think Judaism has no theology but only a law. Of course, once one asks them the source of this law's authority, and they answer "it is the law of God," their very justification of what they accept as normative can be made only in theological terms.[12] Nevertheless, most of these religious Jews do not see any need at all to talk theology with non-Jews, especially Christians. What does a Jewish theologian like myself and a few others say to the people we worship with about our theological involvement with you Christians? What is our Jewish justification for the enterprise to which every speaker at this conference testifies by his life and work?

To eschew theological conversation with Christians, especially with those Christians who accept our most basic self-assertion of our chosenness, is to assume that we have nothing to say to the world outside our-

10. See *Beresheet Rabbah* 39.2.

11. Williamson, *A Guest in the House of Israel* (Louisville: Westminster/John Knox Press, 1993), p. 250.

12. My late revered teacher, Abraham Joshua Heschel (d. 1972), called such Jewish myopia "pan-halachism" or "religious behaviorism." See his *God in Search of Man* (New York: Farrar, Straus & Cudahy, 1955), pp. 320-35.

selves. Many religious Jews have accepted the argument made by the late Rabbi Joseph B. Soloveitchik, who was a Jewish theologian par excellence, that theological discourse is totally self-referential, and that each religious tradition is like a Leibnizian monad, that is, each exists alongside the other, but there are no cognitive bridges between them.[13] In other words, when it comes to theological discourse, however defined, Jews can talk only to other Jews — and, it must be added, only to those other Jews who still believe that God elected Israel and revealed the Torah to her forever. But this assumes that Jews can make intelligible theological claims only on each other. The fact is, though, that even the most religious Jews make — indeed, have to make — theological claims on the outside world. What are those theological claims? I would say that there are two such basic claims, one minimal and one maximal.

The minimal claim Jews have to make on the world is to allow us room to live our life as God's covenanted people. Now who in the world can understand this claim of ours, let alone justifiably respect it? And by "the world" I do not mean lone individuals in the world, which is surely an abstraction invented by modern liberalism, but rather communal persons, who we all are by nature. Therefore, the question is: Which members of which communities/traditions can understand, let alone respect, the minimal Jewish claim on the world for our communal survival, which is in essence a theological claim? Like Blanche DuBois in *A Streetcar Named Desire*, none of us could survive without "always depend[ing] on the kindness of strangers."

The maximal claim Jews have to make on the world is to be "a light to the nations" (Isa. 42:6; 49:6), which means that the Jews are to be attractive to the gentiles because of our public teaching of the Torah and our observance of its commandments. And even though, for a variety of reasons, both political and moral, Jews have not engaged in active proselytizing for centuries, we have never ceased to accept converts from the gentiles.[14] In other words, we have cautiously welcomed those non-Jews who believe themselves elected as we have been elected by God. Indeed, one of the improvements of our living in liberal-democratic states, as opposed to either Christendom or Islam, is that we can now accept converts to Judaism without any political reprisals by the majority religions. However, it is the minimal claim rather than the maximal one that immediately figures in the current level of theological discourse between Jews and Christians in

13. See Novak, *Jewish-Christian Dialogue*, pp. 3-9.
14. See Novak, *The Election of Israel*, pp. 177-88.

our society. Later, though, I shall briefly return to the question of Jewish proselytism.

Getting back to the minimal claim Jews make upon the outside world, it would seem that modern Jews have lived alongside those whose communal identity is either (1) fascist, or (2) communist, or (3) Islamic, or (4) liberal-democratic, or (5) Christian. Which community understands our claim for communal survival best, and which community can respect it most consistently?

We can certainly eliminate fascist communities from Jewish consideration since they have inevitably violated our basic human right to exist as persons, let alone to exist as a community. Communist societies have barely let us exist as persons, but certainly have done everything humanly possible to destroy our traditional/communal existence. As for Islamic communities, there was a time, not so long ago in fact, that Jewish communal claims were well understood by Muslims and fairly well respected by them. Because of that, there was a long history of successful Jewish communities in Islamic societies. Nevertheless, because of contemporary Jewish claims to national sovereignty in the land of Israel, which is seen as being within Islamic territory *(daar al-Islam),* almost all of contemporary Islamic territory is a place from which most Jews have chosen to flee. That is because of the inherently Islamic inability of most contemporary Muslims to understand, much less recognize, our claims to national sovereignty.

The vast majority of Jews today have seen our best chances for communal survival to be in liberal-democratic societies, in which our communal survival is tolerated as an essentially private matter. As for Christian societies, of which there are virtually no nation-states anymore, most Jews have bitter memories of our marginalization and vulnerability, both communal and individual, in the *ancien régime,* formerly known as "Christendom." Nevertheless, I would argue that Jewish communal existence, which is inherently and coherently covenantal, is also highly vulnerable in a liberal-democratic state that is not dependent on a larger religious culture. And in the West, that larger religious culture could only be predominantly Christian. In other words, Jewish communal existence functions best in a liberal-democratic state nurtured by a religious culture — and that is even true for Jewish communal existence in the State of Israel.

Moreover, since many Christians now recognize their inability to unilaterally constitute a culture that can nurture a liberal-democratic state without being subordinated to it, many Christians now realize that their cultural survival requires a new rapprochement with the Jews. Hence, the term "Judeo-Christian morality" — even "Judeo-Christian culture" — is not at all disingenuous. In political terms alone, this means that Jews, who are about 2 percent of the population of North America, now become 50 percent of the influence of the culture that surrounds the civil society and its states. But Jews cannot be an effective partner in that cultural enterprise unless we engage Christians theologically. That means we need a Jewish theology of Christianity, which is both true and politically beneficial, just as we need to encourage Christians themselves to develop a Christian theology of Judaism for the very same reasons. And that enterprise cannot be sustained, much less accomplished, unless we are in regular and deeply challenging theological conversation with one another.

Let me cite a concrete example of how Jews need to make a theological case to Christians for a matter of communal/covenantal survival in a liberal-democratic society, and why we need to do so before we can make an effective case in secular space. In Canada, where I now live, there is a public movement to outlaw the circumcision of infant boys. It is being promoted by some extreme civil libertarians and some gay men. I suspect some of the motivation for this novel prohibition is anti-Semitic since Jews would be its most conspicuous targets. Nevertheless, I can only guess at the anti-Semitism here and must, therefore, address myself to the public reasons given by the proponents of this radical legal innovation. They argue that circumcision is a form of mutilation, which can never be fully remedied. Even on medical grounds, they argue that the value of the procedure is too questionable to allow it to be performed on an unwilling infant. For this reason, it should be performed only on consenting adults. In fact, there are some men in Canada, who were circumcised as infants, who are already suing those who circumcised them for civil damages. Were the circumcision of infant boys to be proscribed by law, then those who circumcise or authorize others to circumcise their infant male children would be subject to criminal penalties as well. Of course, at present, this movement is little more than a journalistic curiosity. Nevertheless, considering the fact that numerous other religiously based social institutions — like marriage, for instance — are being radically redefined before our very eyes, today's journalistic curiosity becomes tomorrow's political and legal fact.

If this were to happen — God forbid — then no self-respecting Jew could remain in Canada with integrity, unless he or she wanted to have outlaw status. We Jews cannot survive as a covenanted community anywhere we are not allowed to circumcise our infant boys, in order "to bring them into the covenant of Abraham our father" *(le-hakhniso be-vrito shel*

Avraham avinu), as the prayer recited by a Jewish father at the circumcision *(berit milah)* of his infant son states it.[15] It is an irrevocable commandment of the God who elected us and gave us the Torah forever. Since Canada is not the only place Jews can live today, leaving Canada to live somewhere else for this reason would be a real political option. It would seem morally preferable for a practicing Jew to opt for a society where he or she can be a law-abiding citizen over a society where his or her Judaism can be practiced only as a criminal act. Thus, when King Ferdinand and Queen Isabella outlawed the practice of Judaism in Spain in 1492, those Jews who quickly left Spain were far more morally admirable than those Jews *(Marranos)* who wanted it both ways by remaining in Spain and practicing Judaism in undetectable privacy.[16] Those who left as Jews survived as a Jewish community — former Spanish Jews became *Sephardim* — but those who remained in Spain could not maintain the communal presence that individual Jews require for them and their children to survive as Jews.

For Jews to attempt to make our initial case to liberal democrats (and by that I mean a much bigger group than the members of a particular American political party) for our communal right to circumcise our infant sons is a mistake. It is a mistake because the adherents of a liberal-democratic political ideology have no way of dealing with communal rights because they have no way of dealing with familial rights. A community, certainly for Jews, is the extension of a group of families into a clan. Every infant Jewish boy has the right to be circumcised on the eighth day of his life (barring medical complications), and therefore his father has the duty to circumcise him or authorize someone more skillful than himself to circumcise him. In the absence of a father to fulfill that duty, the community is obliged to do so *in loco parentis*.[17]

Since the Jewish communal/covenantal claim on the larger public for the exercise of the duty of circumcision is now being publicly challenged, to whom should the Jews first look for support? Muslims are an obvious choice since they too practice infant circumcision. Indeed, a Jewish-Muslim alliance on this issue might even contribute to a better atmosphere for lessening the political tensions between Jews and Muslims over the current situation in the land of Israel. Nevertheless, there are two problems with this suggestion. First, there is the political problem. As it

---

15. B. Shabbat 137b.

16. See Cecil Roth, *A History of the Marranos* (Philadelphia: Jewish Publication Society of America, 1941).

17. B. Kiddushin 29a.

stands now, there is such hostility between Jews and Muslims over the current situation in the land of Israel that any alliance seen to be of lesser political import is quite unlikely. Second, there is the theological problem. The problem is that Jews and Muslims circumcise infant boys for very different reasons. For Jews, circumcision is a direct command of God (*mitsvah d'oraita*).[18] For Muslims, on the other hand, circumcision is only a matter of custom *(hadith).*[19] Muslims can have a communal life even without circumcision. Thus in Indonesia, which has a very large Muslim population, the vast majority of Muslim men are uncircumcised, I am told. But such a situation would be unthinkable in Judaism. (Even the early Reform Jews in the middle of the nineteenth century, with their radical rejection of large parts of the Jewish religious tradition, quickly restored the obligation of circumcision after a very short period in which some of them criticized its necessity.)[20] Moreover, this has a lot to do with the fact that Judaism is a covenantal religion, whereas Islam is a voluntary religion. Islam has no theological notion of election. In Judaism, circumcision is "the sign of the covenant" *(ot ha-berit).*[21]

Ironically, though, Christians, whose religion has consciously changed circumcision from a religiously mandated act to at best a medical option, can fully understand its covenantal significance for Jews. Indeed, Jesus himself had to have been circumcised on the eighth day of his life in order to be able to say that he "fulfilled" (Matt. 5:17) the Law.[22] Perhaps Christians who are supersessionists would be unlikely to support the right of Jews to circumcise their sons since Jews ought not to be keeping their eschatologically obsolete Torah and its tradition. If the covenant between God and the Jewish people is over, in the eyes of these Christians, then there can be little interest in, perhaps even hostility to, the circumcisional claim of the Jews. But those Christians who have truly overcome the errors of supersessionism, on the other hand, can certainly understand, respect, even actively support the right of the Jews to remain faithful to

18. Lev. 12:3. Circumcision is even to be performed on the Sabbath if this is when the eighth day of the infant boy's life occurs (B. Shabbat 132a). See L. A. Hoffman, *Covenant of Blood* (London and Chicago: University of Chicago Press, 1996).

19. See J. Morgenstern, *Rites of Birth, Marriage, and Kindred Occasions among the Semites* (New York: KTAV, 1973), pp. 48-66.

20. See M. A. Meyer, "*Berit Mila* within the History of the Reform Movement," in *Berit Mila in the Reform Context,* ed. L. M. Barth (Cincinnati and New York: Berit Mila Board of Reform Judaism, 1990), pp. 141-51.

21. See B. Nedarim 31b-32a.

22. See Luke 2:21.

God's irrevocable covenant with us. That is the case because Christians have the only communal tradition in the world which, like that of the Jews, requires them to understand themselves covenantally.

But, in order for Jews to be able to make this argument to Christians in a cogently convincing way, there must be both a Christian theology of Judaism and a Jewish theology of Christianity in place. Jews need to recognize that a Christian theology of Judaism can cogently recognize the continuing validity of the Torah and its commandments for the Jews. And, if this Christian theology of Judaism is theologically foundational and not just an apologetics, then Jews need to know quite a lot about Christian theology to recognize such authentic Christian theology when we see it. Moreover, for the very same reason, if this Jewish theology of Christianity is theologically profound and not just good public relations, then Christians need to know quite a lot about Jewish theology. This need becomes especially acute when it is recognized from within that there is a need to call upon the other community, our nearest communal neighbor, for help during the precariousness of this yet-to-be-redeemed world. Members of the covenantal religions of Judaism and Christianity should be sensitive to the dialectic of theology and politics that constantly takes place within a covenant. That is, the transcendent thrust of politics — the way we order our human lives together — becomes most evident when we have to raise a theological issue in public. And the communal focus of theology becomes most evident when we have to raise a political issue for theology. One might well say: politics without theology is blind; theology without politics is dumb.

Thus, if there is to be a Christian theology of Judaism that learns of Judaism from Jews who are very much present and active, then it must be able to see why Jewish adherence to the commandments is not law in place of grace but, rather, a faithful Jewish response to God's most gracious commandments. As our teacher and colleague, George Lindbeck, writes,

> What is the nature and function of Torah? It is in the New Testament custodial in Israel and fulfilled in Christ, but what does this imply for later Christianity and its relations to Judaism? Is not Torah by analogical extension both custodial and fulfilled for Christian communities in this age before the end when fulfillment is not yet final; and does this not make Christians much closer to Jews than they have generally thought?[23]

23. Lindbeck, *The Nature of Doctrine* (Philadelphia: Westminster, 1984), p. 123.

Antecedents, Consequents, Parallels

So far we have seen how the consistent and persistent renunciation of supersessionism by Christians and counter-supersessionism by Jews enables both Christians and Jews to discover deeper truths of Christianity and Judaism respectively. And that effort could not have been possible, let alone effective, if Christians had been thinking only of Judaism without real Jews, and Jews had been thinking about Christianity without real Christians. We have also seen how this is good for the political survival of both Jews and Christians in the contemporary world, and that it is beneficial because it is theologically truthful and not in spite of theologically accessible truth. Nevertheless, after all this is acknowledged and thought out, both Christians and Jews can fall into an easy error which, if left uncorrected, will lead both of us right back to the supersessionist dilemma. That error seems, at first, to be a new source of mutual respect, for it is found in the assertion of Christians to Jews, "We came out of Judaism," and the counter-assertion of Jews to Christians: "You came out of Judaism." These correlative assertions seem to be quite hopeful when first made; indeed, they seem to flatter both Jews and Christians. Yet they turn out to be erroneous on both historical and theological grounds.

Historically, these assertions are erroneous because the Judaism we know today, namely, Rabbinic Judaism — the Judaism of the Talmud and its ongoing tradition of interpretive application and expansion — is in many significant ways not identical with the Judaism out of which Christianity emerged. Instead, Christianity emerged out of the Old Testament as it was read in the last days of the Second Temple, especially by the Pharisees. This is the Judaism that later Rabbinic Judaism, the Judaism of the post-Temple period, succeeded.[24] Thus it can be said, with a certain degree of historical confidence, that Christianity *and* Rabbinic Judaism are two different traditions that emerged at roughly the same time, and they were both responses to the imminently future or imminently past destruction of the Temple as the center of the covenant between God and Israel. Historically, it is inaccurate to say that Christianity "came from Judaism," if one means the Judaism developed in the Talmud and related writings. Historically, our Judaism is no older than your Christianity; and your

24. Thus the rabbinic teaching that the separate Oral Torah is normatively equal to, if not superior to, Scripture or "the Written Torah" (see, e.g., B. Gittin 60b re Exod. 34:27) is considered to be a doctrine fully formulated and emphasized after the rise of Christianity. Whether this was in reaction to Christianity or not, however, is debatable. See E. P. Sanders, *Jewish Law from Jesus to the Mishnah* (London: SCM, 1990), pp. 97-130.

Christianity is no newer than our Judaism. Both Christianity and Judaism — and I mention Christianity before Judaism because the New Testament is an older text than either of the two Talmuds and the Midrashim — presented themselves as new revelations.

This point might become more clear if I explain my use as a Jew of the Christian term "Old Testament" when referring to what for me are *kitvei ha-qodesh,* "the Sacred Scriptures." Among ourselves, of course, we Jews would not use the term "Old Testament." And by now even Jewish scholars who interact with Christians do not have to say the "Old Testament" because these Christian scholars recognize it to be a problematic term for Jews. So, most of us use the neutral academic term "Hebrew Bible," which is a term that is neither Jewish nor Christian and therefore could be both. However, when Jews understand how Christian theology constitutes the relation of the New Testament and the Old Testament for Christians, we can see then how that relation is strikingly parallel to the relation, for us, of the Oral Torah (Talmud) and the Written Torah (Scripture). And when Christians understand how Jewish theology constitutes the relation of the Oral Torah and the Written Torah, they can then see how that relation is strikingly parallel to the relation of the New Testament and the Old Testament for them. In fact, what I want to suggest is that the Hebrew Bible functions very much like an "Old Testament" for the Jews too. Let me begin with the relation of the new and the old.

We usually assume that the new follows the old. If the new replaces the old, then the new has ontological priority over the old like the end has priority over the means.[25] If, on the other hand, the new simply emerges out of the old, then the old has priority over the new like the cause has priority over the effect.[26] This understanding of the relation of the new and the old is what lies at the heart of supersessionist and counter-supersessionist logic. That is, if the New Testament *replaces* the Old Testament and the Church *replaces* the Jewish people as Israel, then the old has been overcome — that is, *has been superseded* — by the new. Thus Christians saying "We came out of you Jews" cannot escape the strong practical conclusion: "So why have you Jews remained behind?" But if the New Testament only *emerges* out of the Old Testament and the Church *emerges* out of the Jewish people as Israel, then the new has usurped the old. Thus Jews saying to Christians "You came out of us" cannot escape the strong practical conclusion: "So why have you Christians broken so far away?"

25. See Aristotle, *Posterior Analytics*, 85b29-35.
26. See Kant, *Critique of Pure Reason*, B124.

But for Christianity, at least as I have learned of it, the New Testament does not *follow* the Old Testament and the Church does not *follow* the Jewish people in a necessary logical sequence, neither as a replacement nor as an emergence. Instead, the prime locus of authoritative revelation is in the New Testament. When that is fully established, Christians are then to look back to the Old Testament, not as the source or ground of that Christological revelation but rather as the set of conditions that made acceptance of the Christological revelation possible. In other words, the "Old Testament" is "old" retrospectively, not as earlier "potential" or as a prior "cause." (Here is where philosophical terminology and conceptuality are important for theology, Christian or Jewish.) Here is where one can locate and intelligently refute the theological error of assuming the derivation of Christianity from Judaism. Thus both Judaism qua Oral Torah and Christianity qua New Covenant are *novi testamenti,* as it were.

This understanding of the old making the acceptance of the new *possible* enables Christians to see the New Testament as its original (as in the German *Ursprung*) revelation without a Marcionite rejection of history. The Old Testament's "oldness" is not that of either potentiality or causality; rather, it is the "oldness" or historical priority (as in the German *Anfang*) of a necessary precondition, but one whose necessity is not known until after the fact of the truly original revelation.[27] Looking at the relation of Old and New Testaments in this way enables one to see "old" as meaning neither "passé" nor "sufficient." In talmudic logic this is called *bereirah,* that is, when the present defines the past in a way in which the past could never define the present.[28] Later talmudic logic called this process *asmakhta,* namely, the "association" of norm and text, which is neither the derivation of the norm *from* the text nor the overcoming of the text *by* the norm.[29]

In this way, one can see how the New Testament is a *midrash* necessarily connected to the Old Testament. A *midrash* appears to be a rabbinic commentary on the text of the Bible. Nevertheless, very little *midrash* is what we would call "commentary" in the strict sense. (That had to wait for post-talmudic Jewish exegesis of the Bible, especially in the Middle

27. This distinction is based on the ontological differentiation made by the Jewish philosopher Hermann Cohen (d. 1918). See his *Logik der reinen Erkenntnis,* 3rd ed. (Berlin: B. Cassirer, 1922), pp. 36, 79; also, *Religion of Reason out of the Sources of Judaism,* trans. S. Kaplan (New York: Frederick Ungar, 1972), p. 69.

28. See, e.g., B. Eruvin 36b.

29. See, e.g., B. Hullin 17b.

Ages.)[30] Instead, most *midrash,* especially that which deals with immediately normative scriptural texts, is the attempt to *relate back* to scriptural foundations what had already been accepted in practice as the content of the Oral Torah *(torah she-b'al peh).*[31] Thus the later practices *(halakhot),* which were very much considered to have been revealed as far back as the time of Moses, are the prime locus of the life of the covenanted community.[32] As the Jewish theologian Yeshayahu Leibowitz vividly put it, "The Oral Torah includes within itself the Written Torah."[33] That is why the very acceptance of one version of the biblical text as opposed to another is determined by the Oral Torah.[34] Indeed, the very sanctity of a written Torah scroll, whether it is fit to be read in the synagogue or not, is determined by the Oral Torah for the Written Torah, not by the Written Torah for itself.[35] And how intriguing it is to consider that Jesus of Nazareth, the word made flesh, and Rabbi Akibah, the greatest embodiment of the Torah, both died martyrs' deaths at the hand of the Romans.[36]

So, if Christians see Jesus to be the embodiment of the truly prior Oral Torah — "the word became flesh" (John 1:14) — then the Old Testament is what has made that possible for Christians to accept. And this is quite similar to the way the Written Torah is what has made the acceptance of the Oral Torah possible for Jews to accept. That is why both Christians in their way and Jews in theirs have been engaged in the midrashic process of relating the new to the old in our respective new revelations and traditions. In that way, then, the Hebrew Bible is very much your Written Torah as it is our Old Testament. But it is only in the thorough theological renunciation of supersessionism and counter-supersessionism that Jewish and Christian scholars can exchange this type of textual and historical information in a way that is neither adversarial nor capitulating. So, I would say: Christianity today need look to Judaism today as its source no more than Judaism today need look to Christianity today as its outcome. Both Jews and Christians today do, however, need to look to our common historical roots in the Old Testament and the Pharisaic Judaism of the

---

30. See David Weiss Halivni, *Peshat and Derash* (New York: Oxford University Press, 1991), pp. 52-88.

31. See, e.g., B. Kiddushin 41a re Deut. 24:1.

32. See B. Menakhot 29b.

33. Leibowitz, *Judaism, the Jewish People, and the State of Israel* (Heb.) (Jerusalem and Tel Aviv: Schocken, 1976), p. 348.

34. See B. Sanhedrin 21b-22a.

35. See Maimonides, *Mishneh Torah: Sefer Torah,* 10.1.

36. See B. Berakhot 61b.

late Second Temple period. And some of that theological research can be done mutually to the deep benefit of both communities in our perpetual search for the truth.

What we see from all of this is that it is best, both historically and theologically, to look upon ourselves as two traditions, related to the same sources, which have developed, often in the same worldly locations, with a striking parallelism. Being parallel to one another, our theological logic in talking with one another should be that of analogy rather than that of either causal inference or teleology. Analogy may not be as conclusive as deduction, and it may not be as comprehensive as teleology. Nevertheless, analogy has an openness and a range of possibilities that make it more attractive for truly personal discourse.

The Specter of Proselytism

Finally, let me make one last point about supersessionism, counter-supersessionism, and proselytism. Christian supersessionism lends itself to an easy way to proselytize Jews. It simply tells Jews that they are living in an irretrievable past. It thus tells Jews to become "full Jews," that is, to become Christians and leave Judaism behind. Even though Jewish proselytism is much more subtle and covert, it can use counter-supersessionism just as effectively. It can simply tell Christians to come home like prodigal sons. Thus, when a formerly Protestant friend of mine told me how by becoming a Catholic he felt as though he had come home, I had the temptation — and it was only a temptation — to tell him, "not quite." Now the renunciation of Christian supersessionism and its Jewish antithesis makes Christian or Jewish proselytizing of each other much harder. We cannot use either teleological or causal logic. That does not mean, of course, that either of us could abandon proselytism. Christians must hope that everyone will accept Christ. All Christians are to be seen as "born again" (anagenesis). And Jews need proselytes to remind us that being chosen is best appreciated when our chosenness is what we would want for ourselves over and above the necessity of our birth to a Jewish mother. Indeed, Sarah, the first Jewish mother, is the archetypal convert: One "born again" (ke-qatan she-nolad).[37]

There is always the chance that some Jews will finally accept the Christian revelation as original just as some Christians will finally accept the

---

37. B. Yevamot 22a and parallels.

Jewish revelation as original. That is a chance we take in mutual theological discourse. It could even be a danger, and that is the reason why many traditional Jews want no part of our enterprise. Nevertheless, the renunciation of supersessionism by Christians suggests that Christians have no more arguments for our conversion than we have arguments for their conversion. That opens the ground for God to make the truly final demonstration of an end that will include us all, making our presently parallel lines converge in eternity.[38]

38. See Novak, *Jewish-Christian Dialogue,* pp. 155-56.

Avoiding Charges of Legalism and Antinomianism
in Jewish-Christian Dialogue

Note: The following essay is a theological background paper written for a project, "A Jewish Statement on Christians and Christianity," sponsored by the Institute for Christian and Jewish Studies (Baltimore), and directed by Tikva Frymer-Kensky (University of Chicago), David Novak (University of Toronto), Peter Ochs (University of Virginia), and Michael Signer (University of Notre Dame). This statement, signed by a number of Jewish scholars, was published in September 2000. It was followed shortly thereafter by a book, *Christianity in Jewish Terms* (Radical Traditions Series of Westview Press), where a number of Jewish thinkers explored the themes of the statement, along with responses from other thinkers, both Jewish and Christian.

Some Presuppositions of Jewish-Christian Dialogue

To sustain the new dialogue that has emerged between Jews and Christians, each side must be willing to see the other side from the best possible vantage point within its own tradition, but without any compromise of the truth claims of its own tradition.[1] True dialogue requires each side to constitute a theological vision of the other that carefully avoids the theological dangers of hostility, capitulation, syncretism, and relativism. The

---

1. See David Novak, *Jewish-Christian Dialogue: A Jewish Justification* (New York: Oxford University Press, 1989), pp. 14ff.

This essay previously appeared in *Modern Theology* 16, no. 3 (July 2000): 275-91. It is reprinted here with permission.

proper conduct of the dialogue is itself a theological issue for Jews and Christians. It can only have serious meaning, therefore, when conducted on a theological level, with integrity from both sides.

Hostility would present the truth claims of each tradition to be so mutually exclusive at every level of comparison that dialogue either would be explicitly disputational (as it usually was in the Middle Ages) or would at least strongly imply a proselytizing agenda from one side or the other or both. Capitulation would be acceptance of the proselytizing agenda of one side by the other. Considering the respective sizes and political strengths of the Jewish people and the Christian Church, plus the asymmetric possibility of Judaism being sublimated into *(aufgehoben)* Christianity in a way Christianity could not possibly be sublimated into Judaism, Jewish capitulation to Christianity rather than Christian capitulation to Judaism has been the more tempting historical possibility during much of the last two millennia.

Syncretism would lead each side to overcome the exclusivity of its truth claims by discovering a new truth for both. But that would necessarily involve the overcoming of the earlier truths each tradition has received by divine revelation. Such a new universality (one thinks of the rational religion envisioned by Spinoza that incorporates Jewish and Christian elements after having deconstructed them both), by its inventive superseding of both Jewish and Christian revelations, would thereby destroy the very basis of the truth claims of both Judaism and Christianity.[2] Hence it would leave nothing authentically Jewish or Christian in its wake. Indeed, both Judaism and Christianity would have to see such a fundamentally human constitution of the relationship with God as a form of idolatry. Idolatry is as much the worship of the right God the wrong way as it is the worship of the wrong god whatever way. Whereas Scripture usually speaks of the worship of "other gods" (Exod. 20:3) or "a strange god" (*el zar* — Ps. 81:10), the Rabbis usually speak of idolatry as "strange worship" *(avodah zarah).*[3]

In the atmosphere of modern secularism, where religious claims are taken to be basically private preferences, relativism is especially dangerous on the part of either side. Relativism makes any truth claim irrelevant, thus making both Judaism and Christianity irrelevant in the most basic existential claim each makes on its own adherents: a Jew or a Christian is

---

2. See David Novak, *The Election of Israel: The Idea of the Chosen People* (Cambridge: Cambridge University Press, 1995), pp. 40ff.

3. See Lev. 10:1; R. Judah Halevi, *Kuzari,* 1.97; also, M. Halbertal and A. Margalit, *Idolatry,* trans. N. Goldblum (Cambridge, Mass.: Harvard University Press, 1992), pp. 186ff.

to die as a martyr rather than accede to the ultimate truth claims of any other faith community, especially those of Christianity made to Jews or those of Judaism made to Christians.[4] Why would anyone be willing to die for anything less than what he or she believed to be the highest truth one could possibly know in this world? Martyrdom is the most demanding, hence the most serious, of all the commandments. Without its possibility, Jewish or Christian piety is ultimately negotiable, even trivial.

Furthermore, the universal truth claims made by Judaism and Christianity are presupposed by the reality of conversion in both traditions. Indeed, Christians must understand that even though Jews have not engaged in the type of proselytizing in which many Christians do engage, we have always accepted converts, and most of those converts have been former Christians. Proselytism presupposes conversion, although conversion does not entail proselytism. Nevertheless, the ubiquity of conversion, in one form or another, throughout Jewish history, certainly does not rule out proselytism, at least de jure.[5]

The willingness of Christians to accept converts from Judaism and of Jews to accept converts from Christianity is a matter of theological rivalry, which means that one cannot assume that the faith position of either side is simply relative. Relativism would annul the proper assertion of Judaism or Christianity to be the most adequate fulfillment of the ultimate requirement of human nature in this world, which is to be related to God.[6] Such truth claims about human nature are necessarily universal.[7] To

4. See R. Abraham Gumbiner, *Magen Avraham* on *Shulhan Arukh:* Orah Hayyim, 128.37 re *Babylonian Talmud* (hereafter "B."): Sanhedrin 74a.

5. See, e.g., *Pesiqta Rabbati,* chap. 35 re Zech. 2:15, ed. Friedmann, p. 161a, and chap. 40 re Lev. 23:24, p. 167b; *Tanhuma:* Tsav re Lev. 8:1, ed. Buber, p. 9b; Maimonides, *Teshuvot ha-Rambam,* 1, no. 149, ed. Y. Y. Blau (Jerusalem: Meqitsei Nirdamim, 1960), pp. 284ff.

6. Cf. the "pluralistic hypothesis" of John Hick, *A Christian Theology of Religions: The Rainbow of Faiths* (Louisville: Westminster/John Knox Press, 1995), pp. 28-29, viz., that all religions are equally human approximations of "the Real as humanly perceived," and behind all of them is "the Real *an sich.*" He bases this on Kant's distinction between the phenomenal and noumenal realms. But, whereas for Kant, the truth of phenomena is bespoken by human reason, in Jewish and Christian (and Islamic) revelations, God speaks the truth of Himself. Furthermore, even for Kant the truth of phenomena is still enunciated in universal categories; hence the structures of experience are not pluralistic. Hick's epistemology by its very pluralism eliminates the question of truth altogether, which is, of course, central to the religions of revelation as it is to human reason. On the moral/political level, however, pluralism is valid by advocating that acceptance of truth cannot be coerced but can only be freely received when one is persuaded by reason or believes the witness of revelation.

7. See *Mekhilta:* Yitro, ed. Horovitz Rabin, p. 205 re Exod. 19:2 and p. 222 re Exod. 20:2; cf. Philo, *De Decalogo,* 1.2/181.

relativize the universal truth claims of Judaism or Christianity would mean either that there is no human nature and hence no truth to be asserted about it, or that Judaism and Christianity address concerns less than those of human nature and any universal truth that can be asserted about it. Such relativism, of either form, would make the claims of Judaism and Christianity merely customary.[8] But, surely, Judaism and Christianity affirm a human nature, and that the pinnacle of this nature is for all humans to be related to God. That is what is meant when they both proclaim that all humankind is created in the "image of God" (Gen. 1:27) and in the End Time "the Lord will be king over all the earth" (Zech. 14:9). And, surely, Judaism and Christianity are primarily concerned with truth. This is what is meant when they both proclaim "the truth [*emet*] of the Lord is forever" (Ps. 117:2).[9]

At the ultimate level, no matter how worthy they deem dialogue to be, Jews and Christians have to recognize that their truth claims are not only different, they are mutually exclusive. The highest form of worship of the Lord God of Israel is *either* by the Torah and the tradition of the Jewish people *or* by Christ and the tradition of the Church. One cannot live as a Jew and as a Christian in tandem, that is, by the normative criteria of either Judaism or Christianity. At this level, one simply cannot have it both ways. One makes a choice for one faith rather than the other in a way that is essentially unlike any other option presented to Jews or to Christians by any other faith. In this way, Judaism could well be considered the greatest temptation to Christians, and Christianity the greatest temptation to Jews. This fact explains why the stakes in the Jewish-Christian relationship are so high.

8. That is precisely what the Jewish philosopher Moses Mendelssohn (d. 1786) did to Judaism when he asserted that the "Israelites possess a divine *legislation* . . . but no doctrinal opinions, no saving truths, no universal propositions of reason. These the Eternal reveals to us and to all other men at all times . . ." *(Jerusalem; or, On Religious Power and Judaism,* trans. A. Arkush [Hanover, N.H.: University Press of New England, 1983], p. 90). Mendelssohn assumed that all universal propositions are necessarily those of reason; hence he denied that Judaism could make universal claims let alone does actually make them. But a revelation to a specific community can still have universal intention. See, e.g., B. Kiddushin 31a re Ps. 138:4.

9. In Hebrew *emet* basically means "faithfulness" (see, e.g., Gen. 47:29). For the connection between God's faithfulness as the source of truth as correspondence and coherence, see Novak, *The Election of Israel,* pp. 126-27. For the important argument that this truth is only validated within the universe of discourse constituted by revelation and sustained by tradition, that it is validated neither by objective (ordinary) experience (what is best named by the German *Erfahrung*) nor by subjective (existential) introspection (what is best named by the German *Erlebnis*), see George A. Lindbeck, *The Nature of Doctrine: Religion and Theology in a Postliberal Age* (Philadelphia: Westminster Press, 1984), pp. 16ff., 30ff.

The recognition that the ultimate claims of Judaism and Christianity are mutually exclusive need be the basis of hostile disputations only when it is assumed that Judaism and Christianity have no commonalities at all. However, not only is that historically false, it is also practically dangerous inasmuch as it invites animosity in our interrelations where none need exist. As such, it is important to carefully distinguish between the ultimate level of truth where we are presently at an impasse (and which cannot be resolved by human politics, human philosophy, or human textual exegesis) and the penultimate level where there is rich commonality. And this rich commonality can be respected without necessarily falling into capitulation, syncretism, or relativism. Jews and Christians must always be aware of the ultimate impasse their rival universal truth claims make. But that impasse can be cogently bracketed in order to deal with what is less than those claims and which also has great theological and ethical import. Indeed, this tension between the ultimate and the penultimate in the Jewish-Christian relationship makes all discourse about it dialectical rather than merely straightforwardly assertive. It is never just a comparison of this and that, but this in response to that and that in counterresponse to this. Our historical entanglement from the very beginning makes our encounters far more than exercises in comparative religions.

The impasse at present is ultimate, but it ought not be seen as final, a point most profoundly seen by Franz Rosenzweig, who could well be considered the greatest Jewish theologian in modern times and the most profound Jewish thinker about Christianity.[10] Jews and Christians can certainly see even the present ultimate impasse against an eschatological horizon, toward an End Time when all differences of faith between all humans will be overcome at last in a final divine act of redemption of Israel, of humankind, indeed of the entire created universe. Thus the claims of each community are not absolute in the sense of their being perfectly sufficient for human existence insofar as human existence is still unfulfilled. These claims do intend a transcendent realm, even if what lies on its other side is now still ineffable.[11] The eschatological horizon of all Jewish and

10. See Novak, *Jewish-Christian Dialogue*, pp. 93ff.

11. Along these lines, Jewish or Christian philosophical theology must deal with Wittgenstein's implicit critique of Kant in *Tractatus Logico-Philosophicus* (London, 1961), 5.61, viz., we cannot speak of the limits of our knowledge unless we know *what* limits it from "the other side." Jews and Christians, however, can respond from our revealed eschatologies *that* there will be a judgment of God in the future (see Job 19:25-27) even though we could not possibly say here and now *what* it will actually do then, i.e., *how* it will operate then (see B. Berakhot 34b and 2 Cor. 2:9 re Isa. 64:3). As such, it functions very much like Kant's *Ding*

Christian witness and striving in this world should guard each community from succumbing to the temptation of triumphalism in its witness of the truth given to it.

Legalism and Antinomianism

For too long, it has been assumed by many Jews and by many Christians that a part of the ultimate impasse between Judaism is over what Jews call *mitsvah* (commandment) and what Christians call "the Law" *(ho nomos)*. Many Christians have assumed that Jews believe that the successful keeping of the commandments of the Torah automatically leads to salvation, to full reconciliation with God in the world-to-come. This is seen to be "Jewish legalism," which is criticized as "works righteousness," namely, that which ignores the human propensity for sin and is, in effect, idolatrous self-creation. Many Jews have assumed that Christians have rejected the law of God in favor of a human creation, the Church, even deeming its law and worship idolatrous.[12] Clearly, for any religion based on biblical revelation, invoking "idolatry," even if only by connotation, is a trump against any empathetic appreciation of that other on theological grounds. The dialogue, even at the level of ultimate impasse let alone at lower levels where there is more commonality, must overcome even the implication of idolatry by either side against the other if it is to be cogent.

Christians can recognize that the Jewish devotion to the commandments of the Torah, including our ongoing tradition of interpretation and application, is not a human construction of the kingdom of God. There is much in the Jewish tradition that looks upon the transcendent intention of the keeping of the commandments as being a response to God's revealing presence rather than being some sort of human succes-

---

an sich, which to me seems to be something only God *could* know here and now, viz., qua *ens creatum,* even for Kant. See *Kritik der reinen Vernunft,* B125, where Kant separates the phenomena we experience causally from what is "vermittelst des Willens." Whose will could possibly have this power sui generis except God's? Where will is primary, it locates *what* is *then* to be found *therein*. It is like the categorical difference between the poetic knowledge of a creative artist that *informs* his or her painting and the theoretical knowledge of an art critic perceiving *that* form already within the frame the artist has put that painting into. Our belief *that* God *will* judge our present claims at the Eschaton thereby limits any finality for them here and now.

12. See Maimonides, *Mishneh Torah:* Avodah Zarah, 1.3-4. For Maimonides' seeming changed view of Christianity, however, see Novak, *Jewish-Christian Dialogue,* pp. 57ff.

sion of God's creativity.[13] The very need for forgiveness of and atonement for sins indicates that keeping the commandments is a human participation in a larger covenantal reality, which human effort alone could neither initiate nor fulfill. In this sense, the final redemption is the final atonement. Neither redemption nor atonement is an essentially human achievement. Thus our keeping of the *mitsvot* is something begun and ended by God, for which we are grateful to God for allowing the people of Israel to be, at best, his junior partners. "I am the first and I am the last, and there is no God other than Me" (Isa. 44:6).

Christians are certainly justified in questioning whether this Jewish keeping of the *mitsvot* is adequate even here and now as the highest and most complete worship of the Lord God of Israel, whom both Jews and Christians acknowledge to be the one true God. If Christians did not question this, they would have to become Jews in good faith (which has always been a historical possibility). That is because Judaism and Christianity are the only two historical options for the worship of the God who stated about Himself "I am the Lord your God, who took you out of the land of Egypt, out of the house of bondage" (Exod. 20:2).[14] Nevertheless, Christians can very well recognize in good faith that the central Jewish concern with keeping the *mitsvot,* including the very legally oriented tradition *(halakhah)* that so carefully structures that practice, is not legalism but, rather, a genuinely theological enterprise from beginning to end.

In fact, one could very well say that part of the great divide between Judaism and Christianity is not whether law is or is not part of the relationship with God. Instead, it is better to say that the need for law, for the keeping of the commandments of the Lord God of Israel, is what is common to both Judaism and Christianity. How could the Lord God of Israel, the creator of heaven and earth, whom both Jews and Christians worship, not command us? Is not every act in relation to this God of normative significance? Is not our relationship with this God a covenant? And is not a covenant a political reality? And could there be any polity not governed by law? So, the divide (what could be called *la différence même*) between us is not over law per se. The divide is over *what* those immutable commandments are, which entails *when* and *where* one hears them and *how* one is to do them. Judaism or Christianity provide the only historical locations for hearing the commandments of the Lord God of Israel and responding to them in a covenanted community.

13. See *Mishnah:* Avot 2.15-16.
14. See Halevi, *Kuzari,* 1.25.

It is only when Christians overcome the false charge against Judaism of legalism that Jews can better appreciate the fact that Christianity is not antinomian. Thus Christian questioning of the sufficiency of "the Law" as the content of God's commanding presence is not a rejection of law per se, which can only be the law of God for anyone recognizing the authority of God to be the one absolute any human can affirm in this world. God commands us for the sake of the covenant. The question for human beings is what the content of the covenant truly is. The answer to this question is not the result of philosophical abstraction (which does have other important theological functions) but, rather, concrete historical identification.

Christians can no more be antinomian than Jews can be legalistic with theological cogency. At the key point of human action, both of these extremes substitute man for God by replacing the divine with the human. The legalist errs by placing the kingdom of God in human hands; the antinomian errs by denying there is any kingdom at all in his or her radical individualism. The Rabbis saw antinomianism at the heart of the rejection of God's authority. The antinomian lives in an ultimately absurd universe, acting as if "there were no law *(din)* and no judge *(dayyan)*."[15] He or she is the immoral "fool [*naval*] who says in his heart there is no judging God [*elohim*]" (Ps. 53:2). The task for Jews who wish to appreciate Christianity with authenticity, both in terms of the norm of the Torah and the fact of Christianity, is to understand how Christian lawfulness can be seen as consistent with Jewish normativeness without, however, being made subordinate to it.

Noahide Law

From rabbinic times on, Jews have developed a rubric for dealing with the issue of gentile normativeness. That rubric is the concept of the "seven commandments of the children of Noah." The seven commandments are seen to be the following: (1) the mandate for a society to set up courts of justice; (2) the prohibition of blasphemy; (3) the prohibition of idolatry; (4) the prohibition of killing innocent human life; (5) the prohibition of the sexual practices of incest, adultery, homosexuality, and bestiality; (6) the prohibition of robbery; (7) the prohibition of tearing a limb from a living animal for food. This concept along with discussions

15. See *Targum Jonathan ben Uzziel:* Gen. 4:8.

of the various commandments themselves are found in many places in rabbinic and post-rabbinic writings. They are seen as being addressed to the "Noahides" *(bnei Noah),* that is, all humankind, who after the Flood are the descendants of Noah.[16] All of them are based on if not actually derived from Scripture. And it is important to note that the three most central of these seven commandments are taken to be the prohibitions of idolatry, killing innocent human life, and sexual immorality.[17] These three prohibitions admit of no exceptions, and a Jew is to die as a martyr rather than transgress them.[18] In other words, the *conditio sine qua non* of Judaism is the very same one Judaism constitutes as that of the gentiles as well. This is the most fundamental of all commonalities between Judaism and any gentile tradition on earth.

Since Christians base their morality on the Scripture they call the "Old Testament," and since all the Noahide laws found in Scripture do pertain to humankind per se in one way or another, Christians are the most likely candidates for the category of "Noahides." In fact, when Maimonides designates those gentiles whom he considers worthy to join "all Israel" in the world-to-come, he specifies that they are those who "accept and practice them [the Noahide laws] because God commanded them in the Torah and let us know through Moses our master that the children of Noah were commanded concerning them beforehand."[19] Do not Christians best fit this description? They have the only non-Jewish tradition that sees its morality as being fundamentally biblical in origin. That is important to bear in mind since Maimonides (and others) also regards these laws as being rationally discernible. Therefore, even though other gentiles can live a moral life that is consistent with what Jews regard to be minimal non-Jewish morality, one could very well say that Christians are the only gentiles who are part of the transcendent trajectory that Jews see as the ultimate end of all human striving, striving that begins with devotion to justice in this world.

Some Jewish and Christian advocates of a richer Jewish-Christian relationship than had been possible in the past have been wary of using the concept of the Noahide and Noahide law for this purpose. They have seen it as being much too minimal in scope and even in depth to account for the richness of the commonalities and parallels between Judaism and

16. See David Novak, *The Image of the Non-Jew in Judaism: An Historical and Constructive Study of the Noahide Laws* (New York and Toronto: Edwin Mellen Press, 1983), chap. 1.

17. See B. Sanhedrin 57a.

18. See B. Sanhedrin 74a and parallels.

19. *Mishneh Torah: Melakhim,* 8.11.

Christianity.[20] However, they have missed the reason for which, it seems, the Rabbis conceived the concept of the Noahide and of Noahide law altogether. To be sure, there have been Jewish thinkers who conceive of the Noahide as a real historical status, separate from either Christianity or Islam or any other religious tradition.[21] They have also conceived of Noahide law as comprising a "code" unto itself.[22] Nevertheless, most Jewish thinkers have used these concepts differently. In most of the sources, these concepts are used more heuristically than descriptively, that is, they are used to discover what is the *conditio sine qua non* for a community of gentiles with whom Jews can interact out of genuine respect and not just political or economic necessity. But they are not seen as comprising the actual content of the religious and cultural life of a community that truly accepts them in principle. In other words, they are regarded as the necessary but not sufficient condition for any human community to be considered as living according to divine law. Noahide law is too "thin" to constitute the "thickness" of a historical tradition like Judaism or Christianity. No human community could live by Noahide law alone, but no human community who does not affirm it is worthy of the loyalty of humans created in the image of God.

The best way to see this point is to look at how the Rabbis deal with gentile idolatry. The Noahide *(ben Noah)* is considered to be that gentile who has discovered that the prohibition of idolatry is universal in scope, and that therefore gentiles as well as Jews, at least in principle, are obligated to uphold it. For the Rabbis, it is quite clear that their main concern was whether any gentile whom they confronted was or was not an idolater. In fact, in later versions of rabbinic texts, gentiles who are penalized in one way or another in Jewish law are generically termed "idolaters" *(ovdei avodah zarah).*[23] It seems that the Rabbis thought that once idolatry had been rejected by gentiles, acceptance of the other moral laws would inevitably result therefrom. On the other hand, though, it also seems that when the Rabbis saw gentile respect for the other Noahide laws, especially

20. See Clark M. Williamson, *A Guest in the House of Israel: Post-Holocaust Church Theology* (Louisville: Westminster/John Knox Press, 1993), pp. 129-30.

21. See R. Elijah Benamozegh, *Israel and Humanity,* trans. M. Luria (New York: Paulist Press, 1995).

22. See, e.g., J. D. Bleich, "Abortion in Halakhic Literature," in *Jewish Bioethics,* ed. F. Rosner and J. D. Bleich (New York: Sanhedrin Press, 1979), p. 162.

23. For the influential efforts of R. Menahem ha-Meiri in the fourteenth century to distinguish between "idolaters" mentioned in the Talmud and contemporary Christians and Muslims, see Novak, *The Image of the Non-Jew in Judaism,* pp. 351ff.

the respect for human life involved in the prohibition of bloodshed, they had a tendency to regard any cultural vestiges of idolatry in such societies quite leniently. This indicates the close relation Jews have always seen between theology and ethics. Theology entails ethics as ethics presupposes theology in any monotheistic system based in revelation (namely, Judaism, Christianity, and Islam).

In order to constitute properly a Jewish appreciation of Christian normativeness, it must be emphasized at the outset what the political context of that normativeness is. All law structures a political reality, even if that reality is the human world in general as it is in the covenant between God and the earth through the Noahides or humankind. The acceptance of Noahide law is, then, the acceptance of natural law. Minimally, it is natural law in the sense that it is so closely related to universal human nature that it is taken to be a universal requirement here and now. On that point, all those Jewish thinkers who accept the idea of universal human nature would have to agree in their discussion of Noahide law.[24] It applies to all humankind, to all those deemed to partake of human nature, who are the descendants of the first man and the first woman.[25] Maximally, however, Noahide law is natural law in the sense that it is accessible to human reason, that it can be known when human beings truly ponder what it means to be human and what makes a society worthy of the loyalty of the human beings who comprise it. In this Jewish point of view, revelation of basic moral law in Scripture is a confirmation and deepening of natural law. Neither natural law qua general revelation nor scriptural law qua special revelation, though, are products of human reason. In the case of general revelation, *anybody* can discover the law for himself or herself. In the case of special revelation, the law discovers *somebody,* who then holds fast to it in trust until *everybody* accepts it.[26]

Jews can very well see in Christians those human beings outside the people of Israel who have understood these truths best. I think a natural-law perspective best explains the normative commonalities between Judaism and Christianity, but one can still recognize these commonalities even if one assumes that moral law must be originally located in special revelation and a tradition that passes on its content.[27]

24. For the absence of an idea of universal human nature in kabbalistic theology, see David Novak, *Natural Law in Judaism* (Cambridge: Cambridge University Press, 1998), p. 145.

25. See *Palestinian Talmud:* Nedarim 9.4/41c re Gen. 5:1.

26. See Deut. 4:6-8; Isa. 43:7-10 and 55:6-7; Mic. 4:1-3.

27. To answer the Barthian charge that asserting general revelation ties one to "natural theology" and all that it presupposes and entails, see Novak, *Natural Law in Judaism*, pp.

The humanly inhabited world is the most general political context of Noahide law, including some basic recognition of God as sovereign. Only a sovereign can make law that is to be obeyed by his subjects. The idea of law as divine law in essence and human law as a participation therein or an elaboration thereof seems to involve a notion of divine kingship, however remote that king is before covenantal revelation occurs. A community who sees the authority of the Lord God maker of heaven and earth as being supreme, which is a community having a cosmic intention, is a community Jews can respect in principle.[28] And it can be respected in fact when recognition of God's supremacy includes respect for the historical claims of the Jewish people, claims that are seen as being of cosmic significance. For Christians, for whom the Lord God maker of heaven and earth is manifest as the Lord God of Israel, those historical claims of the Jewish people are more readily intelligible than they are for anyone else.

The Law of a Gentile Community

Both Jews and Christians can agree that Christianity has only appropriated part of the law of the Torah for herself. The part appropriated has been the moral law of the Torah in general — including basic obligations of love and respect first to God and then to fellow humans. The part of the Torah not appropriated by Christianity has consisted of those commandments that are addressed to the people of Israel in their very separateness, such as the purity laws pertaining to diet, dress, and marital relations. It also includes those practices like Passover that celebrate pre-messianic events in the life of the people of Israel. These commandments have been replaced by the Church with the sacraments that celebrate the life, death, and resurrection of Jesus.[29] Here the Church seemed to have based herself on an ancient Jewish belief that when the Messiah comes, the more ethnically specific parts of the Torah will have already fulfilled their function and thus be overcome, that is, no longer binding on Israel of the new (better, renewed) covenant *(brit hadashah)*.[30] Perhaps because of its use by

---

142ff. For a Christian answer, see Oliver O'Donovan, *Resurrection and Moral Order: An Outline for Evangelical Ethics* (Grand Rapids: Eerdmans, 1986), pp. 86-87.

28. See Maimonides, *Guide of the Perplexed*, 2.40.

29. See Thomas Aquinas, *Summa Theologiae* 2/1, q. 98, a. 5.

30. See *Tosefta:* Berakhot 1.12-13 re Jer. 23:7-8. Regarding the *renewed* covenant, see 1 Sam. 11:14-15; Jer. 31:30-33.

Christianity in its separation from Judaism, this view of the temporal limit of at least some of the Torah became bracketed in almost all post-Christian Jewish theology.

Even the appropriation of part of the law of the Torah has not been without debate in the history of Christianity. Very early in Christian history, the monk Marcion advocated a total break with the Jewish legacy of the Church, and that included a total break with Jewish law. The fact that Marcionism was declared the very first heresy by the early Church itself indicates that despite her ultimate differences with Judaism, the Church did not want to break away from her Jewish origins, and that included her partial connection to Jewish law, at least in its scriptural core, the Ten Commandments. Thus whenever Christians have had to consider what a Christian polity would actually be like, they have had to return to the law of the Old Testament. This, in turn, has frequently led Christian scholars to seek out Jewish interpretations of scriptural law for their own enlightenment. Even today, when most Jews and Christians have accepted the necessity of a secular polity, Jews and Christians have discovered important commonalities in their attempts to influence moral and political issues because of that basic connection.

The key problem with Christian normativeness for Jewish theology is the partialness of the Christian appropriation of Jewish law. In fact, one of the reasons given for why the reading of the Ten Commandments is no longer a feature of the daily liturgy (although still read within the full cycle of scriptural readings in the synagogue) is because of the "charges of the sectarians" *(minim)*. These charges are that "only the Ten Commandments were given at Sinai."[31] Even though the meaning of "sectarians" is often unclear, it seems clear from this talmudic discussion that the Rabbis had the Jewish Christians in mind. This diminution of the full range of the binding norms of the Torah is seen as the prime reason for the rabbinic rejection of the Christianity of these Jews as an acceptable form of Judaism itself. For Christians, of course, this is not a diminution of God's law inasmuch as what had been superseded in the Old Law had been only a temporal preparation for the full law of God in the New Law of the New Covenant. At this point, anyway, there seems to be an unbridgeable gap between partialness and fulfillment.

Nevertheless, the way to get over this impasse depends on the essential status of the Christian community, the Church herself, in Jewish eyes. When the Church *(ekklēsia)* was a predominantly Jewish community, one

---

31. *Palestinian Talmud:* Berakhot 1.8/3c re *Mishnah:* Tamid 5.1.

made up of persons whom the Rabbis had to consider bona fide Jews plus some questionable converts, the Christian attitude to the law of the Torah had to be seen as an unacceptable deviation from Judaism by a group of Jewish sectarians. However, the reverse became the case when the Church soon became an essentially gentile community.

This transition had to happen. Beginning from the time of Paul, the Church was becoming a more and more gentile community. Moreover, the reason that the Church in the time of Paul decided not to require gentile converts to the Church to go through a fully Jewish conversion (requiring circumcision and full acceptance of theretofore extant Jewish law) might well be because of the isolation in Jewry of even the Jewish Christians. Since the Church was already considered a deviant Jewish group by the vast majority of the Jews, a view justified by their rabbinical authorities, even if she required fully Jewish rites of conversion, it is unlikely that these same Jewish authorities would accept the power of such a deviant group to "make Jews."[32] The vast majority of Jews would most likely have looked upon these converts as still being gentiles. Thus the Church seemed to be faced with the option of either returning to Pharisaic Judaism, which would mean abandoning the messianic claims of and for Jesus, or moving herself out of the Jewish people politically and legally, even if not out of "Israel" as an eschatologically verified community *(verus Israel)*.

Jews began to deliberate about Christian normativeness in the Middle Ages, by which time the Church was an undeniably gentile community both by her own criteria and by the criteria of Judaism. There is a fundamental difference between a group of Jews lessening the number of the commandments of the Torah they consider binding on themselves and a group of gentiles adopting some of the commandments of the Torah as binding on themselves, especially those commandments of the Torah the Jewish tradition considers binding on both Jews and gentiles universally here and now.[33] Such a group of gentiles are moving away from zero normativeness upward as opposed to the earlier group of Jews who were seen as moving toward zero normativeness downward. The Jewish group is to be discouraged by Jews; the gentile group is to be encouraged by Jews. That is why Judaism could assign a valid status for gentile Christians for the opposite reason it could not do so for Jewish Christians. Jews who practice Christianity are for Jews apostates *(meshumadim)* just as Christians who practice Judaism are for Christians apostates. To employ a met-

---

32. See B. Yevamot 47a re Deut. 1:16. Cf. Acts 15:1-29.
33. See *Tosefta:* Sotah 8.6 re Deut. 27:3.

aphor, the difference between Jewish Christians and gentile Christians is like the difference between seeing a glass as half empty or half full. It depends on who is drinking from the glass. Is it someone who once had more and has now taken less, or is it someone who had less and has now taken more?[34]

At this point, though, there seems to be a fundamental asymmetry in the Jewish-Christian relationship. This asymmetry is of great normative significance. It concerns the political difference between Jewish law and Christian law in relation to one another, namely, that Judaism and Christianity cannot comprise a polity together without the unacceptable subordination of one community to the other. Jews and Christians cannot both comprise the people *Israel* in a cogent way. That is why, I think, the legal commonalities between Judaism and Christianity are best negotiated and developed in secular political space, where both Jews and Christians are struggling to survive in similar ways for similar reasons and neither could or would seize political power for itself. This is best seen by contrasting what has been in the past with what might have been.

From a Jewish perspective, the only way Christians could live in a Jewish polity — governed by Jewish law, that is — would be in sort of resident-alien status, a status held by one whom Scripture calls "the sojourner in the city" (Exod. 20:10) and whom the Rabbis called the *ger toshav*. In ancient Israel, these tolerated gentiles lived under Jewish rule with definite rights and responsibilities. By some type of formal acceptance, these persons confirmed a status of being both subjects and objects of a definite segment of Jewish law. However, there was no doubt at any time that they were a subordinate group of second-class citizens. In fact, a good case could be made that most of these tolerated gentiles eventually assimilated into the Jewish people altogether.[35] After all, if such assimilation is possible, whether by a transgenerational process or what later became an actual event of conversion *(gerut)*, it would seem that such persons would want to become full members of their host society, full members of some other society, or full members of their own society (as was the case with Jews themselves in proto-Zionist Jewish messianism). For many, no doubt, being a resident gentile alien among the Jewish people was a historical stopping point on the way to full Judaism. Jews themselves could well recognize the meaning of such a compromised status since they often had to

---

34. This is best expressed by the talmudic principle "One is to be raised *[ma'alin baqodesh]* not lowered in holiness" (B. Yoma 12b and 73a).

35. See Novak, *The Image of the Non-Jew in Judaism*, pp. 14ff.

make the same type of arrangements with the gentile societies that tolerated them. But such arrangements are the result of political necessity rather than being any sort of desideratum. Neither Jews nor Christians can cogently desire to be "sojourners" in each other's house, even if that is the best the other community can do for them in good faith.

This is the problem with Paul's famous metaphor of the Church as "the branch grafted onto the tree" (Rom. 11:17-24). The metaphor would be apt if Christians (gentile Christians, that is) simply regarded themselves as a group subordinate to the Jews because of their adoption of some of Jewish law, indeed, that segment of Jewish law that also pertains to the gentiles. But the fact is that Christians have regarded themselves as a community that has superseded the Jews.[36] And even if that supersessionism (consistent with Paul's refusal to give up on the Jews in his view of Israel) does not reject the Jews from being forever *part of* Israel, it still has to assert two things: one, the Jews are no longer solely identical with Israel; two, the Church does have the more authentic definition of Israel than Judaism has. The more radical Christian supersessionism has the Church replacing the Jewish people altogether in the covenant. The more conservative supersessionism sees the Jews as the original stubborn settlers of the polity, whom the newer settlers realize cannot be displaced without recognizing the probability that they too could suffer the same fate from even newer settlers feared to be massing just beyond the horizon. Nevertheless, to bring Paul's ancient agricultural metaphor up to date with a modern urban one: even if the suburbs of the new settlers do not displace the old inner city altogether, they certainly displace its normative centrality in the urban scheme of things.[37] Needless to say, though, no Jew who is loyal to Judaism could possibly accept such a subordinate role for Judaism in good faith. That is why there would be hardly any Jews at all who would look forward to any return of "Christendom" in any

36. For the most impressive contemporary attempt to present a non-supersessionist Christian theology, see Paul van Buren, *A Theology of the Jewish-Christian Reality,* vol. 1 (San Francisco: Harper & Row, 1987); and most recently, R. K. Soulen, *The God of Israel and Christian Theology* (Minneapolis: Fortress Press, 1996), and Scott Bader-Saye, *Church and Israel after Christendom: The Politics of Election* (Boulder, Colo.: Westview Press, 1999). However, I think as Christian theologians, van Buren, Soulen, and Bader-Saye only make a convincing case against the more radical type of Christian supersessionism. But that is all Jews can really ask Christians to do as Christians. It certainly makes a new form of dialogue possible from the Christian side.

37. See Wittgenstein, *Philosophical Investigations,* 2d ed., trans. G. E. M. Anscombe (New York: Macmillan, 1958), 1.18.

form whatsoever.[38] It also explains why Christians would have a problem living in any Jewish polity fully governed by Jewish law. Christians would have as hard a time with the political privileging of Judaism as Jews have had with the political privileging of Christianity.

Normative Commonalities

It is better to see the normative commonalities between Judaism and Christianity as a matter of significant overlappings than as related species in a single genus "Israel." That is because seeing Judaism and Christianity as species of a single genus would make the commonalities greater than the difference.[39] However, that would surely supply the rationale for the assimilation of the weaker species by the stronger species, a kind of theological "survival of the fittest." That would be done by the assertion, explicitly or even only implicitly, that the survival of the genus itself would be better served by the consolidation of the species themselves, which would mean the incorporation of the smaller into the larger. The fact that Judaism precedes Christianity and Christianity succeeds Judaism historically, and the fact that Christianity has been much more successful politically than Judaism, would give Christianity a decided edge in any sort of "genetic" process of mutual self-definition with its built-in temporal trajectory.

The logic of overlapping, on the other hand, provides a much more even playing field for the new encounter between Judaism and Christianity, which must always immediately involve a new normative relationship between Jews and Christians themselves.[40] That is because in this more dialectical interrelationship, there need not be prior agreement on first principles or agreement on final conclusions. The recognition of commonalities can lead to the subsequent enunciation of principles, although agreement on first principles a priori is beyond the grasp of human intelligence here and now. As for final conclusions, they are still only tentative insofar as they are still hidden behind an eschatological horizon. Only when we know the end will we thereby know the beginning. Law and com-

---

38. Cf. Oliver O'Donovan, *The Desire of the Nations: Rediscovering the Roots of Political Theology* (Cambridge: Cambridge University Press, 1996), pp. 224ff.

39. See Aristotle, *Categories*, 2b15-20.

40. For the political significance of a logic of "overlapping," see John Rawls, *Political Liberalism* (New York: Columbia University Press, 1993), pp. 35ff. Jews and Christians, of course, have overlappings on the deeper ethical level and the even deeper ontological level, which are far more important than what a secularist like Rawls could admit.

mandments are especially well suited to be the subject of this new relationship between Jews and Christians because they lie in between the foundations that are their source and the *telos* that is their final intention. The process of recognizing and developing commonalities takes two forms.

First, the recognition of normative commonalities is located in the broad area of ethics: the proper structure of human relationships. Here the common reliance on the Hebrew Bible, the *Tanakh* or the Old Testament, is most evident. It is not a matter of adjudicating cases of moral difficulty according to biblical law as much as it is a matter of discovering the underlying principles of the way Scripture judges human personhood and human community. This can be done when we return to the three most basic Noahide laws (or, better, normative categories): the prohibitions of idolatry, bloodshed, and sexual immorality.

Regarding idolatry, this means that Jews and Christians need to be especially sensitive to the manifestations of idolatry in our own time. While a universal ethics cannot prove the existence of God, much less constitute what the human relationship with God is to consist of, it must still argue against those modern ideologies of absolutized individuals or absolutized collectives which by definition make no room for any relationship with the Lord God creator of heaven and earth, be it by their explicit or implicit atheism. It is no accident that the most prominent of these ideologies, Communism and Fascism, have directed their particular attacks on Judaism or Christianity or both. It is also no accident that although it has not been the basis of atrocities, as has been the case with Communism and Fascism, doctrinaire liberal secularism has been almost as hostile to Judaism and Christianity, at least in principle. It is the ethical task of Jews and Christians together to see religious liberty as the most basic of all rights in a secular society, and to recognize that the denial or belittling of the human quest for God entails an assault on human dignity and destiny.

Regarding bloodshed, this means that Jews and Christians need to work together for the broadest possible definition of human personhood in order to include everyone genetically human within the prohibition of homicide. As long as there is some agreement about the uniqueness of human personhood, it will be hard to argue for any permission of homicide per se (except, of course, by those who see nothing unique in human personhood, labeling it "speciesism"). Because of that, those who have in fact advocated homicide have in principle had to preclude certain segments of humankind from the category of human personhood. That way, they have argued for what they consider the killing of less than human life. But for Judaism and Christianity, anyone descended from human parents, who is thereby descended from the original human couple, is made in the image of God and, hence, the object of special protection and care. Anything less than this definition of humanness/humankind is only based on some features of the human condition, arbitrarily selected by those humans having power over other humans. Ultimately, the criterion of selection turns out to be racism of one form or another. Jews and Christians must become the advocates and protectors of all those who could easily be precluded from human personhood when its essence is taken to be something less than the image of God.[41]

Regarding sexual immorality, this means that what Judaism and Christianity teach to be universally prohibited (incest, adultery, homosexuality, and bestiality) are all for the sake of the family as the core of authentic human community. All of the prohibited sexual acts contradict the claims of the heterosexually constituted family to be the exclusive arena for sexuality, with the purpose of the conception, birth, and rearing of children (including the lifelong identification of children with their parents' union, even when they themselves are adults). Jews and Christians need to be advocates of family life in the face of an unprecedented assault on sexual morality, one that sees sexuality as a private preference between consenting adults or a matter of natural determinism. Seeing sexuality as either private preference or natural determinism makes sexuality per se amoral: the former by denying it universality; the latter by denying it freedom of choice.[42] It is no accident that, for Jews, Jewish identity is primarily familial; and it is no accident that, for Christians, Jesus was raised in a traditional family.[43] This indicates how familial identity lies at the core of our religious identities as Jews and as Christians.

Finally, the recognition of commonalities in some ways must be more analogous than identical. These analogies are more in the area of cult and ritual, what the Jewish tradition calls the area "between humans and God," that is, those acts like prayer and worship which have God as their direct object. Here Jews and Christians cannot develop a common life together without sliding into capitulation of one side to the other or into

41. See Novak, *Natural Law in Judaism*, pp. 164ff.

42. See David Novak, "Religious Communities, Secular Society, and Sexuality: One Jewish Opinion," in *Sexual Orientation and Human Rights in American Religious Discourse*, ed. S. M. Olyan and M. C. Nussbaum (New York: Oxford University Press, 1998), pp. 17ff.

43. See Matt. 1:1-25; Luke 1:5-2:21. For a very different Christian view of sexuality and family by a learned and insightful theologian, see Eugene F. Rogers Jr., *Sexuality and the Christian Body: Their Way into the Triune God* (Oxford: Blackwell Publishers, 1999).

syncretism. Nevertheless, we Jews and Christians can still learn a great deal from each other's "religious" beliefs and practices. That goes far beyond the discovery of "interesting" similarities and differences between Judaism and Christianity, something that could be the case between any two religions or philosophies. Instead, we can learn much from each other, even up to the point of empathy, because our religious ways of life are both developments of God's covenant with Israel. Worshiping the same God as we do, and reading the same Book *(biblos)* as we do, it is inevitable that our religious ways of life are often parallel. Indeed, throughout our historical interaction, Christians have learned significant things from Jewish piety, and Jews have learned significant things from Christian piety. That is because we have been commanded by the same God. Thus it is the centrality of the *mitsvah* to us both that offers the greatest content and the greatest hope for our relationship in this world and the next.

Law and Eschatology:
A Jewish-Christian Intersection

The Doctrinal Dialectic between Judaism and Christianity

One can look at the differences between Judaism and Christianity as being centered on the quintessential question: What is the most correct way to be in faith with the Lord God of Israel? Two more specific questions within this largest question have been over the role of law and the role of eschatology in the life of faith, especially how the two are interrelated. It is usually assumed that Christian notions of law and eschatology have been formulated out of earlier Jewish notions, and that these notions have been subsequently developed in contradistinction to the views of those Jews who refused to see these Christian notions as a legitimate development of traditional Jewish doctrine. Many Christians have assumed that Christianity moved forward while Judaism remained in the past. This, of course, has been the basic assumption of Christian supersessionism. Many Jews have responded to this type of supersessionism by arguing that what Christians consider to be the upward development of Jewish doctrine, Jews consider to be a deviation away from the purity of that doctrine. In other words, they have accepted the notion of the timeless quality of Judaism, only differing from the Christian conclusion from it. So, along these lines one could ask: Is Judaism proto-Christianity or is Christianity quasi-Judaism? Are those Jews, indeed most of the Jews, who have continually refused to become Christians, fixated in past tradition or faithful to its source?

This essay previously appeared in *The Last Things: Biblical and Theological Perspectives on Eschatology*, ed. Carl E. Braaten and Robert W. Jenson (Grand Rapids: Eerdmans, 2002), pp. 90-112.

Another assumption of this kind of historiography of doctrine is that Christianity has developed out of Judaism and then beyond Judaism, whereas Judaism developed only up to the point of the Christian schism, and then remained frozen in time, as it were, purposefully oblivious to everything that has happened in the world, especially the Christian world after that time. The thesis of this paper, though, is that this represents a large misunderstanding of Judaism and, probably, of Christianity as well, by both Christians and Jews. Here I shall try to show that Jewish doctrine, especially on the issue of law and eschatology, has undergone considerable development over the course of history after the Christian schism. Moreover, I shall try to show that some of the development of Jewish doctrine has not been *apart from* but *because of* the claims of Christian doctrine. That is, the doctrinal intersection of Judaism and Christianity has not been a once-and-for-all matter but, rather, something that began in Christianity's self-differentiation from Judaism and continued in Judaism's self-differentiation from Christianity. One can see this ongoing intersection as dialectical: a constant back and forth, forth and back. Indeed, one can see this process of mutual self-differentiation as continual from the beginnings of Christianity until the present day. It is obvious that Christianity would not be what it is without this process of intersection with Judaism. It has been less obvious, though, that Judaism has had to continually distinguish itself from Christianity, and that this process has had a profound effect on the inner development of Jewish doctrine itself. Nowhere has this been more evident than on the issue of law and eschatology.

Christianity emerged out of a Jewish milieu that was obsessed with eschatology. The condition of the Jewish people under alien Roman rule made hope for a radically transformed future a central issue for Jews. It was, to borrow a term from Spinoza, *the* theologico-political question. This hope for such a future (generally called *l'atid la-vo*) had three interrelated components: the hope for the days of the Messiah *(yemot ha-mashiah)*, the hope for the resurrection of the dead *(tehiyyat ha-metim)*, and the hope for the coming-world *(olam ha-ba)*. Although in medieval Jewish theology there was considerable speculation about how these three components designated three different times or three different realms, it seems that at least in the period of the first century C.E. there was no such differentiation. They were seen as three aspects of one realm. Indeed, one could say that the "coming-world" emphasizes the temporal nature of the End Time: it is a time yet future, not an eternal realm already existent into which the present time is finally included.[1] The resurrection of the dead emphasizes the personal nature of the End Time: it is a time when persons, who in biblical anthropology could not be conceived other than embodied, are fully restored to the coming-world.[2] The days of the Messiah emphasize the political nature of the End Time: it is a time when a polity, with a king at its head, will be the collective form of the coming-world.[3] That is why God's reign is over a collective entity; it is God's kingship and kingdom *(malkhut shamayim)*.[4]

It appears that in this period Pharisaic Jews (out of whose Judaism subsequently came both Christianity and Rabbinic Judaism) believed that when the Messiah comes, he will either be resurrected or resurrect the dead himself in order for the living and the dead to live forever in communion with God their king.[5] On this score, both the books of the New Testament (the earlier literary works) and the Rabbinic Writings (the later literary works) seem to be in accord. The question became, therefore: What is the Messiah to do with the law under whose rule the Jewish people had been living since time immemorial?

Since the New Testament is the earlier text, it seems best to look at some key passages there in order to see, along general lines, just how Christian eschatology dealt with the question of the law. We should then try to discover in some rabbinic texts what seem to be the Jewish doctrines out of which these Christian doctrines emerged. Afterwards, we should look at how it seems these same Jewish doctrines were modified and developed in response to what appeared to Jews to have been Christian dis-

---

1. Under the influence of Platonism, there were medieval attempts to view *olam ha-ba* as the eternal realm, unchanged and unchanging, without an end or a beginning. Its temporality is, therefore, only subjective, viz., the time of the death of the justified person, *when* he or she enters that realm. Maimonides was the most important advocate of this view (see *Mishneh Torah:* Repentance, 8.8). But the earlier rabbinic view of *olam ha-ba* itself being temporal, with a finite beginning at the end of history ("this world," *olam ha-zeh*) and an infinite extension into the future, was always maintained by many post-rabbinic theologians. See David Novak, *The Theology of Nahmanides Systematically Presented* (Atlanta: Scholars Press, 1992), pp. 129-30.

2. I know of no better conceptual representation of this theological anthropology than that of Reinhold Niebuhr, *The Nature and Destiny of Man,* vol. 2 (New York: Charles Scribner's Sons, 1964), pp. 295-97.

3. See *Babylonian Talmud* (hereafter "B."): Berakhot 34b re Deut. 15:11.

4. See, e.g., *Midrash Rabbah:* Genesis, 98.13 re Gen. 49:18. For the use of *shamayim* (lit. "heaven") as a synonym for God, see A. Marmorstein, *The Old Rabbinic Doctrine of God* (New York: KTAV, 1968), pp. 105-7.

5. See Solomon Schechter, *Some Aspects of Rabbinic Theology* (New York: Macmillan, 1909), pp. 97-115.

tortions of them. Finally, I shall speculate a bit about what this intersection with Christianity means for Jewish theology today.

The Fulfillment of the Law

In the New Testament the relation of law and eschatology first appears in the Sermon on the Mount. There Jesus says:

> Do not suppose that I have come to eliminate [*katalusai*] the Law and the Prophets. I have not come to eliminate them but to fulfill them [*plērōsai*]. . . . not even one little letter or one superscription shall pass away from the Law until everything has come to be [*panta genētai*]. Whoever would leave off even one of the least [*elachiston*] of these commandments . . . he is least likely [*elachistos*] to be called into the kingdom of God [*basileia tōn ouranōn*]. . . . I say to you that unless your righteousness [*dikaiosynē*] is greater than that of the Scribes and Pharisees, you will not come into the kingdom of God. (Matt. 5:17-20)

A Jew at the time of Jesus could have very well heard this text to mean the following: The kingdom of God will only come when the righteousness *(tsedaqah)* of the people is sufficient for God to fully complete his rule over Israel, which is when "everything has come to be." That righteousness is the complete response of the Jewish people to God's commandments *(mitsvot)* revealed in the Torah. The Scribes and the Pharisees seem to be those who are most punctilious in their observance of the Torah.[6] But Jesus has come to set an example of greater Torah observance than that of those heretofore recognized as the epitome of piety. Only those who follow Jesus and emulate his piety will be worthy of entrance to the coming kingdom of God. They alone will constitute the "saved remnant of Israel" *(she'erit yisrael)*.[7] "Fulfillment" here would mean complete personal observance. But what is not yet clear is whether the observance of the commandments is to be completed in this world now in order to attain the kingdom of God as its due reward, or whether the observance of the commandments will continue in the kingdom of God when and only when full observance will be possible. As we shall see, this has always been a disputed issue in Jewish eschatology.

6. See E. P. Sanders, *Jesus and Judaism* (London: SCM Press, 1985), pp. 245-69.
7. See B. Yoma 38b re 1 Sam. 2:8.

From what follows later in the Gospel of Matthew, it seems that the observance of the commandments of the Torah is a preparation for the kingdom of God, but when that kingdom is considered to have arrived, the time of the commandments will thereby have passed. The kingdom of God will have arrived when the Messiah makes himself known to Israel. Thus when Pharisees see disciples of Jesus gleaning grain on the Sabbath, and complain to Jesus about this obvious violation of the Sabbath prohibition of work, Jesus adopts two strategies in answering their objection: one strictly legal and the other more eschatological (Matt. 12:1-8). On the legal level, he makes the argument that the disciples were starving and, therefore, the preservation of human life takes precedence over the observance of the Sabbath. Since the time when the Maccabees agreed that not to fight the enemies of Israel on the Sabbath would lead to the wholesale destruction of all those who keep the commandments of God, it became common Jewish (especially pharisaic) teaching that this mandated dispensation applies even to individual Jews in mortal danger, be that danger from human malice or from natural disaster.[8] Human life takes precedence over the prohibition of work on the Sabbath. Jesus surely knew what he was saying and to whom he was saying it. Nevertheless, all of this is simply hypothetical in the light of the categorical conclusion of this whole episode. There Jesus says, "This is because [*gar*] the Son of Man is lord [*kyrios*] of the Sabbath" (Matt. 12:8). In other words, the Messiah has the authority from God to dispense Jews from the observance of any of the commandments. That seems to be an essential privilege of his messiahhood.

From the above answer, one could conclude that this simply means the Messiah *eo ipso* has the authority to dispense some Jews from the observance of the Sabbath ad hoc, not that the Messiah has declared the time of the observance of the Sabbath per se to be over forever. His authority could thus be like the authority the Rabbis later ascribed to a true prophet, namely, he (or she) could dispense people from ordinary rules by virtue of his or her generally accepted status as a prophet. This is unlike an ordinary Rabbi, who would have to give a specific legal justification for any such dispensation.[9] A Rabbi must speak *ad rem;* a prophet can speak *in personam.* Accordingly, could one see the development of Jesus' argu-

8. See 1 Macc. 2:32-42; Josephus, *Contra Apionem,* 2.2 and *Antiquities,* 12.6; also, B. Yoma 85b and parallels. Cf. Mark 2:27 and Luke 6:1-5.

9. See B. Yevamot 90b re Deut. 18:15. Nevertheless, later rabbinic interpretation limited prophetic authority to making ad hoc dispensations from the law (see B. Megillah and parallels re Lev. 27:34). Hence a Sage who interprets God's *perpetual* law could be seen as greater than a prophet (see B. Baba Batra 12b re Ps. 90:12).

ment with the Pharisees moving from the interpretive authority of a Rabbi to the more personal authority of a prophet? Thus, when Jesus begins his argument with the Pharisees over the permissibility or non-permissibility of what the disciples did on *that* Sabbath, he argues with them on their ground, namely, the common assumption that danger to a life requires violation of the Sabbath when that is the only way to save *that* life. His argument up to that point is one that any Rabbi could make with any other Rabbi. However, the question to ask is whether Jesus' messianic authority is something more than the authority of a prophet. Is his personal authority to dispense people from observance of any of the commandments more than just ad hoc?

The pivotal point in the dispute, however, is when Jesus points out how the service of the Temple itself takes precedence over the observance of the Sabbath. Thus the prohibition of lighting a fire on the Sabbath only applies outside the Temple, "in all your dwellings [*moshvoteikehm*]" (Exod. 35:3); but in the Temple itself "the burnt offering of the Sabbath [*olat shabbat*] is offered on each Sabbath [*be-shabbatto*]" (Num. 28:10).[10] After making this point Jesus says, "I say to you that this place [*hōde*] is greater than the Temple. But if you had known what this means, 'kindness not sacrifice do I desire' [Hosea 6:6], you would not have condemned the innocent [*anaitous*]" (Matt. 12:6-7). Of course, one can interpret Jesus' intention here to be that one should judge by standards less stringent than those of the strict law. This would be like a prophet offering an ad hoc dispensation, this time retroactively, which is one way of looking at divine forgiveness and atonement of sins. But if this were so, why would it have been preceded by Jesus' very legal argument just before? Accordingly, it might be more accurate to say that his argument here is that a higher form of sanctity takes precedence over a lower form of sanctity and thereby dispenses one from the obligations of that lower form of sanctity.[11] The grace or "kindness" of God is that higher form of sanctity, namely, the response to the authority of the Messiah himself. It is much more than the human tendency to bend the strictness of the law in extenuating circumstances. It is thus much more than the authority of any Rabbi, even more than the authority of any prophet.

In the case of the Temple, that lower form of sanctity is everywhere outside the Temple precincts.[12] The difference is spatial. But in the case of

---

10. See B. Shabbat 20a re Exod. 35:3.

11. See, e.g., *Mishnah* (herafter "M."): Berakhot 3.1.

12. See, e.g., M. Rosh Hashanah 4.1.

the Messiah, whose time has now come, the difference is temporal. Before the messianic time the commandments were in full force; during the messianic time, which is seen as being now *ad aeternum,* the time of the commandments is over. Keeping the commandments has fulfilled its task in this world, up until the coming-world. Thus the word usually translated as "this place" *(hōde)* can be just as easily translated as "this time" (namely, *kairos*).[13] It is the "when" of the Messiah that now determines the "where" of his rule. Sacred space is no longer confined to the Temple; it is to be extended everywhere. As the end of the Gospel of Matthew indicates, that new "where" is the space-time to be extended "even to the farthest end [*synteleias*] of the world [*aiōnos*]" (Matt. 28:20).

So far we have seen what seems to be a temporal thrust to the New Testament's view of the relation of the law and the End Time. The law is in full force until the End Time arrives in the person of the Messiah. From that time on the Messiah is the norm and it is his life (and death) that is to be emulated by the faithful. However, one does not emulate Jesus' observance of the specific commandments of the Torah; instead, one emulates Jesus' love of God by accepting Jesus himself as the Christ. At this level, Jesus has "fulfilled" the law finally. Nevertheless, it is still unclear what the essential connection between the law and the End Time really is. When the author of the Gospel of Matthew uses the term "fulfill" *(plerōsai)* to describe the law as perfectly observed by Jesus, he is still speaking of Jesus' motivation in that observance, not what the law itself is, that is, what its function is in the salvific order of God. Enter Paul.

In speaking of the relation of the law and the eschaton, Paul introduces a different term. He says "For Christ is the end [*telos*] of the law, leading all who have faith into righteousness [*eis dikaiosynēn*]" (Rom. 10:4). *Telos* is a term that already had a long history in Greek thought. It was taken to mean either the temporal end of all things, that which they inevitably become at the conclusion of their days *after* they have departed the world, or it was taken to mean the purpose of human activity *within* the world itself.[14] It seems that Paul understands *telos* in both the temporal and the purposeful senses; indeed, he seems to combine them both into one meaning: the purpose of the observance of the commandments of the Torah *has been* to bring those observers to salvation at the End Time. Salvation is being saved from

13. See *Theological Dictionary of the New Testament,* ed. G. Kittel, trans. G. W. Bromiley (Grand Rapids: Eerdmans, 1965), vol. 3, pp. 459-62.

14. See Aeschylus, *Agamemnon,* 928; Sophocles, *Oedipus Rex,* 1527-1530; Herodotus, *Persian Wars,* 1.32; Aristotle, *Physics,* 194a30 and *Nicomachean Ethics,* 1100a10-35.

the evils of this world, primarily death, which came into the world because of human sin since the first humans. However, the commandments themselves, according to Paul, could not bring about that salvation because the sinfulness of human nature since the Fall prevents anyone and everyone from the *full* observance of the Torah.[15] (Only Jesus, who was not infected with the sinfulness of human nature, could accomplish that.)

The failure of observance of the Law can only be known after Jesus the Christ has appeared as the righteousness of God, faith in *whom* having been the true *telos*, the true intentionality of the Law all along. The commandments, then, function as a kind of *via negativa*, clearing the way, as it were, for faith's original and everlasting object. Thus Paul praises the Jews for their general purposefulness in trying to keep God's law, while at the same time indicating that they didn't really know the precise object of that trying. "They have a zeal for God [*zēlon theou*], but not because of what they know [*ou kata epignōsin*]" (Rom. 10:2). Then, at this point, Paul uses the term "righteousness" as a *double entendre*, meaning one thing in God's case, another in the case of humans. "They try [*zētousin*] to set up their righteousness [*idian dikaiosynē*], but they do not submit themselves to the righteousness of God" (10:3). Now *dikaiosynē* is the Septuagint's rendition of the Hebrew *tsedaqah*.[16] *Tsedaqah* primarily means what God does graciously for humans. Secondarily, it means the human response to God's grace.[17] Often that response is an act of *imitatio Dei*.[18] So, Paul's *double entendre* in Greek is an insightful exegesis of the correct sense of the original Hebrew term in Scripture. Up until the coming of Christ, the faithful response to the righteousness of God had been the attempt to keep the commandments of the Torah. But with the full revelation of the righteousness of God in the person of Christ, keeping these commandments as salvific is a rejection of the righteousness of God. It is a claim to achieve salvation by the recipients themselves instead of being a response to the source of salvation itself. "When you have faith in your heart that God has raised him [Christ] from the dead, you shall be saved [*sōthēsthē*]" (10:9). Before Christ, the teleology of the Law had been positive; after Christ it is now (and forever) negative, retroactively, that is.[19]

15. See Rom. 8:1-4.

16. See, e.g., LXX on Gen. 18:19; Zech. 8:8.

17. See David Novak, *The Election of Israel: The Idea of the Chosen People* (Cambridge: Cambridge University Press, 1995), pp. 125-38.

18. See B. Shabbat 133b re Exod. 15:2 (the opinion of Abba Saul).

19. For a most comprehensive treatment of Paul's complex relationship with the Law, see E. P. Sanders, *Paul and Palestinian Judaism* (Philadelphia: Fortress Press, 1977), pp. 474-511.

One final point must be made in concluding this brief representation of New Testament teaching about the relation of law and eschatology, and that is to better decide just what Paul means by "the Law" *(ho nomos)*. Does it mean the whole Torah, all the commandments given through Moses and the prophets? Or, does it mean only part of the Torah? If the latter, then we must determine which commandments have been superseded by the coming of Christ and which remain intact. This has been a constant problem for Christian exegesis. On the one hand, it has had to maintain some connection to Jewish law in order to ward off the threat of Marcionism, for the logical conclusion of Marcionism's rejection of the Jewish people and Jewish revelation (and its law) was the rejection of the Lord God of Israel whom Jesus called his father. But Paul himself never severed his ties to either the Torah or to the Jewish people, and he would have certainly been opposed to any Christian doing that.[20] On the other hand, Christian exegesis cannot interpret the New Testament in a way so Jewish that Christianity is seen as nothing more than an offbeat Jewish sect. Traditionally, this latter threat has been known as "judaization."[21] So, in contrast to Marcionism, Christian exegesis of the New Testament, especially the Pauline epistles, has had to affirm some Jewish law as opposed to none; and in contrast to the judaizers, it has had to affirm some Jewish law as opposed to most or all of Jewish law.

What emerges from the Pauline epistles, especially Romans, is that Paul affirms those aspects of Jewish law that are universal in scope. That means the prohibition of idolatry and all that it entails. And it means the virtually intact retention of Jewish moral law in its broad outlines. What distinguishes the Jewish law still to be kept from the Jewish law now taken as superseded is that the former is universal; the latter, by contrast, is what has been legislated based on the unique past experience of the Jewish people. Furthermore, what is universal in scope is that which is known to all humans even before any specific historical revelation. Thus Paul condemns the unrighteousness *(asebeia)* of the gentiles "because [*dioti*] that which is known of God is evident [*phaneron*] to them since [*gar*] God has made it evident to them, since what is invisible becomes evidently known [*nooumena*] from what has been created" (Rom. 1:18-19). In the next chapter, Paul speaks of the gentiles "who have not law but do by nature [*physei*] what the law contains . . . being a law unto themselves [*heautois eisi*

---

20. See Rom. 9-11.

21. See Robert L. Wilken, *Chrysostom and the Jews* (Berkeley: University of California Press, 1983), pp. 66-94, 116-23.

nomos] . . . they bear witness through their conscience [*tēs syneidēseōs*] . . . the law written in their hearts" (2:14-15). It is clear why all Christian natural law proponents have referred to these words of Paul as their prime theological source.[22]

The difference between law retained and law superseded is that law retained pertains to present human nature, whereas law superseded pertains to past Jewish history. The coming of the kingdom of God, which Paul (and all Christians) see as being ushered in by the coming of Christ, introduces a posthistorical time into the world, which is the realm of eternity. The events of the life and death of Christ will be what are now celebrated because of this radical conclusion of all previous history. Nonetheless, it does not introduce a time when acts like murder, fornication, and deceit will now be permitted. That is because human nature still endures, and its redemption can hardly be seen as leading to a moral devolution. Redemption is meant to cleanse human nature of sin, not permit sins against human nature heretofore prohibited by the law, both Jewish and natural. Paul is anything but an antinomian. That is something the Reformers like Luther and Calvin were quick to emphasize when their Pauline-based revolt against the law of the Catholic Church was interpreted by some more radical than themselves to be a revolt against law per se in the name of God.[23]

The Question of the Repeal of the Commandments

In the century or so after the death of Jesus, especially after the destruction of the Second Temple in 70 C.E., Pharisaic Judaism, which is now better named Rabbinic Judaism, was in a process of profound reformulation and reevaluation. Both the loss of the central institution of Jewish national-religious life and the rise of a community that seemed to be deviating more and more from Judaism and the Jewish people called for a critical reexamination of much of the tradition. This was especially the case with eschatology, the issue over which the Christian community was beginning to declare its independence from Judaism. One sees this process of reexamination in the following rabbinic dispute from the second century of the Common Era:

22. See Thomas Aquinas, *Summa Theologiae*, 2/1, q. 91, a. 2.

23. See Paul Althaus, *The Ethics of Luther,* trans. R. C. Schultz (Philadelphia: Fortress Press, 1972), pp. 25-42; John Calvin, *Institutes of the Christian Religion,* 2.7.13-15.

Ben Zoma expounded the verse "that you remember the day you went out from Egypt all the days of your life" (Deuteronomy 16:3): "the days of your life" refer to daytime; "all [kol] the days of your life" refer to nighttime. But the Sages say that "the days of your life" refer to this world; "all the days of your life" refer to the days of the Messiah. Ben Zoma said to them, is the exodus from Egypt to be remembered during the days of the Messiah? Is it not stated, "Behold days are coming, says the Lord, when it will no longer be said 'as the Lord lives who raised the children of Israel out of the land of Egypt,' but 'as the Lord lives who brought the stock of the House of Israel from the land of the North'" (Jeremiah 23:7)? They said to him that mention of the exodus from Egypt will not be extirpated from its place [in the liturgy], but the exodus from Egypt will be supplemental to mention of the [redemption from the rule of the foreign] kingdoms [malkhiyot]. Mention of the foreign kingdoms will be primary [iqqar] and mention of the exodus from Egypt will be secondary [tafel].[24]

There are two basic contexts of this dispute. Both concern mention of the exodus from Egypt, which plays a central role in all Jewish liturgy. Indeed, remembrance of the exodus from Egypt is the uniquely Jewish reason given in the Torah for many of the commandments one today would call "cultic" or "ritual." The first context is a discussion of whether or not mention of the exodus must be a regular part of evening worship. Ben Zoma opts for mention of the exodus being part of evening worship now in contrast to the coming-world when it will be redundant. The second context is in the Passover table service (seder), the question being whether there will be a Passover celebration when the Messiah comes.[25]

Ben Zoma's total elimination of the obligation to mention the exodus from Egypt in the days of the Messiah is clearly the more radical option. However, it is also the one that seems closer to the post-exilic eschatology found in Scripture. There the messianic texts mention a radically changed world, one where the ties to past salvific events will be overcome. Thus Deutero-Isaiah speaks of "the new heaven and the new earth to stand before Me" (Isa. 66:22). Jeremiah speaks of the time when God will make a covenant "not like the covenant I made with your ancestors when I had to force them to be taken out from Egypt" (Jer. 31:31). Ezekiel speaks of the time when God "will open your graves and raise you up from your graves"

24. Tosefta: Berakhot 1.10.

25. See M. M. Kasher, Israel Passover Haggadah (New York: Shengold Publishers, 1964), pp. 54-57.

(Ezek. 37:12). From all of these texts and more one sees that God's fulfillment of the covenant with Israel will so radically alter the world that the normal preconditions for the observance of the commandments of the Torah will be largely gone forever.

The earlier eschatological view is also seen in this rabbinic text. "Rabbi Abba bar Kahana said that God said 'a Torah will go forth from Me' (Isa. 51:4), namely, a new Torah [*hiddush torah*] will go forth from Me. Rabbi Berakhyah said in the name of Rabbi Isaac that God will [*atid*] be making a banquet [*ariston*] for His righteous servants in the coming-future [*l'atid la-vo*], where all who did not eat proscribed foods [*nevelot u-trefot*] in His world [*olam ha-zeh*] will be privileged [*zokheh*] to eat them in the coming-world."[26] From the standpoint of this strand of rabbinic theology, there would be no dispute with the New Testament about the "Son of Man is the lord of the Sabbath." These Rabbis would also agree that the law is overcome in the messianic future. And, obviously, the law to be overcome is the kind of law of which the Jewish dietary restrictions are the prime example. It is the law that has heretofore characterized the uniqueness of the Jewish people. Nevertheless, surely no one would have said that those who did not commit adultery in this world will have their pick of sexual partners in the next world, or that those who did not commit murder in this world will have their pick of victims in the next world.

It is quite clear from these and other similar texts that the coming-world will be based on a future experience so transforming that the very historical identity of the people of Israel will be radically altered, including all those rituals based on past, partially salvific, experiences. The House of Israel will remain because of God's everlasting covenant with her, but her characterizing acts will be fundamentally different. The new manifestation of this covenant in the coming-future will have the effect of attracting many gentiles to join the Jewish people, and that itself might explain why a new Torah will be needed for this radically transformed time.[27] But, surely, a promise that there will be no moral law in the End Time could hardly be an attraction to the same God who gave the Ten Commandments.[28] So, these Rabbis would no doubt agree with Paul that

26. *Midrash Rabbah:* Leviticus, 13.3.

27. See Isa. 2:1-4; 56:6-7.

28. For rabbinic recognition that the Christians (whom they called *minim*, "sectarians") regarded the Ten Commandments as the basic content of the Mosaic Torah to remain authoritative forever, see *Palestinian Talmud:* Berakhot 1.8/3c. For subsequent Christian emphasis of the unique normative status of the Ten Commandments, see Aquinas, *Summa Theologiae*, 2/1, q. 100, aa. 3, 8; Calvin, *Institutes*, 2.8.1.

the messianic time will elevate, not debase human nature, hence the basic law governing interhuman relations will remain intact, both for Jews and for gentiles.[29]

At this level, the debate, indeed the only essential debate, is whether or not Jesus of Nazareth is the promised Messiah of the House of Israel. The Christians say yes; the Jews say no. That difference alone has been more than sufficient to keep Jews and Christians in two separate, indeed competing, communities since the first century. Nevertheless, this difference spawned some corollaries in the history of the Jewish-Christian relationship.

The Transformation of Jewish Eschatology

It seems almost inevitable, though, that with the increasing division between the Jewish community and the new Christian community, the difference over the messiahhood of Jesus of Nazareth would not only be a matter of *who* the Messiah is but it would also become a matter of *what* the Messiah is to do and *why* he is to do it. The original dispute was over whether Jesus of Nazareth was the Messiah or not. One can assume that the older pharisaic position, for the most part, was that the commandments of the Torah will have already performed their propaedeutic function by the time the Messiah ushers in the kingdom of God. However, with the whole negative critique of the law by Paul, who asserted that the main function of the law is to show us how sinful we are rather than positively foreshadowing the kingdom of God, it seems that Jewish thought reasserted the value of the law in response. Any reassertion of a doctrine in the present is always more emphatic than the original assertion in the past.

If one can see the view of the Sages in contrast with that of Ben Zoma as at least a partial reaction against Christian eschatology, then one might reconstruct its logic as follows: We not only say that Jesus of Nazareth was not the Messiah because he did not remove Roman domination over us, but we also say that the very abrogation of the law made in his name also shows us that he was not the Messiah. We assert that the law will be in full force in the kingdom of God. In fact, we see the prime purpose of the kingdom of God to be to enable us to fully observe the commandments.

---

29. The parallel to this in Rabbinic Judaism is that one who converts to the Jewish covenant (and who is "born again," cf. John 3:4-6) is in no way dispensed from moral obligations that Jewish law recognizes as binding on all humans. See B. Yevamot 22a; B. Sanhedrin 59a.

Jesus' assertion that he came to fulfill the law for us instead of enforcing the law for us is a sure sign that he was not the Messiah. A true Messiah would have done the exact opposite. Thus, for example, the Rabbis had to admit that the Jewish revolutionary, Bar Kokhba (ca. 135 C.E.), was not the Messiah because he too failed to remove Roman domination over the Jewish people. Nevertheless, he could have hardly declared the authority of the law to be now past and have, nonetheless, won the support of the leading Sage of his time, Rabbi Akibah ben Joseph, a man who died as a martyr for teaching the law in public.[30] Rabbi Akibah's belief that Bar Kokhba was the Messiah turned out to be a bad political judgment.[31] Yet it was not theologically unsound inasmuch as Bar Kokhba would have no doubt administered the full range of the commandments of the Torah had he been able to assume real messianic power. The most charitable view of Jesus of Nazareth, therefore, would be that he was one more would-be Messiah who failed. The true Messiah, then, would still have to be the object of hope, not memory.

The debate between Ben Zoma and the Sages is essentially over the question of whether or not "the commandments are to be nullified in the coming-future" *(mitsvot betelot l'atid la-vo)*. The following rabbinic text reflects this debate in a new way:

> A garment in which there was detected threads of wool and linen [*kla'yim*] . . . one may make from it a shroud for a corpse. Rav Joseph said that this means that the commandments are nullified in the coming-future. . . . Rabbi Yohanan said that one may do so, and this follows Rabbi Yohanan's view concerning the verse "the dead are free" [*ba-metim hofshi* — Psalm 88:6], which means that a person is free from the commandments [*hofshi min ha-mitsvot*] when he dies.[32]

This text begins with the question of whether the scriptural commandment not to wear a garment in which wool and linen are mixed (*shatnez* — Deut. 22:11) applies to the shrouding of a corpse. Firmly believing in the resurrection of the dead, Rav Joseph infers that if this is permitted, and if corpses are to be resurrected in the clothing in which they were when buried, then the wearing of a forbidden garment could not be a problem at the time of the resurrection.[33] In other words, he gives a theological reason for

---

30. See B. Berakhot 61a-b.
31. See *Palestinian Talmud:* Taaniyot 4.5/68d.
32. B. Niddah 61b.
33. See B. Berakhot 18a. Cf. Berakhot 17a re Exod. 24:11; also, Matt. 22:23-32.

a practical legal ruling. However, the earlier view of Rabbi Yohanan seems to come to the same practical conclusion, but for a different reason. He seems to avoid the theological question of the resurrection altogether and simply assumes that the clothing of corpses is not the same as the clothing of the living.

Whereas Rav Joseph was a Babylonian Sage of the late third and early fourth centuries, Rabbi Yohanan bar Napaha was a Palestinian Sage of the third century. The difference in time and place is very important to bear in mind. Whereas Rav Joseph was a Sage in a time and place where very few Christians were found and where Christianity was not confronting Judaism in any direct way, Rabbi Yohanan (a contemporary of Origen and possibly someone who had disputed with him) was a Sage in a time and place (Tiberius) when Christianity was in major conflict with Judaism. This comes out in the following text on our question of the relation of law and eschatology: "Rabbi Yohanan said that although the Prophets and Hagiographa will be nullified in the [messianic] future, the five books of the [Written] Torah will not be nullified. What is his scriptural support? 'a great voice unending' (Deuteronomy 5:19)."[34] His colleague and brother-in-law, Rabbi Simon ben Laqish, went further and is reported in this same text to have included the book of Esther and the oral traditions (halakhot) in what will remain in force when the Messiah comes. It is doubtful whether Rav Joseph was even aware of the theological basis of Rabbi Yohanan's view since the above text from the Palestinian Talmud or anything like it is not even mentioned in the discussion of shrouds in the Babylonian Talmud.

The reason for the willingness to see no further need for the Prophets and Hagiographa is that their main function is taken to be the enunciation of messianic prophecy. As Rabbi Yohanan is also reported to have said, "all the prophets only prophesied about the days of the Messiah."[35] But, whereas the days of the Messiah will make prophecy's role passé, it will not have this effect on the commandments of the Torah. They are taken to be perpetually binding even — especially — when the Messiah will come. Because of his time and place, it is quite likely that anti-Christian polemic was an important part of Rabbi Yohanan's theological reflections.

---

34. *Palestinian Talmud:* Megillah 1.5/70d.
35. B. Berakhot 34b re Isa. 64:3.

Law and Faith

Rabbi Yohanan's further emphasis on the authority of the law, in both pre- and post-messianic time, is in full accord with the continual rabbinic emphasis on the sanctity of the Torah and the power of the commandments of the Torah to make the Jews who keep them the intimates of God here and now. Later on, in the face of the efforts of the much more politically powerful Christian community to proselytize the Jews in the Middle Ages, some Jewish scholars who were very familiar with Christian texts argued that there is no opposition between faith and the law but, rather, that the commandments themselves are faith-acts.[36] Therefore, anyone who denies the perpetual authority of the law is without true faith. One such scholar was Rabbi Moses ben Nahman of Gerona, subsequently known as Nahmanides, the leading Jewish jurist and theologian in Christian Spain in the thirteenth century. In fact, he was the leading Jewish spokesman in the most famous of the public disputations, commanded by royalty, that pitted Dominican theologians against Jewish theologians to prove — or try to prove — which faith is the true faith. This disputation took place in Barcelona in July of 1263.[37] Over and above the record of this disputation, it is clear from all his writing that Nahmanides knew Christian sources very well. This enabled him to defend Judaism in a most learned way, one showing great insight into the Christian basis for opposition to Judaism.

We see this great insight in Nahmanides' interpretation in his Torah Commentary (his central theological work) of the verse, "cursed is one who does not uphold the words of this Torah to do them" (Deut. 27:26). He writes:

> In my opinion this acceptance means that one acknowledges [the commandments] in his heart and that they are true in his eyes. . . . But if he denies any one of them or they are in his eyes nullified forever [*betelah l'olam*], he is surely cursed. Yet that is not so if he only transgresses one of them . . . for the verse did not say, "cursed is the one who does not do [*lo ya'aseh*] the words of this Torah"; it says "who does not uphold [*lo yaqim*] the words of this Torah."[38]

---

36. See E. E. Urbach, *The Sages,* vol. 1, trans. I. Abrahams (Jerusalem: Magnes Press, 1975), pp. 391-99.

37. See R. Chazan, *Barcelona and Beyond* (Berkeley: University of California Press, 1992), pp. 39-79.

38. *Commentary on the Torah:* Deut. 27:26. See Novak, *The Theology of Nahmanides Systematically Presented,* p. 43.

There is little doubt that Nahmanides is arguing against Paul's interpretation of this verse (Gal. 3:10), for Paul uses it to show that everyone living under the law is cursed because no one can possibly observe all the commandments all of the time. Furthermore, Paul's interpretation uses the Septuagint's rendering of this verse as saying "all [*pasin*] the words of this Torah." The force of Paul's interpretation is that the observance of the law is all or nothing: either totally effecting salvation or totally preventing it, the latter being the curse of which the verse warns at the outset.

But Nahmanides turns Paul's interpretation on its head, so to speak. In his interpretation, faith is faith in the perpetual sanctity and authority in the Torah as a normative whole, even if one cannot possibly observe all of its commandments all of the time. It is not this faith but our human works that always lag behind it. Faith in God's law is itself salvific. For Nahmanides, then, it is not our works that remind us of our sin so much as our works attempt to put our faith in practice, knowing full well that faith in the God who gave the Torah is the same faith in the God who will finally redeem us forever.[39] And, moreover, this salvific faith is extended by Maimonides (d. 1205, and a great influence on Nahmanides' theology) to those gentiles who also accept the law that the Rabbis assumed is binding on them, even without full conversion to Judaism.[40] In the case of these gentiles, what is important is not their perfect observance of the law, but rather their *acceptance* of the law as being from God and not from human invention. For some medieval Jewish authorities, this was the criterion for judging Christianity and Islam to be authentic kinds of monotheism and thus leading to the inference that true Christians and Muslims would indeed be worthy of being included with all Israel in the life of the coming-world.[41] In the case of Christianity, interestingly enough, this meant a Jewish validation of Christianity on Jewish, but certainly not Christian, terms. Whether or not Christians can possibly agree with this Jewish validation of them, at last minimally, is an important question for those Christians now engaged in the new and significant dialogue with Jews.

39. See his *Commentary on the Torah:* Gen. 15:6.

40. *Mishneh Torah:* Kings, 8.9-11 re *Tosefta:* Sanhedrin 13.2.

41. See David Novak, *Jewish-Christian Dialogue: A Jewish Justification* (New York: Oxford University Press, 1989), pp. 42-72.

A Contemporary Review

There are two ways of formulating doctrinal theology: one *sub specie aeternitatis,* the other *sub specie durationis.* The former makes theological statements and insists they be regarded as dogmas, namely, propositions that have always been true and always will be. The latter addresses itself to a specific question arising at a point in the history of the faith-community, drawing upon the tradition's resources and coming to a tentative conclusion. Some doctrinal theologies have assumed that all theological statements must be presented as embodying perpetual truth. For them, all doctrine is dogma without history. Conversely, other doctrinal theologies have assumed that all theological statements can only be presented tentatively, that is, history without truth. They seem to fall into a type of historicism that reduces everything taught by the tradition to the relative meaning of those who have enunciated it, hence leaving it without any perpetual authority. Everything can be changed.

Rabbinic Judaism only assigned perpetual truth to propositions it could assume had the unanimous agreement of all the Sages that it was the teaching of the Sinaitic revelation. This meant that the majority of rabbinic teaching was, at least in principle, subject to subsequent repeal. For this reason, Jewish theology is well advised to draw as much as it can from critical-historical enquiry, so long as it does not adopt the historicist ontology some historians and philosophers have seen as being essential to this enterprise.

In the realm of law, the Rabbis spoke *sub specie aeternitatis* when they insisted that those commandments judged to be grounded in the Pentateuch (Written Torah) and those commandments judged to be undisputed ancient traditions going back to Sinaitic revelation *(halakhot)* are not subject to any possible repeal by anyone in this world.[42] All of these traditions prescribe further details of scriptural commandments that cannot be derived through scriptural exegesis. The number of these scriptural commandments was finally determined to be six hundred thirteen, a determination that itself became very much a Jewish dogma.[43]

In the realm of theology, though, the number of dogmas was much smaller. In fact, one can say that here are really only three undisputed rabbinic dogmas: one, that the Torah is direct divine revelation *(torah min ha-shamayim);* two, that the resurrection of the dead is revealed doctrine

42. See B. Kiddushin 29a re Num. 15:23; B. Niddah 73a re Hab. 3:6.
43. B. Makkot 23b-24a re Deut. 33:3.

(tehiyyat ha-metim min ha-torah); three, that God exercises authority in the world. One who denies the third dogma is deemed an "Epicurean" *(apiqoros),* a follower of someone like the Hellenistic philosopher Epicurus, who could only admit to a totally absent god, which practically means no God at all.[44] The greatest Jewish dogmatist of all time, Joseph Albo, a fifteenth-century Spanish theologian (and the chief Jewish disputant at a famous disputation with Catholic theologians held in Tortosa in 1413-14), summarized these three dogmas more abstractly as being: one, God exists; two, God reveals his law; three, God judges how his law has been kept or violated in the world.[45] Whether or not one wants to limit the number of dogmas to these three (Maimonides posited thirteen), one could hardly argue that any of them had not been a dogma of Rabbinic Judaism.

From this dogmatic constellation, it seems that although the question of the relation of law and eschatology involves the two dogmas of the divinely given law and the final divine judgment of the dead, one cannot insist that the question of whether or not the law will be abrogated in the coming-future admits of dogmatic resolution. As such, it is best to identify a current theological dilemma for Jews and then select which view of law and eschatology seems to better address it than the other.

It has only been since the establishment of the State of Israel in 1948 that Jews have had the power Christians long had, namely, the political authority to enforce their religious law. In the State of Israel today, because of coalition politics, there are areas of Jewish law, especially regarding personal and marital status, that are enforced by the state. This has led to the political problem of the resentment of many secularist Jews and even non-Orthodox religious Jews against the Orthodox rabbinical establishment because of what they consider to be undemocratic religious coercion. This resentment and the counter-resentment of many Orthodox Jews against what they see as antireligious secularism lies at the heart of a major *Kulturkampf* facing Israeli Jews and, by extension, all Jews throughout the world, since the vast majority of all Jews everywhere have long been Zionists. But the problem is more than just political in the usual secular sense. It is theological.

The coercive policies of the rabbinical establishment are frequently justified by a messianic theology. This theology assumes that the main

44. M. Sanhedrin 10.1

45. *Sefer Ha'Ikkarim,* intro., trans. I. Husik (Philadelphia: Jewish Publication Society of America, 1929), 1:3.

function of the Messiah is to be the full enforcement of Jewish law as it pertains to both Jews and non-Jews living under Jewish rule.[46] But if the enforcement of the law is the main function of the Messiah, then it is inferred that one can also say that the further and further enforcement of the law will actually bring the Messiah. Instead of enforcement of the law being a secondary function in a polity of Jews who overwhelmingly want to live under the law, the enforcement of the law in this theologico-political vision is now the prime task of a polity making the Messiah's rule possible, even probable. Needless to say, this greatly enhances the political power of the Rabbis and encourages the most authoritarian tendencies among them. It is a prime recipe for the establishment of a *theocracy,* not in its original sense of being in effect the kingdom of God *(theokratia)* but, rather, a dictatorship of clerics.[47] Such a view, of course, virtually obscures the covenantal thrust of Jewish theology, namely, the view that the relationship between God and Israel functions best when there is a maximum of free persuasion and a minimum of coercion. As a famous rabbinic text teaches, even God could not force Israel to accept his law.[48] Only when the Jewish people accepted it out of the freedom of love did that law assume its true authority in the lives of the people. There is certainly more to the covenant than democracy; nevertheless, there is more of a democratic element in the covenantal reality than contemporary Jewish theocrats can or will see.

Because of the theologico-political dangers of religious coercion, it seems best for Jews today to see the End Time as a totally apocalyptic event, one that will judge all our efforts in this world, not one that will simply extend the authority of the law with the concomitant human authority of interpreting and applying it in the world.[49] This might well be an excellent antidote to any historical triumphalism. Indeed, we Jews have learned the theologico-political dangers of historical triumphalism from the history of Christianity in its Constantinian manifestation. For Jews, the Constantinian notion of "Christendom" was the usual justification for our marginalization, even our persecution, by officially Christian societies. But, the notion of Christendom also led to great spiritual problems for Christians among themselves. This triumphalism led too many Chris-

---

46. See Maimonides, *Mishneh Torah:* Kings, 11.1, 12.1-4.

47. For the original meaning of *theocracy,* see Josephus, *Contra Apionem,* 2.164-67. For a critique of contemporary Jewish theocrats, see David Novak, *Covenantal Rights: A Study in Jewish Political Theory* (Princeton, N.J.: Princeton University Press, 2000), pp. 25-32.

48. B. Shabbat 88a re Exod. 19:17. See Novak, *The Election of Israel,* pp. 163-77.

49. See Novak, *The Election of Israel,* pp. 252-55.

tians to believe that the kingdom of God will only be realized when the power of the Church is justified by political dominion, which always means *a* political regime. But the kingdom of God is not brought about, indeed it might well be impeded by, the mere extension of the power of the religious establishment through its official endorsement of one particular human regime on earth. Have we not seen from the history of Christianity that when the Church officially endorses the state, it ends up by becoming an agency of the state? Isn't it better when the Church is in the world but not of it?

Jews have much to learn about the bad political and spiritual consequences of certain forms of Christian eschatology. Christians have had much more experience with political power than we have had. The political consequences of any form of eschatology should be our prime criterion for selecting one form of eschatology rather than another at the point in history when that theological judgment has to be made, for what we think of the future is an essential factor in how we are to act here and now. And since the messianic element in Jewish theology is so profoundly political in its vision, its present implications cannot help but be profoundly political as well. We have much to learn about this from the political history of Christianity, something that should instruct Christians themselves even more.

The time when Jews rightly thought that they had to maximally distinguish themselves from Christianity is past. We have well survived Christian attempts to theologically incorporate us, and Christian political hegemony over Jews is almost totally passé. We now have as much to learn from our similarities to Christians than we have to learn from our differences with them. The issue of the relation of law and eschatology is a prime case in point. Our more important task today in the world is how to handle our new power here and now. How do we offer it to glorify God's kingship and not use it to enhance our own importance? In the light of this task and the questions it raises, we are better advised, I think, to look to the End Time as the apocalyptic conclusion of the time of the commandments and thus the initiation of a new time "no eye but God's has ever seen" — or even anticipated.[50] Can one think of any better prophylactic against the idealistic and ideological pretensions of all the great movements of modernity, be they secular or religious? At least *sub specie durationis,* theology, especially eschatological theology, might well function best *via negationis.*

50. See B. Berakhot 34b re Isa. 64:3. Cf. 1 Cor. 2:9.

Maimonides and Aquinas on Natural Law

Natural Law and Divine Law

It is indisputable that Moses Maimonides was an important influence on the thought of Thomas Aquinas. Whether agreeing with him or disagreeing with him, Aquinas always refers to Maimonides with the same respect he pays his Christian theological sources and his Greek and Arabic philosophical sources. A number of insightful modern studies have been written that show the depth of that influence and how deeper and more comprehensive understandings of Aquinas's thought must take it into account.[1] Furthermore, Maimonides seems to be the only Jewish thinker Aquinas took seriously, perhaps the only Jewish thinker he had ever read at all.

Most studies of the influence of Maimonides on Aquinas concentrate on metaphysics. There is good reason for that since Maimonides was an important link in the chain that brought the ontological theory of Aristotle to the attention and consideration of Christian thinkers in Europe. In metaphysics, Maimonides added his voice to the *falasifa* of Is-

---

1. See, e.g., Isaac Franck, "Maimonides and Aquinas on Man's Knowledge of God: A Twentieth-Century Perspective," *Review of Metaphysics* 38 (1985): 591-615; Idit Dobbs-Weinstein, *Maimonides and St. Thomas on the Limits of Reason* (Albany: State University of New York Press, 1995). All of the articles collected in *Studies in Maimonides and St. Thomas Aquinas,* ed. J. I. Dienstag (New York: KTAV, 1975), deal with metaphysical similarities and differences.

This essay previously appeared in *St. Thomas Aquinas and the Natural Law Tradition: Contemporary Perspectives,* ed. John Goyette et al. (Washington: Catholic University Press, 2004), pp. 43-65.

lamic thinkers like Ibn Sina. Following the example of his teacher Albertus Magnus, Aquinas was eager to appropriate this great metaphysical tradition into the type of Christian theology that takes philosophy seriously in its own constructive endeavors. As such, Aquinas could not very well ignore how this way of thinking was handled by Maimonides, whom he respectfully calls "Rabbi Moses" at all times.[2] Nevertheless, at the level of metaphysics, it is largely irrelevant whether Maimonides is *Rabbi* Moses or not. In these metaphysical discussions, it makes little difference whether one is a pagan like Aristotle, a Muslim like Ibn Sina, a Jew like Maimonides, or a Christian like Thomas Aquinas.[3] It is only when one gets to the more explicitly theological level, whether that theology be theoretical or practical, that these religious distinctions make a real difference.

Without in any way belittling the metaphysical influence, one could well argue that the influence of Maimonides on Aquinas was far more extensive in the area of practical reason, which covers the joint area of ethics and politics. This is the area where Aquinas works as a Christian moral theologian. Aquinas engages in two types of practical reason and, indeed, contemporary Thomists dispute which is the more important in his moral theology. In the opening questions discussed in the first part of the second section *(prima secundae)* of the *Summa Theologiae,* Aquinas engages in what we would call "virtue-based ethics" today.[4] But, more of the questions discussed in this section of the *Summa* (beginning with question 90) concern what we would call "law-based ethics" today.[5] Even though Aquinas himself did not call this part of the *prima secundae* a "Treatise on Law"

---

2. In the earliest monograph on Aquinas by a Jewish scholar, *Das Verhältnis des Thomas von Aquino zum Judenthum und zur judischen Litteratur* (Göttingen: Vandenhoeck und Ruprecht's Verlag, 1891), Jakob Guttmann noted at the outset (p. 3) how respectful Aquinas was of Maimonides *(ein ehrenvolles Zeugnis).* For Aquinas's views on Jews and Judaism in general, see J. Hood, *Aquinas and the Jews* (Philadelphia: University of Pennsylvania Press, 1995).

3. Thus the great historian of ancient and medieval philosophy, Harry A. Wolfson, wrote, "The same Greek terminology lay behind the Arabic, Hebrew, and Latin terminology. . . . The three philosophic literatures were in fact one philosophy expressed in different languages, translatable almost literally into one another" *(Spinoza* [Cambridge, Mass.: Harvard University Press, 1934], p. 10). For a study that insightfully demonstrates this point in the area of God-talk, see David B. Burrell, *Knowing the Unknowable God* (Notre Dame: University of Notre Dame Press, 1986), esp. pp. 1-18.

4. See, e.g., Daniel Westberg, *Right Practical Reason* (Oxford: Clarendon Press, 1994).

5. See, e.g., Russell Hittinger, "Natural Law and Catholic Moral Theology," in *Our Preserving Grace: Protestants, Catholics, and Natural Law,* ed. M. Cromartie (Grand Rapids: Eerdmans, 1997), pp. 1-30.

as it is frequently called today, one can see why his treatment of questions of law *(de Legibus)* could be seen as a self-contained work by itself. So we need to see how Aquinas structures this part of the *Summa* in order to appreciate the significant role Maimonides plays in it.

Aquinas divides law into six main categories: (1) eternal law, which is the norm whereby God governs the universe, most of which is unknowable by finite human minds; (2) natural law, which is that aspect of the eternal law that is knowable by finite human minds and applicable to human life, what my teacher Professor Germain Grisez calls "an intellect-sized bite of reality";[6] (3) human law, which is how human minds apply the general principles of natural law in particular historical situations; (4) divine law, which is that aspect of the eternal law that is made known to human minds by God through historical revelation; (5) the Old Law, which is that aspect of divine law made known by God through pre-Christian revelation to the Jewish people; and (6) the New Law, which is that aspect of divine law made known by Christ to the Church.

What is most interesting, even surprising, about this arrangement is that Aquinas devotes more time to the discussion of the Old Law than he does to any of the other categories of law. And it is in these questions where we find Maimonides appearing quite regularly. That is not surprising inasmuch as this is Aquinas's most concentrated and extensive treatment of Judaism, and virtually everything he knew about Judaism came from Scripture and the interpretations of Maimonides.[7] (How fortunate for himself and for posterity that Aquinas's engagement with Judaism was located in his engagement with the thinker whom no subsequent Jewish thinker can ever really leave behind when thinking about Judaism.) Here one sees how carefully Aquinas read Maimonides' main work in philosophical theology, the *Guide of the Perplexed*. In his discussion of the Old Law, Aquinas draws much from the third section of that work, which deals with what rabbinic tradition called "the reasons of the Torah" *(ta'amei torah)* and what Maimonides and the medievals called "the reasons of the commandments *(ta'amei ha-mitsvot)*.[8] Yet I can't help thinking how much more Aquinas would have gotten from Maimonides' Jewish jurisprudence if he also had access to Maimonides' encyclopedic codification of all of Jewish law, the *Mishneh Torah*. In the *Guide* Maimonides called

6. Grisez, "The First Principle of Practical Reason," *Natural Law Forum* 10 (1965): 174.

7. See Guttmann, *Das Verhältnis des Thomas von Aquino zum Judenthum und zur jüdischen Litteratur,* pp. 13-15.

8. See *Babylonian Talmud* (hereafter "B."): Sanhedrin 21a-b; Maimonides, *The Book of the Commandments:* Introduction, root no. 5, and *Guide of the Perplexed* (hereafter *Guide*), 3.26.

this work "our great composition" *(ta'alifana al-khabir)*.[9] Aquinas could have well called it *Corpus Juris Judaeorum,* perhaps even *Summa Theologiae Judaicae,* had he been able to read it and not just hear about it.

At this point I would like to consider why Aquinas engaged in this lengthy and detailed treatment of Judaism in his own great composition, which too many forget is a summa of *theology,* not of philosophy, and where philosophy is the servant of theology *(ancilla theologiae),* not its mistress. This consideration begins with the question: Why is Aquinas *qua Christian theologian* interested in natural law? Moreover, what is the connection between natural law and the Old Law? This is important inasmuch as it is in Aquinas's discussion of the Old Law that Maimonides plays his most extensive role in Aquinas's thought.

We need to ask these questions because a theologian's interest in natural law is not the same as that of a philosopher. For a philosopher, whom Maimonides and Aquinas would see as a human thinker to whom revelation is unavailable (or ontologically irrelevant as it was for Spinoza), the prime example being Aristotle and the Aristotelians, the interest in natural law (better "natural right" as *orthos logos* or *recta ratio*) stems from the attempt to know what remains permanent and universal in human nature as opposed to what is ephemeral and parochial in human history.[10] To discover natural law is to discover what is divine within the universe, especially as it pertains to the human condition. It is the very apex of worldly human knowledge. But for a theologian, divine law is more than natural law. As such, it is not discoverable naturally, that is, by universally accessible human reason. Divine law is directly revealed by God in history to an elect community. It is not a dispensable element *within* the human story; instead, it is the preview of the eschatological consummation of history itself. That is why divine law is super-natural, but not irrational.[11] For a philosopher, conversely, natural law is either identical with divine law (as it is for Plato), or divine law is inferior to natural law (as it is for Kant).[12]

9. Maimonides, *Guide,* 1.36. Arabic text: *Dalalat al-ha'irin,* ed. S. Munk (Jerusalem: n.p., 1931), p. 56.

10. See Leo Strauss, *Natural Right and History* (Chicago: University of Chicago Press, 1953), pp. 81-119.

11. See John Courtney Murray, S.J., *We Hold These Truths* (New York: Sheed & Ward, 1960), p. 298.

12. See Plato, *Laws,* 631B-D. Cf. Kant, *Religion within the Limits of Reason Alone,* trans. T. H. Greene and H. H. Hudson (New York: Harper & Brothers, 1960), pp. 169-71. It is questionable, though, whether Aristotle affirmed what we call "natural law," viz., universally valid and cognizable moral norms. Note his hesitation in *Nicomachean Ethics,* 1134b25-34.

For a theologian, natural law is at best an indispensable element within a larger divine story, what some modern theologians have called *Heils-geschichte*.[13]

In Aquinas's thought, grace brings nature to its true perfection.[14] As such, natural law must somehow or other be seen as being contained within the divine law itself. Somewhat similarly, Maimonides had earlier said that "the [divine] Law, although it is not natural, enters into what is natural."[15] Natural law, then, can be seen as the precondition for divine grace, the greatest manifestation of which heretofore is the revelation of divine law. The humanly knowable world into which revelation can possibly enter must be a world in which natural law is discernable and respected.

I would now like to show how the constitution of this relation between divine law and natural law is generally similar in Aquinas and in Maimonides because each theologian had to deal with the question of the natural preconditions for revelation. Nevertheless, there are specific differences between them and these specific differences are important for contemporary theologians, both Jewish and Christian, to consider when rethinking natural law today.

For a variety of reasons, the more theological comparison of the views of Maimonides and Aquinas is of greater contemporary import than the comparison of their more philosophical views. One of these reasons might be that one can still engage in theology, especially moral theology, similar to the way Maimonides and Aquinas engaged in it, whereas it might well be fantastic to attempt to engage in the type of Aristotelian metaphysics that occupied both of them. In moral theology it could be said we are still dealing with the same objects they both dealt with. In metaphysics, however, such objective continuity is rather implausible. In what might be termed their respective "meta-ethics," the ethics is still the same. But in their respective "meta-physics," the physics is radically different. That is a great problem for those philoso-

13. For a study that puts Aquinas's natural law theory in the context of his biblical exegesis, and hence in the context of his understanding of *Heilsgeschichte,* see Eugene F. Rogers Jr., *Thomas Aquinas and Karl Barth* (London and Notre Dame: University of Notre Dame Press, 1995), pp. 46-70.

14. See *Summa Theologiae* (hereafter "ST") 2/1, q. 99, a. 2.

15. Maimonides, *Guide,* 2.40, trans. S. Pines (Chicago: University of Chicago Press, 1963), p. 382. For a fuller discussion of Maimonides' view of nature, see David Novak, *The Image of the Non-Jew in Judaism: An Historical and Constructive Study of the Noahide Laws* (New York and Toronto: Edwin Mellen Press, 1983), pp. 290-94.

phers today who think they can return to a comprehensively Aristotelian position.[16]

First, let us look at how Maimonides constitutes the relation of natural law and divine law. Next, let us look at how Aquinas constitutes that relation. Finally, let us attempt to evaluate the specific differences between their respective approaches to what might be seen as the connection of nature and grace.

Maimonides' Main Statement of Natural Law

The statements on law in the *Guide of the Perplexed* with which Aquinas was familiar are built upon his statements on law in his great legal compendium, the *Mishneh Torah*. (This assertion is controversial inasmuch as the late Professor Leo Strauss and his disciples see a difference in kind between the Maimonides of the *Mishneh Torah* and the Maimonides of the *Guide*. I follow those scholars who see much more unity in Maimonides' theology, the differences between the two main works being much more differences of degree.)[17] Even though Aquinas was not familiar with the earlier and larger work, it is important for us to look at it for Maimonides' most explicit statement of natural law. (This assertion is also controversial inasmuch as the late Professor Marvin Fox, among others, argued that the general difference between Maimonides and Aquinas is that Aquinas has a natural law doctrine whereas Maimonides denies natural law altogether.)[18] One cannot fully appreciate Maimonides' treatment of natural law in the context of the "reasons of the commandments" in the *Guide* without seeing its precedent in *Mishneh Torah*.

Even though Maimonides does not use the term "natural law," it is clear he means something quite similar when he refers to some norms as being required "because of the inclination of reason" *(mipnei hekhre hada'at)*.[19] This term could be literally translated into Aquinas's Latin as

16. See David Novak, *Covenantal Rights: A Study in Jewish Political Theory* (Princeton: Princeton University Press, 2000), pp. 21-23.

17. See David Hartman, *Maimonides: Torah and Philosophic Quest* (Philadelphia: Jewish Publication Society of America, 1976), pp. 22-26. Cf. Leo Strauss, *Persecution and the Art of Writing* (London and Chicago: University of Chicago Press, 1988), pp. 38-94.

18. See Fox, *Interpreting Maimonides* (London and Chicago: University of Chicago Press, 1990), pp. 124-51.

19. *Mishneh Torah* (hereafter "MT"): Kings, 8.11. (The entire *Mishneh Torah* is available in English translation in the Yale Judaica series from Yale University Press.)

inclinatio rationalis, which for humans is the prime *inclinatio naturalis.*[20] This term is employed within a larger discussion of possible Jewish governance of gentiles in chapter eight of "the Laws of Kingship" of *Mishneh Torah.* What are the types of this possible governance?

The most obvious form of Jewish governance of gentiles is when gentiles convert to Judaism. This type of governance is the most complete, so complete in fact that the gentiles cease to be gentiles at all and are totally absorbed into the Jewish people. It is the equivalent in Roman law of someone of non-Roman birth becoming adopted by the people of Rome that he could now say with them "I am a Roman citizen" *(civus Romanus sum).* Maimonides mentions this option (which may not be forced upon gentiles against their will), but that is not his main concern here, which is with the gentile "other."[21] The forms of Jewish governance of the gentile "other" with which Maimonides is concerned here are threefold.

First, according to the Talmud, any gentile living under Jewish rule is required to accept upon himself (or herself) seven norms that are seen as binding on all humankind. They are called "the commandments of the children of Noah" *(sheva mitsvot bnei Noah).*[22] The core of these commandments are three general prohibitions: the prohibition of idolatry, the prohibition of killing innocent human life, and the prohibition of sex outside a permanent heterosexual union.[23] Acceptance of these basic prohibitions is required for any gentile to become a resident-alien *(ger toshav)* in a Jewish polity.[24] Since these requisite norms are administered by Jewish authorities, and since these norms seem to be universally justifiable by reason, several scholars have compared this type of Jewish rule over gentiles domiciled in their midst to the Roman political institution of *ius gentium.*[25] This was the form of law used by Roman officials to govern non-Roman peoples who had long lived under Roman rule. (In later Roman law it designated law seen as internationally prevalent, that is, by *consensus gentium.*) *Ius gentium* was more general and less specific than Roman law for Roman citizens *(ius civile).*

Second, Maimonides speaks of gentiles who accept the Noahide laws,

20. See ST 2/1, q. 91, a. 2. Quotes taken from the Blackfriars edition, Latin text with English translation (London: Eyre & Spottiswoode, 1964-74).

21. MT: Kings, 8.10.

22. *Tosefta:* Avodah Zarah 8.4; B. Sanhedrin 56a-b.

23. B. Sanhedrin 57a. Cf. Ibid. 74a where these same three commandments are designated as those a Jew is to die as a martyr rather than transgress.

24. B. Avodah Zarah 64b.

25. See Novak, *The Image of the Non-Jew in Judaism,* pp. 11-14.

not because of Jewish rule but because of acceptance of what Judaism regards as rationally binding on all humans. These are persons who practice
these basic laws because of "the inclination of reason."[26] Here we have a
distinction between general moral obligation and specific Jewish political
obligation. Those who follow reason need not live under a Jewish regime
at all, and Jewish tradition recognizes their moral status as law-abiding
persons nonetheless. Thus valid morality does not need Jewish enforcement or supervision. Such persons Maimonides calls "their [that is, the
gentiles'] sages."[27] Undoubtedly, this category of persons includes both
those who can arrive at moral truth through their own reasoning as well
as those who follow the teachings of their own sages as participants in a
venerable moral tradition. Some scholars have seen this type of rule to be
akin to the Roman notion of *ius naturale,* which is the law that is prior to
the founding of any human polity.[28]

Finally, there is a third category, and it is quite problematic, being the
subject of great debate among students of Maimonides for centuries.
Here is what Maimonides says:

> Whoever accepts the seven commandments and is obligated [*nizhar*]
> to perform them, this person is one of the pious of the nations of
> the world [*me-hasidei ummot ha'olam*] and has a portion in the world-
> to-come. But this person is one who accepts them because [*mipnei*]
> God has commanded them in the Torah. And He [God] has let us
> know through [*ve-hodi'enu al yedei*] Moses our Master that the
> Noahides had been commanded concerning them in the past [*me-
> qodem*].[29]

Many scholars have interpreted this statement of Maimonides, especially, as the clearest indication that he is opposed to the idea of natural
law. They have read it to mean that only those who accept Mosaic revelation and what it requires of gentiles can be said to be law-abiding gentiles.[30] Furthermore, they accept the reading of the printed texts of
Mishneh Torah, which have Maimonides saying that those who only accept

---

26. For the rabbinic sources of this concept, see *Tosefta:* Hullin 8.1; *Palestinian Talmud:*
Sanhedrin 1.1/8b; also, M. Guttmann, "Maimonide sur l'universalité de la morale
religieuse," *Revue d'études juives* 99 (1935): 41.

27. MT: Kings, 8.11.

28. See David Novak, *Natural Law in Judaism* (Cambridge: Cambridge University Press,
1998), pp. 122-42.

29. MT: Kings, 8.11.

30. See Fox, *Interpreting Maimonides,* pp. 130-39.

the Noahide laws because of rational inclination are "neither pious nor wise" *(ve-lo me-hakhmeihem)*. Spinoza made much of this text, using it to show that there is no universal ethic in Judaism, indeed, that such an ethic could not be constituted even by one so committed to the reconciliation of Scripture and reason as was Maimonides.[31]

In this view, the only law-abiding gentiles, for Maimonides, are those who are willing to live according to that department of Jewish law designated for them. That would include any gentiles actually living under Jewish political rule, or any gentiles willing to accept the moral authority of Jewish teaching from books. This latter type of law-abiding gentile might also include Christians, who see the general moral teachings of the Old Testament to still be authoritative even after the coming of Christ and the New Covenant.[32] And, by a somewhat more inclusive reading, it might even include Muslims, whose basic morality seems to be close enough to that of Judaism, and who also revere Moses as a genuine prophet.[33] Nevertheless, it would not include those whose morality stems from their own rational discovery of natural law. A more careful reading of this text, however, plus a look at the overall *Tendenz* of Maimonides' understanding of practical reason, give a different impression altogether.

First and most important, Maimonides says that some of the laws of the Torah are rationally evident (what Aquinas would call *ratio quoad nos*), and that the seven basic Noahide laws fall into this category.[34] Second, the best manuscripts, unlike the printed texts, do not have Maimonides' saying that those who keep the Noahide laws are not even wise. Instead, they have Maimonides saying that those who keep these laws because of rational inclination may not be pious "but they are wise" *(ela me-hakhmeihem)* nonetheless.[35] This makes much more sense in the context of this whole chapter in the *Mishneh Torah* about gentile obligations. The lowest level of gentile is one who accepts what Judaism regards as universally

31. Spinoza, *Tractatus Theologico-Politicus,* chap. 5, trans. S. Shirley (Leiden: E. J. Brill, 1991), pp. 122-23.

32. See David Novak, *Maimonides on Judaism and Other Religions* (Cincinnati: Hebrew Union College Press, 1997), pp. 4-10; also, David Novak, *Jewish-Christian Dialogue: A Jewish Justification* (New York: Oxford University Press, 1989), pp. 57-72.

33. See David Novak, "The Treatment of Muslims and Islam in the Legal Writings of Maimonides," in *Studies in Islamic and Jewish Traditions,* ed. W. M. Brinner and S. D. Ricks (Chico, Calif.: Scholars Press, 1986), pp. 233-50.

34. See ST 1, q. 2, a. 1.

35. See I. Twersky, *The Code of Maimonides* (London and New Haven: Yale University Press, 1980), p. 455n.239.

mandated because that is the way for him or her to gain a permanent and protected status in a Jewish polity. This makes one eligible to become a resident-alien (ger toshav). The next highest level is one who accepts what Judaism regards as universally mandated because that is what he or she reasons is right. This makes one a wise Noahide. The highest level is the one who accepts what Judaism regards as universally mandated because he or she believes this is a divine law. This makes one pious. Only this last person is worthy of the world-to-come along with all Jews who accept (or, minimally, do not deny) the Mosaic Torah to be divine law. But, it is important to keep in mind, this pious gentile does not have to convert to Judaism in order to attain the world-to-come.

After this analysis of the text, it would seem that Maimonides does affirm natural law and that the natural law is known by practical wisdom. The only difference between one who keeps natural law and one who keeps divine law is that the keeper of natural law only has a respected status in this world, but the keeper of divine law also has a respected status in the world-to-come. It would seem that the difference between the two is that the keeper of divine law must accept it via Mosaic revelation, whereas the keeper of natural law need only keep it via rationally perceived human nature. However, even this distinction may not be what Maimonides means.

A careful reading of the text shows that Maimonides is not saying that the pious gentiles are pious *because* they accept Mosaic revelation. He only says Mosaic revelation "informs us" — the Jews — *that* the universal moral laws have already been accepted as divine law by humankind in the past. In other words, the *Torah* they discover need not be the specifically Mosaic Torah. As such, the Mosaic Torah given to the Jews confirms what the gentiles have or could have been doing since time immemorial (*me-qodem*). It is not that the Noahides need to learn their basic morality *from* Jewish revelation; Jewish revelation need not be prescriptive for them. Instead, Jewish revelation is simply descriptive of what has been prescribed for the gentiles elsewhere. And, if they accept divine law from this other source, then they are worthy of joining normative Israel in the world-to-come. But, what is this other source? Haven't we already eliminated both reason and Mosaic revelation? Must it be some other revelation like that of Christianity or Islam, or is there another alternative?

The only key we get from this text in our quest to answer the above questions is that Maimonides says that the Jews know about Noahide/human normativeness from what God revealed to us through Moses. But where is this to be found in Mosaic revelation? The few biblical verses brought by the talmudic Rabbis when explicating these commandments are only allusive rather than being strictly prescriptive.[36] That is undoubtedly why Maimonides does not cite them. So, what Maimonides means here by Mosaic revelation is the Oral Tradition, which for him is the long history of Jewish teachers reasoning about what the meaning and application of the Torah is to be.[37] That reasoning sometimes even includes speculation as to what the universal preconditions for the acceptance of the specific Mosaic Torah must be. This discursive tradition is initiated by Moses, and it is carried on by all who participate in it and contribute to it. They are functioning as Moses did, and with Mosaic warrant.[38]

I do not think it is implausible to infer from his words about Mosaic revelation that Maimonides might mean that Jews learn of what the Noahides have been commanded by reasoning about what are the basic requirements of a decent life for any human being. Those are the things which, according to the Talmud, "had they not been written, they would have to have been written *(hayu le-kotvan)*."[39] Indeed, according to rabbinic tradition, the Jews themselves were Noahides before their status was elevated when they accepted the Written Torah (that is, the fundament of Scripture) at Mount Sinai.[40] In other words, Jews learn about the obligations of Noahides/humans the same way all humans are to learn of their moral obligations, that is, by reasoning about what the fulfillment of human nature essentially requires. This is taken to be divine law when one reasons that this must be what God intended for humans to do by creating them. But, if that is so, why does Maimonides dismiss rational inclination as a sufficient way to learn how to attain the world-to-come?

36. See B. Sanhedrin 56b-57a.

37. See Novak, *Natural Law in Judaism,* pp. 95-99.

38. MT: Rebels, chap. 1.

39. B. Yoma 67b. In his comments on an earlier draft of this paper, Prof. Martin D. Yaffe points out that Maimonides cites this very talmudic text to argue against the "dialectical theologians" *(mutalkallimun)* who speak of "rational commandments" *(mitsvot sikhliyot).* Based on this text (*Commentary on the Mishnah:* Avot, Introduction [*Eight Chapters*], chap. 6), Prof. Yaffe concludes, "This passages alone evidently decides the question of whether Maimonides has a natural law teaching. By his own lights, at least, he does not." However, considering the earlier distinction between rational commandments and revealed commandments *(mitsvot shimi'yot),* could Maimonides, who continually emphasizes the reasons of the commandments, not affirm rational commandments? So, it seems that it is better to interpret Maimonides' criticism of the distinction of the earlier theologians as being that they limit the category "rational" to only some of the commandments. However, a more sufficient metaphysical foundation would have enabled them to affirm, as does Maimonides himself, that all the commandments are rational, albeit some having reasons more evident than others. See Novak, *The Image of the Non-Jew in Judaism,* pp. 285-87.

40. B. Nedarim 31a.

The answer to this last last question cannot be inferred from the texts we have been examining so carefully. For this answer we must turn to the *Guide,* the Maimonidean work Aquinas knew quite well, and where Maimonides himself is much more explicit philosophically. What we see from the *Guide* is that there are two distinct types of human reason, and their respective use determines what kind of law we get.

> Accordingly, if you find a law the whole end of which . . . [is] directed toward the ordering of the city . . . you must know that that Law is a nomos. . . . If, on the other hand, you find a Law all of whose ordinances are due to attention being paid . . . to the body and also to the soundness of belief . . . with regard to God . . . and that desires to make men wise . . . you must know that this guidance comes from Him, may he be exalted, and that this Law is divine [*al-shariyah al-alahiyah*].[41]

What we see from this is that ordinary human reason, which is directed to purely political matters, might satisfy the immediate practical demands of rational inclination, but it does not lead rational inclination to its true object. That true object of the intellect is apprehending that what is good for human life is the result of the divine governance of the whole universe. I think Maimonides would have agreed with Bernard Lonergan when he said, "One can go beyond common sense and present science, to grasp the dynamic structure of our rational knowing and doing, and then formulate a metaphysics and an ethics."[42] For Maimonides, that metaphysics and that ethics are "natural," understanding the *nature* that makes them *natural* to be cosmic and not just the general structure required by earthly politics. For him, the world-to-come is not a future historical event; instead, it is the eternal realm of God which those of highest rational ability can apprehend even while they are living in the physical world.

Some scholars have seen this higher type of reason to be a more Platonic than Aristotelian correlation of practical and theoretical reason.[43] The Judeo-Christian-Islamic idea that nature is the lawful creation of the divine creator/lawgiver gives a new and more satisfying grounding to the

---

41. Maimonides, *Guide,* 2.40, pp. 383-84 = Arabic, p. 271.

42. Lonergan, *Insight* (New York: Harper & Row, 1978), p. 635.

43. See Shlomo Pines' introduction to *Guide,* p. lxxxviii. Cf. Aristotle, *Nicomachean Ethics,* 1177a25-30; Thomas Aquinas, *Commentary on Aristotle's Nicomachean Ethics,* 10.2087-97, trans. C. I. Litzinger, O.P. (Notre Dame, Ind.: Dumb Ox Books, 1993), pp. 624-26.

process whereby ethics presupposes metaphysics and metaphysics entails ethics.[44] This is a far cry from the type of practical reasoning that is satisfied with what appears to be politically useful. It is also a far cry from the type of theoretical reason that sees the universe as a place indifferent to what humans do or do not do. And, even though these truths are available to human reason, since they are not evident to most human minds, Jewish and Christian and Islamic revelations (the only historically recorded revelations of the one creator God) make them dogmatically, even if not demonstrably, available for large communities of humans.[45]

Finally, as a Jewish theologian, Maimonides believes that Judaism presents the divine law in the best possible way, that it is the best coordination of theoretical and practical wisdom available in the world. It is rationally knowable, even if not immediately evident (what Aquinas would call *ratio per se*).[46] However, as his most astute commentator noted, when Maimonides indicated that the attainment of the world-to-come does not require conversion to Judaism (although apostasy from Judaism could forfeit it), he was accepting one rabbinic view over its opposite.[47] The opposite view is a Jewish version of *extra ecclesiam nulla salus,* namely, only Jews can attain the life of the world-to-come.[48] Maimonides clearly denies that.

At most, Judaism's superiority to the other monotheistic religions and to the philosophical coordination of ethics and metaphysics is one of degree rather than one of kind. Prophetic revelation is a propensity of human nature, and only philosophers can become prophets, even though there is no natural necessity that they actually do become prophets.[49] Prophecy is not confined to Israel (as Maimonides' predecessor, Judah Halevi, had argued), but Moses is unique among all the prophets and will never be surpassed.[50] The recognition of natural law, especially as it operates in human nature, is the beginning of a process that could possibly end in prophetic revelation, which grants us vision of the larger created nature of which human nature is a part. But to see natural law apart from its metaphysical

44. See Novak, *Natural Law in Judaism,* pp. 113-21.

45. See M. Kellner, *Dogma in Medieval Jewish Thought* (Oxford: Oxford University Press, 1986), pp. 10-49.

46. ST I, q. 2, a. 1.

47. Joseph Karo, *Kesef Mishneh* on MT: Kings, 8.11.

48. See *Tosefta:* Sanhedrin 13.2 and B. Sanhedrin 105a re Ps. 9:18.

49. See Novak, *Jewish-Christian Dialogue,* pp. 129-38.

50. MT: Foundations of the Torah, 7.1-6; Maimonides, *Guide,* 2.36, 39. Cf. Halevi, *Kuzari,* 1.95, trans. H. Hirschfeld (New York: Pardes, 1946), p. 31.

ground is to make human reason rather than divine wisdom the measure of all things. That is why Maimonides is reticent to treat natural law apart from the full Law itself. To concentrate on what is only immediately evident could easily lead to the erroneous conclusion that what we call natural law at the political level is not only necessary but sufficient for the fulfillment of human nature. Natural law can be abstracted from the full Law itself, but it cannot be constituted in any adequate way independent of it. As Maimonides notes with good Aristotelian reasoning, the natural/Noahide law is "completed" (ve-nishlamah) by the Torah of Moses."[51]

Aquinas on the Old Law

Although Aquinas was unaware of Maimonides' constitution of Noahide law as natural law (since Maimonides does not discuss Noahide law in the *Guide*), one could make the following analogy: Maimonides' view of the relation of Noahide law to Mosaic law is logically quite similar to Aquinas's view of the relation of the Old Law to the New Law. That general similarity is best seen in the fact that like Maimonides, Aquinas regards the relation of the earlier law to the later law to be one of potency and act. That is, the Old Law functions as potential for its full actualization in the New Law. Both of them learned much from Aristotle in their respective teleologies.

As a Christian theologian, Aquinas had to deal with a problem that has troubled Christians ever since the time when Christianity separated itself from Judaism. One might see this problem as how does a Christian steer clear of the Scylla of Marcionism and the Charybdis of judaization. Because Christianity's claims are primarily based on the revelation of the Old Testament (the "Jewish" Scriptures), to advocate the total supersession of Judaism, as did Marcion and his followers (in all ages), is to destroy the very basis of Christianity. That basis is the claim that Jesus of Nazareth is the promised Messiah of Israel, and that God became incarnate in the body of this Torah-observant Jew.[52] (That is why the core of the Jewish-Christian debate is located in the rival claims made by Jews and Christians about the meaning of the Hebrew Bible as the prime criterion of truth: *torat emet.*) Something significantly Jewish must remain within Christianity and its teaching. On the other hand, if Christianity is not selective in its incorporation of Judaism, then how can it be regarded as any-

51. MT: Kings, 9.1.
52. Matt. 5:17.

thing more than an heretical Jewish sect (since the vast majority of Jews have refused to accept Christian claims upon them)? So, where does a Christian theologian draw this crucial line?

In Aquinas's view, Judaism's continued validity for Christians lies in its superior constitution of natural law. Natural law is what humans discover in their "natural inclination to know the truth about God and to live in society; and in this respect, whatever pertains to this inclination belongs to natural law."[53] Aquinas says that "the Old Law was in accordance with reason," and that "the Old Law was good, but imperfect."[54] The imperfection of the Old Law is not seen, however, until the revelation of the New Law in the same way, let us say, the immaturity of an acorn is not seen until it grows into a mature oak tree. In other words, the imperfection of the old is only seen retrospectively after the appearance of the new. Taken in and of itself, the Old Law intends "a sensible and earthly good, and to this man was directly ordained."[55] In fact, Aquinas is so serious about the earthly sufficiency of the Old Law that he argues, "the Old Law is said to be forever *(esse in aeternum)* unqualifiedly and absolutely as regards its moral precepts."[56] Moreover, "it is clear that the Old Law provided sufficiently concerning the mutual relations of one man with another."[57] Indeed, it is only because there are "things in which human reason may happen to be impeded" that natural law had to be given the stamp of divine (that is, revealed) law in ancient Israel.[58]

Aquinas insists that natural law is "fully contained" not only in the New Law, but even in the Old Law.[59] Indeed, it might even be more evident

---

53. ST 2/1, q. 94, a. 3.

54. ST 2/1, q. 98, a. 1.

55. ST 2/1, q. 91, a. 5.

56. ST 2/1, q. 103, a. 3 ad 1. See also ST 2/1, q. 100, a. 1.

57. ST 2/1, q. 105, a. 2. See also ST 2/1, q. 91, a. 5.

58. ST 2/1, q. 99, a. 2 ad 2. In his comments on an earlier version of this paper, Prof. John Goyette rightly points out that Aquinas saw the need for natural law to be part of the revealed Old Law (citing ST 1, q. 95, a. 1): "Because of original sin . . . man does not possess the knowledge he needs to fulfill the natural law and it was necessary, therefore, for God to give the Old Law to the Jews so that nature might be restored." But for Maimonides, conversely, it would seem that if there is any "original sin," it is the falling away of Adam (and his descendants) from the *vita contemplativa* and being solely concerned with the bodily goods that are the subject of the *vita activa* (see *Guide,* 1.2). Hence, there is a natural cure for this human predicament. Nevertheless, for a rabbinic view of original sin and the need for grace/revelation to cure humans of its consequences, see B. Yevamot 103a-b re Gen. 31:24.

59. ST 2/1, q. 94, a. 4 ad 1. Cf. John Calvin, *Institutes of the Christian Religion,* 2.7.10 and 4.20.16.

in the Old Law than it is in the New Law inasmuch as Aquinas goes so far as to suggest that "the form of government established by the divine law" (that is, the divine law as the Old Law) was the best example in human history of a mixed political constitution, combining what is best in monarchy, aristocracy, and democracy.[60] That is highly significant inasmuch as it could be argued that the New Testament itself has no distinct political teaching. Jesus proclaims to Pontius Pilate, the representative of Roman imperial authority, "my kingdom is not of this world."[61] Before that he differentiated between the this-worldly realm of Caesar and the otherworldly realm of God.[62] Both Peter and Paul advocate obedience to temporal authority as long as one is still living in this world.[63] At most, beginning with Augustine, especially, one can see Christian political theory as functioning as a negative limit on the authority of the state whenever it tends to regard itself as divine.[64] That is why Aquinas seems to suggest that it is a good thing for an earthly sovereign to attempt to positively model his realm on biblical ideas of polity and its structures, as long as he does not present this political program as a literal reinstitution of the Old Law per se.[65]

Aquinas's selectivity of the Old Law is seen in the way he divides its precepts into three categories: moral, ceremonial, and judicial. Only the moral precepts, which turn out to be those contained in the Decalogue, are seen as the perpetual precepts of natural law, which have in no way been superseded by the precepts of the New Law. The ceremonial precepts and the judicial precepts, conversely, have been superseded by the New Law, but they have been superseded by it in quite different ways.

The ceremonial precepts of the Old Law have been superseded by the sacraments ordained by the New Law, which is the New Testament as interpreted by the *magisterium* of the Church.[66] In the past these ceremonial precepts functioned as the way Israel legitimately worshiped God, that is, until the coming of Christ. As such, their meaning today is that of a memory of God's faithfulness to Israel by seeing how God enabled Israel to worship Him in great detail. And, even more importantly, they are to be seen as a foreshadow of the complete worship of God brought about by Christ's in-

---

60. ST 2/1, q. 105, a. 1.
61. John 18:36.
62. Matt. 22:21 and parallels.
63. Rom. 13:1-7; 1 Peter 2:13-17.
64. See *De Civitate Dei,* 19.17.
65. ST 2/1, q. 104, a. 3. See also ST 2/1, q. 98, a. 5.
66. ST 2/1, q. 104, a. 3.

stitution of the sacraments. In this view, their meaning is symbolic, in contrast to the sacraments whose meaning, for Christians, is literal, even if mysterious by the standards of this world.[67] However, since they have been practically superseded in toto by the sacraments, Aquinas insists that it would be spiritual regression to observe them after the coming of Christ in the way they were (properly) observed before the coming of Christ. In fact, "it would be a mortal sin now to observe those ceremonies which the fathers of old fulfilled with devotion and fidelity," and thus they are "not only dead, but deadly *(mortifera)* to those who observe them after the coming of Christ."[68] Here Aquinas's intention seems to be directed against those Christians who think they can practice Judaism and Christianity in tandem. (It is hard to ascertain, however, what he thinks of the legitimacy of Jews continuing to practice these commandments.)

The judicial precepts, though, have not been superseded as much as they have been relativized. That is, their connection to the everlasting moral precepts can be seen as their having been historically relative means to absolute ends. Their function must be seen as what some Aristotelians have called "instrumental ends."[69] Regarding the Old Law, Aquinas speaks of the judicial precepts as "the determination of those things . . . according to the different states of mankind."[70] By *determinatio,* he means something similar to what Kant meant by "schematization," namely, "the *application* of a category to appearances."[71] These judicial applications are much closer to the perpetual precepts of natural law that govern inter-human relationships than the ceremonial precepts are to the perpetual precepts of natural law that govern the divine-human relationship. One needs to see this view of the historical function of the judicial precepts and their closer connection to the moral precepts as originating in Aquinas's natural law theory per se.

In writing about the precepts of natural law, which are known in

---

67. ST 2/1, q. 104, a. 4.

68. ST 2/1, q. 104, a. 3.

69. See Aristotle, *Nicomachean Ethics,* 1094a1-5. There Aristotle distinguishes between ends where the activity per se is the end per se and ends where the activity is a means to something separate from it. Clearly the former are superior to the latter; in fact, if all ends were instrumental, we would be left with the absurdity of an infinite regress (see *Metaphysics,* 994b10-15). For further clarification, see Aquinas, *Commentary on Aristotle's Nicomachean Ethics,* 1.12-14, pp. 4-5.

70. ST 2/1, q. 104, a. 3 ad 1.

71. Kant, *Critique of Pure Reason* B177, trans. N. Kemp Smith (New York: Macmillan, 1929), p. 180.

themselves *(per se nota)*, Aquinas does not want to claim that these precepts are sufficient to govern any real human society in history.[72] They require precise application to the moral/political situation at hand. Thus he writes that "those things which are derived from the law of nature *(lege naturae)* by way of particular determination belong to the civil law, according as each state decides on what is best for itself *(aliquid sibi accomode)*."[73] Here I think we need to make a clear distinction between the specificity of laws and the particularity of cases. For Aquinas, it seems, civil law is derived from natural law in the institution of specific laws in a specific society. They are designed to function as means to the general ends of justice. Civil law is then applied to particular cases within that specific society.

The choice between good and evil is occasionally so stark that one's moral decision can be made on the basis of the primary precepts of natural law. But in most cases these primary precepts need to be mediated by the specifics of the civil law. And the civil law is the human law that is necessary for the proper administration, legislation, and adjudication of justice. Whereas "the natural law contains universal precepts which are everlasting *(quae semper manent)*, human law contains certain particular precepts, according to various circumstances *(secundum diversos casus qui emergent)*."[74] As such, the determinations of the natural law are formulated in an historically contingent way by human authorities. And "these determinations which are made by human law are said to be, not of natural, but of positive law *(de iuro positivo)*."[75]

Nevertheless, positive law is not confined to human law. There is also a divinely ordained positive law *(ius divinum positivum)*.[76] Picking up on his statement about human law just quoted above, Aquinas says "so the determinations of the precepts of natural law effected by the divine law are distinct from the moral precepts which belong to natural law."[77] Therefore, there is some divine law that is perpetual because it is identical with either natural law or the supernatural reality of Christian revelation (the difference being between earthly and heavenly ends), while there is some divine law that is brought by prophets for a limited period of time.[78] This aspect of divine positive law, in the form of the judicial precepts, may even

---

72. ST 2/1, q. 100, a. 4.

73. ST 2/1, q. 95, a. 4.

74. ST 2/1, q. 97, a. 1 ad 1. See also ST 2/1, q. 96, a. 2; q. 98, a. 2 ad 1.

75. ST 2/1, q. 99, a. 3 ad 2. See also ST 2/1, q. 108, a. 2 ad 4.

76. ST 2/1, q. 104, a. 1.

77. ST 2/1, q. 99, a. 3 ad 2.

78. ST 2/1, q. 102, a. 2.

have great analogical (as distinct from symbolic) meaning as long as it is justified by natural law rather than by pre-Christian revelation. After Christ, for Aquinas, only one revelation qua revelation is immediately normative.[79] That revelation, together with the precepts of natural law, is now totally sufficient to attain both earthly and heavenly ends.

The Differences between Maimonides and Aquinas

The main point in common between Maimonides and Aquinas is their admission, *mutatis mutandis,* that the divine law contains the natural law. Both Maimonides and Aquinas had to battle against the fideists in their respective communities, those who seemed to think that ascribing reason to God's law limits the infinity of God's power and will.[80] And both Maimonides and Aquinas have been suspected by subsequent fideists in their respective traditions as being too philosophical to be trusted by the faithful.[81] This commonality of both their friends and their enemies should not be underestimated. Any retrieval of natural law by either Jews or Christians has a lot to learn from Maimonides and Aquinas and the roles they played in history, both in their own times and in later times. Nevertheless, their differences must be appreciated in order for Jews and Christians to be able to have a greater diversity of teachers about natural law. What are these differences?

The first difference is not only theological, it is religious. As a post-talmudic Jew, Maimonides could not very well accept a new law to supersede the Torah of Moses (and the whole Jewish tradition built upon it). The law of God, centered in the Torah of Moses, is permanent and perfect, from its most general precepts to its particular minutiae.[82] Rejecting one earlier rabbinic view that those aspects of the Torah which Aquinas (and others) called "ceremonies" will be abrogated when the Messiah comes, Maimonides stressed that God will never change any aspect of His law.[83] (And, moreover, he denied that Jesus of Nazareth was the Messiah.)[84] In

---

79. ST 2/1, q. 103, a. 3 ad 4; q. 103, a. 4; q. 107, a. 2 ad 1.

80. See *Guide,* 3.31.

81. See J. Sarachek, *The Conflict over the Rationalism of Maimonides* (New York: Hermon Press, 1970).

82. See Maimonides, *Commentary on the Mishnah:* Sanhedrin, chap. 10: Foundations, no. 8.

83. MT: Kings, chap. 11 (uncensored edn.), ed. Y. Rabinowitz (Jerusalem: Mosad ha-Rav Kook, 1962), p. 416.

84. MT: Kings, chap. 11, ed. Rabinowitz, p. 416.

fact, the role of the Messiah is not to abrogate the Law but, rather, to provide the political realm in which the Law can and will be fully observed in every detail. For him, then, there is no normative difference between the moral precepts and either the ceremonial precepts or the judicial precepts. There is no divine positive law in the sense of positive law being law that admits of abrogation or repeal. It is only that the present political circumstances of the Jews do not enable them to observe some aspects of the Law like the Temple rituals, for example. However, the reign of the Messiah will once again enable the Jews to observe all the precepts of the Law, which themselves have never lost their perpetual normative force.[85]

The positive law of revelation, as distinct from the natural law in revelation, mostly pertains to certain details of the law, especially in its ritual aspects, which cannot be rationally inferred from the overall ends of the law.[86] As for their nonrational (although never irrational) character, Maimonides and Aquinas would be in agreement. Their difference here would be whether this nonrationality makes them temporary (which would be Aquinas's view) or not (which would be Maimonides' view).

Positive law in any temporally limited sense is only human. For Jews, it is the law made by the Rabbis functioning as the legislators of and for all Israel.[87] (And it is clear from the history of Jewish law, this rabbinic authority had to be responsive to popular needs in the formulation of the law and to popular opinion in the persuasion of the community to accept the law.)[88] Furthermore, these human-made laws admit of repeal if and when it is decided subsequently that they no longer serve the end for which they were originally formulated.[89] (After the demise of the Sanhedrin as the central legislative-judicial body of the Jewish people, repeal de jure became impossible. However, repeal de facto took the form of more conservative judicial review and reinterpretation of the old laws.) For Maimonides, the only thing roughly comparable to Aquinas's notion of divine positive law would be the ad hoc commandments found in Scripture that are addressed to particular prophets for their particular times.[90] Jewish tradition does not consider them to be among the six hundred thirteen permanent commandments of the Written (Mosaic) Torah. But one would have to see these commandments as being particular applica-

85. MT: Kings, 12.1.
86. Maimonides, *Guide,* 3.26.
87. See MT: Rebels, chaps. 1-2.
88. See B. Avodah Zarah 36a-b.
89. See *Mishnah:* Eduyot 1.5.
90. See *Book of the Commandments:* Introduction, root no. 3.

tions of more general principles rather than being specifications of them in the form of common laws. Sometimes they are even particular dispensations from Torah laws, which are requited for very limited situations, what the Rabbis called "decrees of the hour" *(hora'at sha'ah)*.[91]

The second difference between Maimonides and Aquinas is theological, and it is one where Maimonides not only differs from Aquinas, but where he also differs from some other important Jewish theologians. Unlike Aquinas, it seems that Maimonides would make no real distinction between natural law and supernatural law. Such a distinction, as we have seen in Aquinas, is teleological. For Maimonides, natural law leads to natural ends attainable either physically or spiritually. The life of the world-to-come is attainable by ordinary acts of body and soul that are performed in this world. Indeed, it seems that Maimonides saw the world-to-come as the highest aspect of nature, being what is everlasting and beatific.[92] In principle, all the laws of the Torah have universalizable reasons that can be rationally intended here and now. All of them are, thus, natural law in principle. But in this type of rationalism, Maimonides was very much opposed by the kabbalistic theologians. For a few of them, such as Maimonides' most systematic theological critic, Nahmanides (d. 1270), while some of the commandments pertaining to interhuman relationships do have mundane reasons, almost all of the commandments pertaining to the divine-human relationship have supernatural reasons.[93] That is, their effects must be considered the work of grace, not nature. From this perspective, Maimonides elided the difference between theology and philosophy.

For many of the kabbalists, however, the difference with Maimonides is even greater. All of the commandments are the work of grace, not nature. In fact, in what could be termed their acosmic theology, there is no nature at all; everything real is a direct participation in the life of God. All of reality is panentheistic.[94] Everything is very much what Aquinas would call a sacrament.[95] And even those kabbalistic theologians, like Nahmanides, who did recognize the limited reality of nature, are highly critical of what they see as Maimonides' pan-naturalism/pan-rationalism. In Nahmanides' case, that allowed him to affirm natural law, but it was a

---

91. See B. Yoma 69b; also, B. Sanhedrin 46a.

92. See MT: Repentance, chap. 8.

93. See David Novak, *The Theology of Nahmanides Systematically Presented* (Atlanta: Scholars Press, 1992), pp. 107-13. Cf. ST 2/1, q. 91, a. 4; q. 100, a. 5.

94. See Novak, *The Image of the Non-Jew in Judaism,* pp. 265-68.

95. See ST 3, q. 62, a. 1. Cf. ST 3, q. 62, a. 4.

much more minimal natural law than that affirmed by Maimonides (and, for that matter, even by Aquinas). Finally, even those Jewish theologians who would not see the commandments as sacraments in the kabbalistic sense (which also tends to ascribe theurgic powers to them) would ascribe to them a far greater historical particularity than would Maimonides. And since that historical particularity intends a salvific consummation of all human history, it does not share the pitfalls of modern historicism and the relativism it so obviously presupposes. In this view, *Heilsgeschichte* fulfills nature; it does not destroy it or deny it. But Maimonides refuses to assign any supernatural significance to history, even to sacred history.[96]

The Contemporary Retrieval of Natural Law

Natural law theory lies at the border of philosophy and theology. Without theology, it tends to become the type of rationalism that overlooks the fundamental religious thrust of human nature, that humans are essentially and uniquely God-seeking creatures. Without philosophy, natural law theory tends to become a mere apologetics for specifically religious doctrine, namely, rationalization rather than reason in its teleological quest.[97] By concentrating our look at the natural law theories of Maimonides and Aquinas in their understanding of the normative significance of the Hebrew Bible, Jews and Christians have the most to learn from both of them. After all, the most basic claims of Maimonides' Judaism and Aquinas's Christianity come from the common and rival interpretations of that book. Since that book teaches us about the creation of the world and, especially, the creation of the human person having one nature and one destiny, natural law theory by Jews and Christians must ultimately find its theological justification there or nowhere at all. Who understood that better than Moses Maimonides and Thomas Aquinas?

96. See David Novak, "Does Maimonides Have a Philosophy of History?" *Proceedings of the Academy for Jewish Philosophy,* ed. N. M. Samuelson (Lanham, Md.: University Press of America, 1984), pp. 53-68.

97. See Novak, *Natural Law in Judaism,* pp. 174-78.

Buber and Tillich

Précis

This article attempts to show that the deep spiritual and intellectual relationship between Martin Buber and Paul Tillich can be the basis of a dialogical legacy for Jews and Christians in the present if their thoughts are seen as complementary. The article concentrates on their respective interpretations of Exodus 3:14 ("I am who I am"), showing how the respective philosophical exegeses of Buber and Tillich enrich and expand each other. The article shows that Tillich's critique of Buber's limitation of the God-human relation to the I-Thou relationship continues (probably unknowingly on Tillich's part) an important aspect of kabbalistic teaching that Buber neglected in his thought. The article concludes with a suggestion that Jewish-Christian dialogue is most intellectually fruitful when engaging in philosophical exegesis of the Bible.

Relationship and Interrelationship

Jewish-Christian dialogue in modern times has reached great heights when it has occurred between a great Jewish thinker and a great Christian thinker. One recalls Moses Mendelssohn and Gotthold Ephraim Lessing,

This essay originated as an address at the November 1990 meeting of the North American Tillich Society in New Orleans. It previously appeared in the *Journal of Ecumenical Studies* 29, no. 2 (Spring 1992): 159-74.

Hermann Cohen and Wilhelm Herrmann, Franz Rosenzweig and Eugen Rosenstock, Abraham Joshua Heschel and Reinhold Niebuhr. To this illustrative list should be added the names of Martin Buber and Paul Tillich.

Buber and Tillich, both of whom died in 1965, knew each other for over forty years, beginning in Germany in the tumultuous period after World War I. Although they were contemporaries, Buber (b. 1878) being only eight years older than Tillich (b. 1886), it seems that their relationship was one of teacher and student: Buber the teacher and Tillich the student.

On the personal level, the relationship between the older Buber and the younger Tillich is best illustrated by the following story that I heard from someone who was in attendance at a lecture Buber delivered at Union Theological Seminary in New York in 1952, during his first visit to America, a visit in which he made a profound impression on American intellectual circles. At the end of the lecture, Buber indicated that he would entertain questions from the audience. From the back of the crowded lecture hall, Paul Tillich arose and quite respectfully (as was his usual manner) addressed a rather complicated question to Buber. According to my reliable informant, Buber looked up from his text and said, "Ah, Paulus, it is you." Then he walked down the aisle and stood directly in front of Tillich, who was considerably taller than he, raised his index finger up at Tillich's startled face and said, "Paulus, Paulus, you asked me the same question in Germany thirty years ago. Don't you remember what I answered you then?!"

On the level of ideas, Buber's faithful disciple and biographer, Maurice Friedman, reported in his massive biography of his teacher that, at a conference of religious socialists in Germany in the early 1920s, Tillich had suggested that a word should be found to replace "God" in order to include believers as well as nonbelievers in the socialist cause. At that point in the proceedings, Buber arose and emphatically proclaimed, *"Aber Gott ist ein Urwort!"* (God is a primordial word!). As Friedman put it, "You cannot do away with a primordial word like God, said Buber, even for the sake of attaining unity. 'And he was right!' Tillich exclaimed."[1]

So it seems that, throughout their long relationship, it was Buber who was reminding Tillich not to stray from the Hebraic roots of Christianity, for, as Friedman again reports, Tillich stated "that he was undoubtedly more Greek than Buber" at a dinner held in Buber's honor at Brandeis University in 1952.[2]

---

1. Maurice S. Friedman, *Martin Buber's Life and Work,* 3 vols. (Detroit: Wayne State University Press, 1988), vol. 2, p. 99.

2. Friedman, *Martin Buber's Life and Work,* vol. 3, p. 265.

As a model for Jewish-Christian dialogue, this role that Buber played for Tillich's own thought is not to be underestimated, for, at the most fundamental level, the Hebrew Bible is the locus for the Jewish-Christian relationship. Only Jews and Christians regard the Hebrew Bible to be the word of God, however differently that designation is explicated by Jewish and Christian thinkers, respectively. Jews need to remind Christians of that truth, and of late many Christians have indeed gladly and creatively been so reminded.[3] In this context, then, Buber's Hebraic influence on the more "Greek" Tillich can be quite instructive, one to be studied with great profit. By itself, it is an impressive example of an older brother teaching a younger brother about their common source and origin.

Nevertheless, if an interrelationship, with its mutuality and reciprocity, is the desideratum for Jews and Christians to live and think together twenty-five years after the departure of both Buber and Tillich, then what transpired between them is problematic. For, although it is obvious, even documented, that Buber influenced Tillich, it is not at all obvious, much less documented (to my knowledge anyway), that Tillich influenced Buber. As such, we only have an example of a Christian thinker learning from a Jewish thinker but not *vice versa*. Although the legacy of this one-way influence is important, Jewish thinkers must find some way also to learn from Christian thinkers, especially from a Christian thinker like Tillich, who was so eager to engage Judaism on its own terms, without the triumphalist claims and demands too often presented to Jews by Christians. Interrelationship must move in two directions, not just one. Is there any resource in the Tillich-Buber relationship for that?

The Philosophical Understanding of Exodus 3:14

Although there is no evidence that Tillich influenced Buber during their lifetime, the fact is that, now that both men are dead, all we have from them are their written thoughts. As such, those of us still learning from their respective writings can compare their thoughts on a common issue or, even better, on a common text, especially a common biblical text that has been very important in the development of both Jewish theology and Christian theology. In the process of this comparison, done for the sake of our own theological clarity and progress, we can perhaps ourselves consti-

---

3. See David Novak, *Jewish-Christian Dialogue: A Jewish Justification* (New York: Oxford University Press, 1989), pp. 141ff.

tute the reciprocal mutuality between Tillich's and Buber's thoughts, something that eluded them when they were still alive. Indeed, there is a great advantage to having the shoulders of giants to stand on.

In this article I would like to analyze a profound critique of Buber made by Tillich and to show how Jewish thinkers can learn much from that critique precisely because it has remarkably strong affinities to a part of Jewish tradition itself, one that Buber himself unfortunately ignored for the most part. Hence, Jewish thinkers who have learned much from Buber can complement and correct what we have learned from him with what we can now learn from Tillich.

In order to understand the significance of Tillich's critique of Buber, we must begin by examining one of the most theologically charged texts in the entire Hebrew Bible, Exodus 3:14. This important text is the basis for a tradition of theological interpretation that is the historical context for both Buber's and Tillich's philosophical exegesis: "And God said to Moses, 'I shall be who I shall be' [*ehyeh asher ehyeh*]. Thus say to the children of Israel, 'I shall be' [*ehyeh*] has sent me to you." The key philosophical question about this verse's proclamation of God's identity is whether that designation is a statement about a property of God or a relation of God.

The most influential of the classic rabbinic interpretations of this verse sees the statement as one of relation, paraphrasing it as "God says to Moses, 'Say to them that I shall be with you [*ehyeh immakhem*] in this bondage, and I shall be with you in the bondage into which they will be going.'"[4] Thus, we see, to use modern philosophical language appropriated by both Buber and Tillich, that God is stating that God's being-there (*dasein*) is God's being-with (*mitsein*) God's people. Conversely, the classic Hellenistic interpretation in the Septuagint of this verse sees the statement as denoting the divine property of absolute being: "I am he who is" [*eimi ho ōn*], or "I am Being."[5] In and of itself, either interpretation is incomplete, both in terms of the meaning of the overall biblical text and in terms of the subsequent theological ramifications.

The Hellenistic interpretation is incomplete because it does not indicate just how the children of Israel are related to this Absolute Being and

---

4. *Shemot Rabbah*, 3.6, ed. Shinan (Jerusalem and Tel Aviv: Dvir, 1984), p. 128.

5. This whole tradition of identifying God and being is best expressed by Thomas Aquinas, *Summa Theologiae* 1, q. 13, a. 11: "This name, HE WHO IS [*Qui est*], is the most proper name of God.... For it does not signify some form, but being itself.... The being of God is His very essence (which can be said of no other being) . . ." (*The Basic Writings of Saint Thomas Aquinas*, vol. 1, edited and introduced by Anton C. Pegis [New York: Random House, 1945], p. 131).

this Absolute Being to them. Surely, the covenantal character of the narrative is essential. Thus, it is immediately preceded, indeed introduced, by the words, "And God remembered his covenant [*berito*] . . . and God saw the children of Israel and God perceived [*va-yeda*]" (Exod. 2:25). But, what did God perceive? "For I perceive [*yad'ati*] their pain" (Exod. 3:7). Buber and his collaborator, Franz Rosenzweig, translated the Hebrew verb *"yado'a"* with the German verb *"erkennen"* — hence, my English translation of "perceive," meaning direct and intimate knowledge rather than indirect and constituted knowledge, connoted by "cognition" or *"wissen."*[6] Finally, the very verb *"ehyeh"* (I shall be), just before its definition in Exod. 3:14, is used in verse 12 to express the intimate relationship between God and Moses: "For I shall be with you [*ehyeh immakh*]." Buber and Rosenzweig translated this into German as *"Wohl, ich werde dasein bei dir"* (I shall surely be there with you).[7] Buber said about this translation that, in the context of the covenantal urgency of this narrative, it would have been trivial for God to express the eternity of God's being *per se (Aus-sich-Selbtsein)*.[8] Rosenzweig said, in a remark Buber coupled with his own, "What good would it have been for these unfortunates to have a lecture about God's necessary existence?"[9]

However, the Hellenistic interpretation of Exodus 3:14 is not as farfetched as it seems. Contrary to Buber's and Rosenzweig's objections, the narrative itself does require a statement of God's being, not just God's relationality, for the narrative clearly intends not only to declare God's relationality but also to distinguish God from the Egyptian gods.[10] That is why Moses assumes that the people will ask, "What [*mah*] is his name?" (Exod. 3:13). God is more than correlated with God's people. God's very ability to save them from another people and its gods who are mightier than Israel is precisely because of God's transcendence. Not only does Israel have to be aware of God's nearness to it; Israel has to be just as much aware with whom this relationship is to be. Furthermore, contrary to the

---

6. Franz Rosenzweig and Martin Buber, *Die Fünf Bücher der Weisung* (Cologne and Olten: Hegner, 1954), p. 157.

7. Rosenzweig and Buber, *Die Fünf Bücher der Weisung*, p. 158.

8. Martin Buber, *Zu einer neuen Verdeutschung der Schrift* (Olten: Hegner, 1954), p. 28.

9. Franz Rosenzweig, *Kleinere Schriften* (Berlin: Schocken, 1937), p. 188.

10. Even Buber, however, had to admit that *ehyeh asher ehyeh* is not a totally relational statement: ". . . ehje . . . meint: bei jemand da sein, ihm gegenwärtig sein, ihm bei-stehen, nur dass hier das Verb absolut gebraucht wird, ohne dass also hinzugefügt würde, *bei wem* der Daseiende da ist" (Buber, *Königtum Gottes,* 3rd rev. ed. [Heidelberg: Lambert Schneider, 1956], p. 69).

assumption of the antimetaphysical bias of the rabbinic tradition, in the very rabbinic text where "I shall be who I shall be" is emphasized as God's *mitsein* (being-with), another rabbi makes this very metaphysical paraphrase of the verse: "I am he: I am he who was; I am he who is now; I am he who is future."[11]

The biblical text and its subsequent theological development requires, therefore, a constitution of a dialectic, as it were, between divine being *per se* and divine relationality *ad extra*.

The Hellenistic development of this text begins to connect the Septuagint's *"eimi ho ōn"* (I am he who is) with Plato's designation of the Forms as *"ontos ōn"* — being *per se*.[12] Thus, God is seen as eternal *(aiōn)*, beyond any temporal limitation. All lesser being, subject to temporal limitation and thus only *becoming*, only exists at all because it is related to the eternal divine being.[13] When this lesser being is conscious, as it is in its human manifestation, this subordinate relationship is one that can be known. *Nous* is thus able to apprehend, if not comprehend, the *ontos ōn*.[14] Hence, the relationship is always present as an object is always present. Its absence is only an experience due to a subjective lack in the human knower.[15] To borrow from Aquinas's language: God is always *"ratio per se"* (intelligible in Himself) with regard to human noetic potential; God is only *"ratio quoad nos"* (intelligible to us) with regard to actual human knowledge.[16] The actualization of human knowledge is essentially an issue for humans as temporal existences in the process of becoming; it is not essentially an issue for the eternal, unchanging God.

The amazing thing to note is that, despite Buber's *I and Thou*'s being thought of as an "existentialist" classic, one that expresses the radical antimetaphysical primacy of temporal relationality, in the first edition of the work in 1923 Buber's interpretation of Exodus 3:14 was still remarkably similar to the Hellenistic interpretation. As he wrote there:

> Only one You never ceases, in accordance with its nature [*seinem Wesen nach*] to be You for us. To be sure, whoever knows God also knows

---

11. *Shemot Rabbah,* 3.6, p. 127.

12. See *Wisdom of Solomon* 13:1; Philo, *Quod Deter.,* 160; cf. Plato, *Phaedrus* 27E; and Harry Austryn Wolfson, *Philo: Foundations of Religious Philosophy in Judaism, Christianity, and Islam,* 2 vols. (Cambridge, Mass.: Harvard University Press, 1947), vol. 1, pp. 19-20, 210.

13. See Plato, *Timaeus* 35A.

14. See Plato, *Republic* 511D-E.

15. See Plato, *Republic* 514Aff.

16. See Aquinas, *Summa Theologiae* 1, q. 2, a. 1.

God's remoteness . . . but not the loss of presence [*Präsenlösigkeit*].
Only we are not always there [*nur wir sind nicht immer da*].[17]

So we see that, for Buber, at this central point in the development of
his thought, God had a nature, and that nature was to be all-present. All-
presence is eternity; that is why Buber called God "the eternal You [*das
ewige Du*]," which "is You by its very nature [*seinem Wesen nach*]." God's all-
presence cannot be lost but only not-experienced by human consciousness because that human consciousness has removed itself away from the
reality of thou-ness "into the It-world and It-speech." That removal is the
separation of appearance from reality. Indeed, in the 1923 edition of *I and
Thou,* Buber translated Exodus 3:14 as *"Ich bin der ich bin"* (I am what I
am).[18] Thus, if God is the *eternal You,* then God cannot be other than *there.*
There for the real eternal being is ubiquitous; it is the omnipresence of medieval rational theology. Only appearance — that which is less than real
eternal being — is subject to the mixture of being-there and not-being-
there, the mixture of presence and absence.[19] How Platonic!

17. Martin Buber, *I and Thou,* translated and with a prologue by Walter Kaufmann (New
York: Charles Scribner's Sons, 1970), p. 147 (cf. German: *Ich und Du* [Heidelberg: Lambert
Schneider, 1962], p. 100).

18. See Buber, *I and Thou,* p. 160, and Kaufmann's n. 1 thereon. In *Königtum Gottes,* Buber
wrote, ". . . also nicht 'Ich bin der Ich bin' oder dergleichen . . . nicht in Existenzialsinn . . .
wohl aber 'werden geschehen, gegenwärtig werden, da hier sein' . . . der Daseiende da ist"
(p. 69).

19. See Plato, *Republic* 534A. It was the Septuagint that translated the Hebrew of Exod.
15:18 (*l'olam va'ed*) as *ep aiōna kai eti,* literally "unto eternity and beyond." However, the use of
"eternity" makes the use of "beyond" redundant. What could be beyond eternity?
Rosenzweig and Buber (in their *Die Fünf Bücher der Weisung,* p. 193) captured its true meaning somewhat better with their *"in Weltzeit und Ewigkeit."* Nevertheless, even here the use of
Ewigkeit (eternity) still reflects the Platonic distinction between time and eternity (see Plato,
Timaeus 37Dff.). A better German translation of the Hebrew would have been *in Weltzeit und
weiter* or *in Weltzeit und jenseitig* ("in the time of the world and beyond"). In the Hebrew Bible,
God is clearly *everlasting,* in the sense of being both in the world and beyond it, not being
limited by time or space. However, God is not *eternal* in the sense of being unchanged and
unchanging. (See Abraham Joshua Heschel, *The Prophets* [New York: Harper & Row; Philadelphia: Jewish Publication Society of America, 1962], pp. 221ff.) Buber was still following
Luther's *immer und ewig* translation, which itself follows the Vulgate's *in aeternum et ultra*
and, ultimately, the Septuagint. For Rosenzweig's reservations about *Ewigkeit/der Ewige* at
the end of his life, see his essay written in 1929 (the year of his death), "Der Ewige," in
Rosenzweig, *Kleinere Schriften,* p. 197.

The New Understanding of Exodus 3:14

Contrary to the usual assumption that everything Buber wrote after 1923 is only a footnote to the first edition of *I and Thou*, he did change his interpretation of Exodus 3:14, and that changed interpretation is indicative of a major shift in his thought, a shift away from the Platonic-like approach just seen.

In the 1957 edition of *I and Thou*, Buber still referred to "the eternal revelation which is present in the here and now," but he then continued: "The word of revelation is: I am there as whoever I am there [*Ich bin da als der ich da bin*]. That which reveals is that which reveals. That which has being is there [*Das Seiende ist da*], nothing more."[20]

Nevertheless, there is no thirty-four-year empty hiatus between this new translation and the original one. Already in 1928, in his Bible translation with Rosenzweig, we find the translation *"Ich werde dasein, als der ich dasein werde"* (I shall there-be as I shall there-be).[21] The implication of this new translation, it seems to me, is that God's *Dasein*/presence is in a dialectical relation with God's *Ab-sein*/absence. What appears there rather than always being found there can just as easily not appear there, if being is taken as temporal presence.

Certainly, it is quite plausible to see this new use of *Dasein* as stemming from the influence of Heidegger's new use of that term in his 1927 work, *Sein und Zeit*. The *da* ("there") of *Dasein* emphasizes a temporally self-electing presence rather than the ubiquity of *Sein* ("Being") in the old metaphysics.[22] Now God's absence is no longer just a matter of the limits of finite human consciousness. Rather, it is an aspect of the Godhead itself. However, unlike Heidegger — with whose thought Buber struggled and against whose thought Buber cogently argued — God's *Sein* (being *per se*) is just as much a factor as God's *Dasein* (being-there).[23] God still transcends the limits of temporality. Indeed, with *Dasein* alone, there is no transcendent God at all as Jews and Christians have traditionally known

20. Buber, *I and Thou*, p. 160 (*Ich und Du*, p. 113).

21. Rosenzweig and Buber, *Die Fünf Bücher der Weisung*, p. 158.

22. See Martin Heidegger, *Sein und Zeit* (Tübingen: Niemeyer, 1979), p. 250. For the close affinities between Heidegger's thought and that of Rosenzweig, even though Rosenzweig emphasized temporality and eternity, see Karl Löwith, "M. Heidegger and F. Rosenzweig or Temporality and Eternity," *Philosophy and Phenomenological Research* 3 (September 1942): 53-77.

23. See David Novak, "Buber's Critique of Heidegger," *Modern Judaism* 5 (May 1985): 125-40.

God — which, parenthetically, should indicate how selective Jewish and Christian thinkers have to be in appropriating Heideggerian terms, let alone Heideggerian concepts (and, certainly, Heidegger himself, considering his thoroughly odious moral character).

The proof that I am not reading into this new translation more than Buber himself intended is brought out by his own remarks in his 1951 essay, "Religion and Modern Thinking," an essay subsequently published in the book *Eclipse of God:*

> Let us ask whether it may not be literally true that God formerly spoke to us and is now silent, and whether this is not to be understood as the Hebrew Bible understands it, namely, that the living God is not only a self-revealing but also a self-concealing God. Let us realize what it means to live in the age of such a concealment, such a divine silence. . . .[24]

In this explicit reference to a self-concealing God, Buber's note cited Isaiah 45:15: "Therefore, You are a self-concealing God [*El misttatter*], O saving God of Israel." In his Isaiah translation, he translated the key Hebrew term here as *"eine verborgene Gottheit"* (a concealed deity).[25]

The question that now faced Buber was that heretofore in his thought he had cogently explained how the relationship with the self-revealing God was to be conducted, whereas now he had not explained how the relationship with the self-concealing God was to be conducted — indeed, if there *were* any relationship with this aspect of the Godhead at all.

If Buber could not somehow indicate how this relationship was to be constituted, then he could not in truth constitute divine transcendence. Without this constitution, the relationship with the self-revealing God would become a correlation or a symbiosis. For Buber and his school, this should be an especially vexing problem because the early impetus of his theological career was to move beyond what he considered to be the limitations of the rationalist theology of the nineteenth century, especially that of the Jewish neo-Kantian philosopher Hermann Cohen, whose

24. Martin Buber, "Religion and Modern Thinking," trans. Maurice S. Friedman, in Martin Buber, *Eclipse of God: Studies in the Relation between Religion and Philosophy* (New York: Harper & Brothers, 1952), p. 89.

25. Martin Buber, *Das Buch Jeschajahu* (Berlin: Schocken, n.d.), p. 187. The use of the term *Gottheit* strongly suggests the influence of Meister Eckhardt on Buber's thought. See Maurice S. Friedman, *Martin Buber: The Life of Dialogue* (Chicago: University of Chicago Press, 1955), pp. 27-28.

thought dominated Jewish thinking in Germany in the early years of the twentieth century before World War I.[26]

Cohen, in his ongoing polemic with Spinoza, constituted God's transcendence of nature alone but coupled it with at least a functional identification of God with morality. God, for Cohen, was Being-per-se qua Absolute Ideal.[27] Thus, in his 1915 book *Der Begriff der Religion im System der Philosophie* (The Concept of Religion in the System of Philosophy), Cohen stated that we are not concerned "with God alone and himself *per se* [*an sich*], but always in correlation to man [*zum Mensch*] . . . not with man alone, but equally [*zugleich*] always in correlation with God [*mit Gott*]."[28] Unlike the case of the human being, Cohen was willing to admit that God did have an identity *(An-sich-heit)* beyond morality. That is why God was not only *with* the human — unlike the human, who can never be more than with God.

In his posthumously published 1919 work, *Religion der Vernunft aus den Quellen des Judentums (The Religion of Reason out of the Sources of Judaism),* Cohen wrote about the attributes of God as moral examplars for humankind, that they "are contained in the essence of God, but it is impossible to imagine that they could exhaust this essence: they could have been conceived for man only."[29] Nevertheless, Cohen did not show how there could be any relationship at all with this transmoral God. As such, this admission is quite similar to Kant's recognition of the *Ding an sich* (thing-in-itself) as being a surd.[30] But Cohen could not very well

26. For Rosenzweig's acknowledgment of Buber's freeing Judaism from being a *reductio ad Kantium,* see Franz Rosenzweig, "The Builders," trans. William Wolf, in Franz Rosenzweig, *On Jewish Learning,* ed. N. N. Glatzer (New York: Schocken Books, 1955), p. 77.

27. See Hermann Cohen, *Religion of Reason out of the Sources of Judaism,* translated and with an introduction by Simon Kaplan (from 2d rev. ed. of 1929) (New York: Frederick Ungar Publishing Co., 1972), pp. 35ff.

28. Hermann Cohen, *Der Begriff der Religion im System der Philosophie* (Giessen: Toppelmann, 1915), p. 32 (my translation).

29. Cohen, *Religion of Reason out of the Sources of Judaism,* p. 95. This, however, is the only place in Cohen's writings (to my knowledge, anyway) where he made this kind of admission. Even in this last book he otherwise followed his theory of correlation consistently. Thus, on p. 109 he wrote, "There is no other morality but that of man, which even includes the morality of God. And there is no other holiness of God but that of man." Rosenzweig's contention that Cohen himself had gone beyond his lifelong Kantianism (see his introduction to Cohen's posthumously published *Jüdische Schriften,* ed. Bruno Strauss [Berlin: Schwetschke, 1924], pp. xlff. [also in Cohen, *Kleinere Schriften,* pp. 328ff.]) was greeted with convincing skepticism by Julius Guttmann in his *Philosophies of Judaism,* trans. D. W. Silverman (New York: Holt, Rinehart & Winston, 1964), p. 366.

30. See Immanuel Kant, *Critique of Pure Reason,* B167.

constitute any such function for this *Ding an sich*–like state in his thought, since in his Neo-Kantian philosophy he argued against the recognition of the *Ding an sich* altogether, thus breaking with Kant on this key point.[31]

I mention all of this because Buber's I-thou relationship faces the same problem as Cohen's correlation between divine Being and human Becoming. Just as for Cohen God cogently transcended nature but not morality, so for Buber God cogently transcended the I-it relationship but not the I-thou relationship. Via Kant (who considered himself a Platonist of sorts),[32] this got Buber back to the Platonic conundrum of all-present being: the *ontos ōn* (being *per se*), which can be apprehended by *nous* (intellect) when *nous* releases itself from the shadows of its own cave of *doxa* — mere opinion based on appearance.[33]

It was at this point that Tillich could come to the aid of those suffering from this Buberian problem, namely, how to constitute the relationship with the self-concealing God.

Tillich and Negative Theology

In his 1959 work *Theology of Culture,* Tillich invoked negative theology in a decidedly non-Platonic way:

> The analysis of the finitude of the finite in the light of the awareness of the Unconditioned . . . this negative way of recognizing the unconditional element in man and his world. It is the most impressive way of introducing people into the meaning of religion — if the fallacious inference to a highest being is avoided.[34]

What Tillich was clearly rejecting here is the whole logic of either the ontological or the cosmological proof of the existence of God. For, in these proofs one infers the ultimate presence of the Absolute from its im-

---

31. See Hermann Cohen, *Logik der reinen Erkenntnis,* 3rd ed. (Berlin: B. Cassirer, 1922), pp. 376-77.

32. See Kant, *Critique of Pure Reason,* B370ff.

33. See Plato, *Timaeus* 28A; also see Plato, *Republic* 514Aff.; and Wolfson, *Philo,* vol. 2, pp. 110ff.

34. Paul Tillich, *Theology of Culture,* ed. Robert C. Kimball (London, Oxford, and New York: Oxford University Press, 1959), pp. 26-27. For his rejection of proofs of the existence of God, see Paul Tillich, *Systematic Theology,* 3 vols. (Chicago: University of Chicago Press, 1951), vol. 1, p. 205.

mediate absence in ordinary human experience: the contingent automatically entails the necessary. From the negative, one directly attains the positive, as in *"malum privatio boni est"* (evil is the privation of good). However, Tillich was not talking about a mere *privatio* but about the authentic experience of *negatio*, which calls for the Infinite but can in no way even apprehend it with certitude by itself.[35]

What Tillich seems to have been saying here (and this becomes more plausible when looking at his fuller discussions of revelation elsewhere)[36] is that, for revelation to be more than a correlation with human action and knowledge, it must be preceded by the experience of finitude, which is the painful absence of God's presence. For God to be present as God, God must be experienced in God's self-concealed absence as well. Without that, God's transcendence gets lost in the intimacy experienced in God's self-revelation as *mitsein* (being-with) in the I-thou relationship.

Further on in *Theology of Culture,* Tillich emphasized the necessity of this duality in the human apprehension of God:

> And so in the symbolic form of speaking about him, we have both that which transcends infinitely our experience of ourselves as persons, and that which is so adequate to our being persons that we can say, "Thou" to God, and can pray to him. And these two elements must be preserved. If we preserve only the element of the unconditional, then no relationship to God is possible. If we preserve only the element of the ego-thou relationship, as it is called today, we lose the element of the divine — namely, the unconditional which transcends subject and object and all other polarities.[37]

Unlike Buber, for whom revelation could have no real preconditions, for Tillich it had to have the precondition of our experienced need to affirm the unconditional, even when we cannot apprehend it.[38] Only in that way could revelation be distinguished from any projection of human consciousness — or even a correlate of it, such as Cohen's Being, or an inten-

---

35. For the philosophical notion of relative non-being *(mē on),* see Aristotle, *Metaphysics* 1069b25-30; and Maimonides, *Guide of the Perplexed* 2.17. The Greek philosophical tradition does not deal with *negatio* qua *ouk on* (*ou/ouk* being the stronger negation in Greek).

36. See Tillich, *Systematic Theology,* vol. 1, pp. 117ff.; also see David Novak, "Theonomous Ethics: A Defense and a Critique of Tillich," *Soundings* 69 (Fall 1986): 443ff.

37. Tillich, *Theology of Culture,* pp. 61-62.

38. See Buber, *I and Thou,* pp. 125, 159; also see Friedman, *Martin Buber's Life and Work,* vol. 3, p. 265.

tion of it, such as Husserl's *noema* (object of knowledge).[39] Only in that way is revelation *from* but not *to* the Ground of Being.

The Polarity of God in Kabbalistic Theology

Buber's disciples have always been quick to decry the impersonal aspect of Tillich's dual approach to God as indicating what Malcolm Diamond has called a "transtheistic position that Buber seeks to avoid."[40] He further charged that "Tillich ultimately subsumes the God of the Bible in an ontological framework that, for all Tillich's protestations to the contrary, is as impersonal as the 'necessary being' of Saint Thomas Aquinas."[41]

However, despite Diamond's innuendo, Tillich's position cannot be characterized — and thus dismissed by Jewish thinkers — as simply that of a Christian Hellenist in contradistinction to that of Buber as a Jewish Hebraist. For, first of all, we have already seen how Tillich's position is decidedly anti-Platonic. Furthermore, the theology that dominated Jewish thought for over six centuries — Kabbalah — which Gershom Scholem especially showed must still be an active component of any comprehensive, creative Jewish thought in the present, provides a truly remarkable precedent for the very point Tillich made against Buber in *Theology of Culture*.[42] Thus, in the *Zohar*, which is the most basic kabbalistic text, assumed by most modern scholars to have been initially written at the end of the thirteenth century, we find the following passage:

> He [*hu*] is concealed not revealed, for the Torah comes from the upper world [*me'alma ila'ah*] and in every place He is the upper world which is not revealed. . . . That is why He is called *He* and not *You* [*attah*]. . . . Everywhere there are two worlds: that which is revealed and that which is concealed [*ve-da b'itkasya*]. And we indeed declare God blessed in these two worlds, as it says in Scripture, "blessed be

39. See Edmund Husserl, *Ideas*, trans. W. R. B. Gibson (New York: Collier, 1962), pp. 235ff.

40. Malcolm L. Diamond, "Dialogue and Theology," in *The Philosophy of Martin Buber*, vol. 12 of The Library of Living Philosophers, ed. Paul Arthur Schilpp and Maurice Friedman (LaSalle, Ill.: Open Court, 1967), p. 245.

41. Diamond, "Dialogue and Theology," p. 245.

42. For Scholem's critique of Buber's virtual dismissal of Kabbalah from his Jewish theology, see David Biale, *Gershom Scholem: Kabbalah and Counter-History* (Cambridge, Mass.: Harvard University Press, 1979), pp. 165-70.

the Lord God of Israel from world to world" (Psalms 106:48). For the upper world we call *He* and the lower world we call *You*.[43]

This distinction between *Deus absconditus* (the hidden God) and *Deus revelatus* (the revealed God) builds upon a stylistic enigma in liturgical Hebrew. Whereas a humanly uttered blessing *(berakhah)* begins with an address to God in the second person: "Blessed are You [*barukh attah*], Lord, king of the universe," the next clause inevitably is a declaration in the third person, for example, "He who has given [*asher natan*] us the teaching of truth [*torat emet*]."[44] At the very same time that the worshiper is affirming his or her intimate relationship *with* God, the worshiper is simultaneously affirming his or her relationship *to* the transcendent source of blessing — and this source of blessing must be acknowledged even when one experiences its results as bad or painful, as in the case of the experience of the death of a loved one.[45]

The danger inherent in Buber's reduction of the God-human relationship to the I-thou relationship is that the God-human relationship becomes enclosed within positive human experience in this world. Granted, Buber carefully distinguished the direct I-thou encounter qua *Gegenwart* (presence) from the indirect, constituted, subject-object experience of I-it qua *Erfahrung*, or even "inner" experience qua *Erlebnis*.[46] Granted, along the same lines, Buber distinguished between direct personal commandments from God and the constituted system of traditional commandments in the system of Jewish law *(Halakhah)*.[47] Nevertheless, he made no provision for the past preconditions of this experience or for the inherent limitations and gaps in this experience in the present or for the future horizon of this experience.

We have already seen, first, how Buber made no provision for the past preconditions of this experience. He seemed to be afraid that the constitution of past preconditions for this experience would automatically de-

43. *Zohar:* Vayetse, 1:156a and 158b (my translation) re *Mishnah:* Berakhot, end. See also *Zohar:* Aharei-Mot, 3:65a-b; and David Novak, "Self-Contraction of the Godhead in Kabbalistic Theology," in *Judaism and Neoplatonism*, ed. Lenn E. Goodman (Stony Brook, N.Y.: State University of New York Press, 1991), pp. 282ff.

44. See R. Moses di Trani, *Bet Elohim* (Venice, 1576): Sha'ar Ha-Tefillah, chap. 5; also see Nahmanides, *Commentary on the Torah* (Jerusalem: Mosad Harav Kook, 1963), ad Exod. 15:26.

45. See *Mishnah:* Berakhot 9.2.

46. See Buber, *I and Thou*, pp. 55-56, 157-58. For Buber's earlier acceptance of *Erlebnis* as a sufficient religious alternative to *Erfahrung*, see Martin Buber, *Ekstatische Konfessionen* (Jena: Diedrichs, 1909), p. 15.

47. See Buber, *I and Thou*, pp. 156-57.

stroy its spontaneity and make it, in effect, a necessary derivative or conse-
quence of these preconditions. However, as I have argued elsewhere, this
fear could well be assuaged by learning from Kant's distinction between a
condition *(Bedingung)* of experience and a cause *(Ursache)* of it.[48] A condition only makes an experience possible; it clears a site for it, so to speak. It
in no way guarantees that it will occur or can be the basis of any inference
when and where it will occur. A cause, on the other hand, necessarily entails its effect. Hence, a recognition of the unconditionality of the Ground
of Being, which is essentially a *negatio,* can function as a precondition for
the positive experience of I-thou without in any way becoming anything
like the necessary inference involved in a proof of the existence of God.

Second, Buber made no provision for the inherent limitations and
gaps in this experience in the present. The fact is that, even in the most exalted experience of God's presence, its temporal limitations and systematic incompleteness are always apparent. Were this not the case, the experience would be a *unio mystica* of one sort or another. This could only lead,
however, to a gnostic disdain for the rest of creation, something that
Buber clearly and with persistence fought against.[49] The apprehension of
the transpersonal being of God enables one to recognize the rest of creation as being related to God in a way not analogous to that of our own
personal experience. As such, our relationship with God is saved from becoming a correlation, where God and the human are solely defined as
functional poles therein.[50]

In Judaism, the kabbalistic emphasis on the infinity of God *(Ayn Sof)*
has always served as a corrective to the type of self-satisfied orthodoxy
against which Buber reacted — perhaps overly so, as Rosenzweig
charged.[51] The Kabbalah has served as a corrective to this self-satisfaction
of the religious by emphasizing that the very affirmation of the transcendent source of the Torah's commandments never allows them to function
merely as parts of some wholly self-contained system of law.[52] The com-

48. See Novak, *Jewish-Christian Dialogue,* pp. 135-37.

49. See Buber, *I and Thou,* pp. 124ff.

50. Even though Tillich used the term "correlation," he explicitly rejected its symbiotic
connotation (see Tillich, *Systematic Theology,* vol. 1, pp. 59ff.).

51. See Rosenzweig, "The Builders," pp. 76ff. For a critique of both Buber and
Rosenzweig on this whole issue, see David Novak, *Law and Theology in Judaism,* vol. 2 (New
York: KTAV, 1976), pp. 10-15; and Novak, *Jewish-Christian Dialogue,* pp. 89-92.

52. For an emphasis of this point by a modern Jewish theologian heavily influenced by
Kabbalah, see Abraham Joshua Heschel, *God in Search of Man: A Philosophy of Judaism* (New
York: Farrar, Straus & Cudahy, 1955), pp. 320ff.

mandments can only be properly understood and properly kept when experienced symbolically — by which I mean in Tillich's sense of the symbolic as that which both *points beyond* itself and *participates in* what is truly and uniquely transcendent.[53]

Finally, Buber made no provision for the future horizon of the I-thou relationship with God. For all intents and purposes, it seems as though God's very being is defined and exhausted by God's being the eternal You. In his *Systematic Theology*, Tillich argued against this temptation as follows:

> Theological criticism of these attempts is easy if the concepts are taken in their proper sense, for they make God finite, dependent on a fate or an accident which is not himself. . . . But this is not the way in which these concepts should be interpreted. They point symbolically to a quality of the divine life which is analogous to what appears as dynamics in the ontological structure. The divine creativity, God's participation in history, his outgoing character, are based on this dynamic element. It includes a "not-yet" which is, however, always balanced by an "already" within the divine life.[54]

If one adopts the triad of Buber's colleague, Franz Rosenzweig — creation, revelation, and redemption — then Tillich's insight here is especially illuminating for Jewish thinkers.[55]

Creation is the "already" within the divine life about which Tillich spoke in the foregoing quotation. It functions as a precondition for revelation in the sense of indicating the utter contingency of all finite being. It makes revelation possible. However, it is not a potential that revelation totally incorporates in the sense of Aristotelian actuality's totally incorporating its own potentiality; nor is it *aufgehoben* (sublimated) in the way lower levels of the Hegelian dialectic of the Spirit are totally absorbed in the higher levels of it. If that were so, creation would lose its radical contingency, the very feature that makes the contrast of the Infinite with the

---

53. See Tillich, *Systematic Theology*, vol. 1, pp. 238ff.

54. Tillich, *Systematic Theology*, vol. 1, p. 246. Tillich's unwitting affinity to Kabbalah might be seen as coming out of his explicit dependence on Schelling, who also had affinities to Kabbalah, a point brought out by Gershom Scholem in *Major Trends in Jewish Mysticism*, 3rd ed. (New York: Schocken Books, 1961), p. 409n.19 and p. 412n.79. Whether Schelling was explicitly influenced by kabbalistic texts that could have been available to him in Latin translation is a point worthy of research.

55. See Franz Rosenzweig, *The Star of Redemption*, trans. William W. Hallo (from 2d ed. of 1930) (New York: Holt, Rinehart & Winston, 1970), pp. 110-11, 250.

finite so overwhelming and so unbridgeable from the finite side. As with Plato's *hypodochē* (receptacle), subsequent structure and content do not contain all of the primordial past.[56]

Revelation is the divine now. It is God's self-presentation in the events of revelation. At this point, a distinction made by my late revered teacher (and a friend and colleague of both Buber and Tillich), Abraham Joshua Heschel, is quite apt. Unlike our usual scientific and historical thinking, from the perspective of the Hebrew Bible events are not components of larger wholes called processes.[57] Rather, they are interruptions of the normal processes of nature and history. They are the unconnected moments when God breaks into nature and history and when the finite is shown to be judged from the perspective of the Infinite, not when it is seen as inevitably adding up to infinity.[58] But revelation only retains its essential symbolic thrust when its God can never be conjured up, not by pre-philosophical incantation, not by philosophical inference, not even by post-philosophical utterance of the most sincere "You." The inner divine dialectic between God as "He" and God as "You," which Kabbalah and Tillich forcefully emphasize, is what saves revelation from reduction to the confines of experience — even the "religious" experience of true dialogue.

Finally, redemption is the "not-yet" within the divine life about which Tillich spoke in the quotation from *Systematic Theology* cited at footnote 54 (above). Redemption, like creation, enables revelation to retain its transcendent thrust, its essential symbolism. For, redemption indicates the basic insufficiency not only of present human efforts at self-fulfillment but even of the presence God has now revealed.

Were revelation to be regarded as self-sufficient, even from God's side, this would imply the triumphalist claim that God's relationship with humankind and, indeed, with all creation is essentially characterized by the situation *here-and-now* of the community that has been so constituted by that revelation — be that community, for us, the Church or Israel. As such, even a renewed and more mutually supportive relationship between the Church and Israel and Israel and the church does not add up to the type of self-sufficiency that could, in concert, exclude the need to take non-Judeo-Christian religions seriously when looking at the horizon of redemption. Redemption indicates that God's full presence has not yet been either past or present, that it is essentially future. Nevertheless, the pres-

---

56. See Plato, *Timeaus* 48Aff.
57. See Heschel, *God in Search of Man,* pp. 209-12.
58. See Heschel, *The Prophets,* pp. 190-91.

ent hope for this as-yet-future era forces us to recognize the partiality, the essential brokenness, of even the best of our lives before God — and even of God's life before us.

In emphasizing the futurity of God, Tillich was, for Jewish thinkers, reiterating the insight of the later kabbalists that redemption is not only the rectification of our broken situation in this world but also the ultimate reconciliation of the Ground of Being with its own exiled and separated being.[59] In that insight, along with the others we have seen, Tillich was both the pupil of Buber and the teacher of those Jewish thinkers for whom Buber has basically established the theological agenda.

Implications for Furthering Jewish-Christian Dialogue

We have seen how Jewish-Christian dialogue was achieved by Martin Buber and Paul Tillich and that the clearest focus of that dialogue might well be found in their respective interpretations (in the broadest sense of the term) of Exodus 3:14. Their Jewish-Christian dialogue can be a paradigm for similar efforts in the present if we realize that it was characterized by three qualities.

The first characteristic of their dialogue was that it was not an "argument" in the sense that one side was convinced it had the truth and that all it had to do was to break down the intellectual resistance of the other side. Both in their interchanges with each other as well as in their interchanges in general, Buber and Tillich were genuinely interested not only in teaching others but in learning from them as well. In the case at hand, our insight into the deeper meaning of Exodus 3:14 is enhanced precisely if we see that Buber had something to add to Tillich's perception and that Tillich had something to add to Buber's. Both thinkers consciously avoided even the hint of triumphalism in their respective works, either oral or written.

The second characteristic of their dialogue was that both Buber and Tillich were open to the possibility that the Bible still speaks truth. Both were opposed to the type of orthodoxy that insists that all the truth of the Bible has already been formulated. Both were just as much opposed to the type of liberalism that insists that whatever truth there is in the Bible is only there because it has been reconstructed by the superior perspective of modernity. The insights we have gained from both Buber's and Tillich's

---

59. See Scholem, *Major Trends in Jewish Mysticism*, pp. 265ff.

responses to Exodus 3:14 would not have been ours had either thinker been "orthodox" or "liberal" in the usual sense.

The third characteristic of their dialogue is that it was enabled by their involvement in philosophy. Although philosophy's influence is more apparent in Tillich than in Buber, neither thinker would have been able to look into Exodus 3:14 without being an active participant in the tradition of philosophical inquiry and speculation. This tradition is not derived from the religious teaching of Judaism or Christianity per se, but, since Philo, it has enabled religious thought to see truth in a way that it could not do without it. Furthermore, philosophy has enabled Jewish and Christian (and Muslim) thinkers to bring the ideas of their respective traditions into the widest possible conversation by seeing them critically interact with ideas from every other source. Without philosophy — most fundamentally, ontology, in its concern with being — neither Buber nor Tillich could have read the Bible the way they both did. Accordingly, they vividly demonstrated that the most intellectually enriching Jewish-Christian dialogue may well be the open philosophical exegesis of Scripture, in which both Jews and Christians have — in one way or another — heard God's word.

Before Revelation:
The Rabbis, Paul, and Karl Barth

Stretching the Parameters of Jewish-Christian Dialogue

The recent experience of theological dialogue between Jews and Christians has convinced many (but not all) of the participants that significant things can be said to each other only when faith is explicit.[1] A significant dialogue can take place, but it is hard. It would seem to be especially hard when the Christian partner in dialogue is under the strong influence of Karl Barth. For other forms of Christian theology — Thomism, Process theology, Tillichian theology, Niebuhrian theology, for example — constitute a realm of nature or being or experience, one that is distinguishable from the singularity of Christian (and Jewish) revelation, a realm where Jews and Christians (and possibly others) can come together as equals. But Karl Barth and his disciples seem vigorously to deny any such possibility, let alone any such reality.

This would seem to be the case because Barth often claims to confine all of Christian doctrine within the singularity of Christological revelation. Since Jews cannot accept the ultimate Christological claim any more than Christians can accept the ultimate claim of the Law, it would seem

1. A philosophical and theological constitution of Jewish-Christian dialogue is presented in my book *Jewish-Christian Dialogue: A Jewish Justification* (New York: Oxford University Press, 1989).

This essay previously appeared in the *Journal of Religion* 71, no. 1 (1991): 50-66. I thank Peter Ochs, now of the University of Virginia, and an anonymous reader for this journal for their helpful comments on earlier versions of this essay. All translations, unless otherwise noted, are mine.

there is no *logos* from which authentic *dia-logue* between Jews and Christians can be constituted.[2]

What I shall argue, nevertheless, is that this impasse is not absolute. There is a point of contact, and that point is the fact that revelation implies preconditions, preconditions admitted and expounded by Karl Barth, despite his continued and vehement rejection of natural theology and natural law. In other words, the theological closure that Barth so strenuously attempted to accomplish in his thought was never really achieved in the absolute way he so explicitly desired. There is an important aspect of his thought that cannot be included in that idealized closure.

Barth's designation and constitution of the key precondition for revelation is strikingly similar to a major trend in rabbinic theology. If this point of contact can now be uncovered, and if it can be shown to be by no means idiosyncratic within Barth's own thought or that of the Rabbis, then it can now be developed in dialogue between Jewish disciples of the Rabbis and Christian disciples of Karl Barth. Furthermore, I shall argue that the recognition of these similar preconditions led both the Rabbis and Barth to draw ethical conclusions from them. As we shall see, this

---

2. Despite this, some modern Jewish thinkers have been influenced by Barth. The one most strongly influenced by him was Hans-Joachim Schoeps, especially in his *Jüdischer Glaube in dieser Zeit: Prolegomena zur Grundlegung einer systematischen Theologie des Judentums* (Berlin: Jüdischer Verlag, 1932). Schoeps's book was, however, subjected to a trenchant critique by Alexander Altmann in an essay entitled "Zur Auseinandersetzung mit der 'dialektischen' Theologie," in *Monatschrift für die Geschichte und Wissenschaft des Judentums* 79 (1935): 358ff. In his critique, Altmann convincingly shows that Schoeps was both uncritical theologically and ignorant of Judaism. Nevertheless, despite his general caution about the relevance of Barth's theology for Jewish theology, Altmann does respectfully note that "Es ist keine Frage, wir können von Barth viel lernen" (p. 359). Barth's influence can also be seen in the work of a most important contemporary Jewish theologian, one who is certainly theologically critical and learned in Judaism, Rabbi Joseph B. Soloveitchik. In his seminal 1944 essay, *Ish Ha-Halakhah* ("Halakhic Man," trans. L. J. Kaplan [Philadelphia: Jewish Publication Society of America, 1983]), one of the very first influences he explicitly mentions is Karl Barth (p. 4). Barth's influence can be especially seen in Soloveitchik's distinction between *homo religiosis* and *halakhic* man, namely, the person who operates solely from a revealed base (see pp. 17ff.). Another contemporary Jewish theologian who explicitly acknowledges Barth's influence on his thought is Michael Wyschogrod. See his article "Why Was and Is the Theology of Karl Barth of Interest to a Jewish Theologian?" in *Footnotes to a Theology: The Karl Barth Colloquium of 1972* (Waterloo, Ont.: Canadian Corporation for Studies in Religion, 1974), pp. 95ff.; and also his *The Body of Faith: Judaism as Corporeal Election* (New York: Seabury Press, 1983), esp. pp. 78-79. For Barth's influence on my own thought, see the chapter in the present volume entitled "Are Philosophical Proofs of the Existence of God Theologically Meaningful?"

bringing together of the Rabbis and Barth is considerably enhanced when we see that Paul was saying some of these same things as were the Rabbis and that Barth's thought stems from his insight into Paul. Moreover, the fuller elaboration of the meaning of these preconditions and their ethical consequences is philosophical rather than strictly theological, for it is not derived from revelation but is presupposed by revelation. This point awaits further constitution. But first it must be uncovered.

Barth's Exegesis of Romans 1:19-21

A comprehensive reading of Barth's large oeuvre shows that he did not have a firsthand experience or understanding of living, postbiblical Judaism.[3] Although he could be quite positive about Judaism and its role in God's plan for creation in his Christian view of it, nonetheless, his view of Judaism was almost exclusively an exegesis of the view of Judaism found in the New Testament, especially in the letters of Paul. However, his exegesis of Paul's letter to the Romans, which, as is well known, launched his theological career in a spectacular way, has been criticized by a number of learned New Testament scholars as being based on ignorance of the postbiblical Jewish context of Paul's teaching. By implication they seem to be saying that Barth's treatment of Paul, although theologically impressive in its own right, is actually a pretext for his polemic against nineteenth-century Christian rationalism and experientialism. I shall argue here, on the contrary, that Barth's reading of Paul is a highly plausible exegesis in the light of one major trend in rabbinic theology. For even though some of Barth's critics among New Testament scholars knew Rabbinic Judaism far better than he did, Barth understood Paul far better than they did, and Paul was closer to Rabbinic Judaism than they were.

This comes out when we look at Barth's exegesis of Romans 1:19-21. The text there states,

> For all that can be known of God is clearly before them; God has shown it to them. Ever since the creation of the world, his invisible nature — his eternal power and divine character — have been clearly perceptible through what he has made. So they have no excuse, for, though they knew God, they have not honored him as God or given

---

3. See F.-W. Marquardt, *Die Entdeckung des Judentums für die christliche Theologie: Israel in Denken Karl Barths* (Munich: Kaiser Verlag, 1967).

thanks to him, but they have indulged in futile speculations, until their stupid minds have become dark.[4]

Now, taken at face value, this passage and what follows it in this chapter and the next seem to be advocating a natural theology as the basis of a natural law ethic. The order of the visible world calls for us to posit an invisible Orderer behind it, and that Orderer has made that world intelligible enough for human intelligences to be able to discover their own natural ends through their intelligent examination of it. The pagans are morally culpable because of their willful ignorance of what should be positively evident to all by inference from the ordered phenomena of nature. Needless to say, someone like Thomas Aquinas made much of this line of interpretation.[5]

Barth, alternatively, interprets this passage not as entailing a positive inference of the existence of God as the Orderer of nature but, rather, as entailing a negative inference, namely, the idolatry of which Paul speaks is the result of the human refusal to infer from its own experience its own nothingness. He writes, "We know that God is He whom we do not know, and that our ignorance is precisely the problem and the source of our knowledge."[6] Elaborating on this line of thought, he continues, "The knowledge of God attainable through a simple observation of the incomprehensibility, the imperfection, the triviality of human life, was not taken advantage of. The invisibility of God seems to us less tolerable than the questionable visibility of what we like to call 'God.'"[7]

Barth's polemic here against natural theology seems to involve a refutation of the assumption that faith in God is prior to the prohibition of idolatry. In other words, the usual assumption is that the negation (idola-

---

4. *The New Testament*, trans. E. J. Goodspeed (Chicago: University of Chicago Press, 1923), p. 290.

5. See *Summa Theologiae*, trans. A. Pegis (New York, 1945), 2/1, 9.91, a.2 re Rom. 2:14 ("When the gentiles, who have not the law, do by nature those things that are of the law"). Barth, conversely, comments thereon as follows: "They [the gentiles] can become God-fearers. . . . They are not lacking in perception of the corruptibility of all things human. . . . They are not without respect for the negation by which the creation is distinguished from the Creator" (Karl Barth, *The Epistle to the Romans*, 6th ed., trans. E. C. Hoskyns [Oxford: Oxford University Press, 1933], p. 66).

6. Barth, *The Epistle to the Romans*, p. 45.

7. Barth, *The Epistle to the Romans*, p. 47. Cf. John Calvin, *Commentary on Romans*, trans. R. Mackenzie (Edinburgh: Oliver & Boyd, 1960; reprint, Grand Rapids: Eerdmans, 1980), pp. 47-49; *Institutes of the Christian Religion*, trans. F. L. Battles (Philadelphia: Westminster, 1960), bk. 2, chap. 7, sec. 10, and bk. 4, chap. 20, sec. 16.

try) presupposes the affirmation (faith) — *malum est privatio boni*. Barth, conversely, seems to be saying that one can already substitute the self and all of its projections for God, even if "God" is only an idea in one's mind, an idea whose real external referent has not appeared in revelation and been responded to in faith. Idolatry is the human refusal to wait for God to fill what is now experienced as a void. It is the human substitution for the *as-yet-unknown* God. That substitution can only be removed by radical existential doubt — *angst* in the Kierkegaardian sense. Without it, faith as the human affirmation of God's truth is impossible. The prohibition of idolatry is, therefore, a *conditio sine qua non* of faith. It is not a corollary of faith; it is its precondition. It is a precondition that in no wise necessitates the presence of faith and its proper object: God.

The Call of Abraham in Rabbinic Theology

Although Scripture does record God's speech to Adam and Noah, numerous rabbinic texts assert that revelation proper, as the content of an everlasting covenant between God and humanity, begins with Abraham — a point that Paul certainly accepted, too.[8] The obvious question is, What did Abraham experience or know that occasioned God to speak to him when and where he did? An important rabbinic text presents the following parable:

> Rabbi Isaac said that it is like one who was travelling from place to place and who saw a palace burning [*doleqet*]. He said, "Could one say that there is a palace without an owner [*manheeg*]?" The master of the palace peered forth [*hetzeetz*] and said to him, "I am he who is the owner of the palace!" So it is that because Abraham our father said, "Could one say the world is without an owner?" that God peered forth and said to him, "I am the owner — the Lord [*Adon*] of the whole world."[9]

To emphasize further the theological meaning of this parable, another version of it quotes the verse "I am the first and I am the last" (Isa. 44:6).

The parable basically admits two divergent interpretations. First, some

---

8. See, e.g., *Babylonian Talmud* (hereafter "B."): Berakhot, ed. Romm (Vilna, 1898): 7b re Gen. 15:2, Jewish Publication Society of America translation (Philadelphia, 1962); also Rom. 4:1ff.

9. *Beresheet Rabbah* 39.1, English translation (New York: Soncino Press, 1977).

interpreters have regarded it as an expression of the so-called argument from design.[10] The "burning palace" means an *illuminated* palace. It is symbolic of both an ordered world (one illuminated for itself) and one that is intelligible (one illuminated for others to see). Such a palace would obviously attract a nomad like Abraham who seems to have come on it after wandering for a long time in the desert. The illuminated palace is not only visible but it is also attractive. It seems to be a place the nomad would want to enter and settle down. God's peering forth to announce his lordship, according to this line of interpretation, seems to be a metaphor for Abraham's having concluded the existence of an Orderer from his experience of order.

Conversely, one can take the "burning palace" to be a symbol of profound disorder. The palace is on fire, and the nomad who has happened on it seems to have nowhere else to go. He is clearly unable to extinguish the fire and, therefore, claim the palace as his dwelling place. He himself is to be part of the conflagration. It threatens to consume him imminently. His question, then, about the owner of the palace is an anguished cry for help from disaster, not a happy conclusion from a situation of order and well-being.[11] There is absolutely no guarantee in advance that any*one* will answer this cry. Moreover, if Abraham had concluded that, somehow, the conflagration would stop on its own and once again the ordered palace would be restored to its former pristine integrity, or that, somehow, he could have autonomously reconstructed the palace based on his new plan for it, if that had happened, then Abraham would have thereby precluded his hearing and understanding God's announcement of God's sole lordship and unexpected redemption of Abraham and of the palace along with him.

Those Jews who are inclined to accept this second, more radical image of Abraham's initial encounter with God can see a strikingly similar theologic in Paul and then in Kierkegaard and then in Barth.[12] All of them are

10. See, e.g., Maimonides, *Mishneh Torah: Laws Concerning Idolatry*, Yale Judaica Series translation (New Haven: Yale University Press, 1949), 1.3. Compare Josephus, *Antiquities*, trans. H. St. John Thackeray, Loeb Classical Library (Cambridge, Mass.: Harvard University Press, 1930), 1:155-56. For other sources, see L. Ginzberg, *Legends of the Jews* (Philadelphia: Jewish Publication Society of America, 1925), 5:210n.16.

11. *Zohar*, 1:78a, English translation (London: Soncino Press, 1931); A. J. Heschel, *God in Search of Man* (New York: Farrar, Straus & Giroux, 1955), pp. 112-13, 367n. 7; also David Novak, *Law and Theology in Judaism*, vol. 2 (New York: KTAV, 1976), pp. 21-22.

12. See Kierkegaard, *Fear and Trembling*, trans. W. Lowrie (Garden City, N.Y.: Doubleday, 1954), pp. 78ff.

asserting a prerevelational norm — the prohibition of idolatry — and all of them are at least implicitly denying that it is in any way inferred from anything like natural theology.

The Critique of Barth's Pauline Exegesis

In the first interpretation of the parable of Abraham and the burning or illuminated palace explicated above, it is not hard to connect the natural theology it expresses with a natural law ethic. The common term is nature in the sense of *physis* as expounded by Plato, Aristotle, and the Stoics. Nature qua *physis* is an ordered world in which humans desire to discover their rightful place. Humans desire to practice the order they perceive in the world around them within their own society among themselves.[13]

Although he does not cite this particular text about Abraham and the palace, W. D. Davies strongly criticizes Barth's interpretation of Paul's statements about the culpability of the gentiles along these general lines. And he does so specifically on the question of the proper relation between theology and ethics.

I shall try to show that Davies is wrong about both Paul and the Rabbis and that Barth is right about Paul and, hence, closer to the Rabbis, as Paul was closer to the Rabbis than was Davies.

Davies in his explicit polemic with Barth writes, "Nevertheless, it would be wrong to conclude . . . that Paul regarded the pagan world as being wholly without some awareness of God's moral demands. . . . Paul presupposes throughout what is the Jewish equivalent of the Stoic doctrine of the Law of Nature: there had been a revelation of God's moral demands prior both to the giving of the Torah of Judaism and to the advent of the Christian Gospel."[14]

Davies is referring to the rabbinic doctrine of the seven commandments of the children of Noah. These seven commandments are derived, either directly or indirectly, from scriptural texts dealing with the human situation before Abraham and even with the Jewish situation before Sinai. These seven commandments are: (1) the positive precept to establish courts of law, and the prohibitions against (2) blasphemy, (3) idolatry,

13. See, e.g., Cicero, *Laws*, 1.7, trans. C. W. Keyes, Loeb Classical Library (Cambridge, Mass.: Harvard University Press, 1928), p. 23.

14. Davies, *Paul and Rabbinic Judaism*, 2d rev. ed. (London: SPCK, 1958), p. 327. For a critique of Davies's use of rabbinic sources in terms of historical methodology, see E. P. Sanders, *Paul and Palestinian Judaism* (Philadelphia: Fortress Press, 1977), pp. 7-12.

(4) sexual immorality (incest, homosexuality, bestiality, and adultery), (5) murder, (6) robbery, and (7) eating a limb torn from a living animal. Davies and a number of other scholars, both Jewish and Christian, have seen this doctrine as being essentially identical with the contemporary Stoic doctrine of natural law or right reason *(orthos logos).*[15]

The important fact overlooked by Davies and others, however, is the negative character of the seven laws. All of them are prohibitions, with the exception of the commandment to establish courts of law. (This commandment is, in fact, an administrative precept, designed to insure the political enforcement of the other six commandments.) Furthermore, in some important versions of these seven commandments, the prohibition of idolatry is presented first.[16] This serial priority is seen as being foundational as well. The prohibition of idolatry is the key to understanding all the other commandments incumbent on the gentiles. There is no commandment for the gentiles actually to have positive faith in God; rather, all that can be expected of them is to avoid idolatry and blasphemy.

By their negative constitution of the prohibitions that pertain to gentiles, the Rabbis were not doing anything like what the Stoics were doing in their natural theology and natural law theories. The Stoics saw evidence of universal reason and morality; the Rabbis emphasized how the gentiles had failed to live up to these minimal moral standards that they should have known.[17] The Rabbis, unlike the Stoics (for whom the very recognition of universal standards was considered morally sufficient), regarded them as necessary but totally insufficient. The acceptance of these standards, furthermore, was the minimal *conditio sine qua non* for Israel later to accept the Torah from God at Sinai. However, the Torah was not seen as a specification of these general standards; which would have made it subordinate to them as parts are subordinate to the whole. Rather, these minimal commandments, all rooted in the prohibition of idolatry,

---

15. See, e.g., *Letter of Aristeas,* trans. M. Hadas (New York: Harper & Brothers, 1951), p. 161.

16. See B. Sanhedrin 56b; also, Maimonides, *Mishneh Torah: Laws Concerning Kings,* 9.1. With respect to the negative status of the six prime Noahide commandments, see B. Sanhedrin 58b-59a.

17. See B. Baba Kama 38a; B. Abodah Zarah 2b-3a. A view of the Noahide laws closer to the Stoic assumption of rational moral sufficiency was put forth by Barth's Marburg teacher, the Jewish neo-Kantian philosopher Hermann Cohen. See his *Religion of Reason out of the Sources of Judaism,* trans. S. Kaplan (New York: Frederick Ungar, 1972), p. 121. For Cohen's influence on the very early Barth, see F.-W. Marquardt, *Der Christ in der Gesellschaft: 1919-1979* (Munich: Kaiser Verlag, 1980), pp. 7-8, 33, 55. (I thank Prof. William Kluback of the City University of New York for this reference.)

simply cleared the ground for the acceptance of God's law revealed in a trajectory from above. Without the serious observance of these commandments, the people of Israel would have been in no position to recognize God's law when it came to them at Sinai.

The question that remains is, How are the other commandments (leaving aside the first positive precept to establish courts of law; see above, p. 115) rooted in the prohibition of idolatry? Furthermore, one can well regard blasphemy as being a subset of idolatry.[18] Finally, the prohibition of robbery can be seen as peripheral inasmuch as definitions of property are so sociologically contingent; and the prohibition of eating a limb torn from a living animal can be seen to pertain largely to a particular period of history: If this is the case, one is then left with the prohibitions of idolatry, sexual immorality, and murder.[19] They alone are truly universal. But how are they related? And, how does the root prohibition of idolatry function as the sine qua non for revelation?

Idolatry, Homosexuality, and Murder

Concerning these three cardinal prohibitions, we can see a striking similarity between the Rabbis and Paul. If the essentially similar point between them is explicated and developed, one can at the same time draw Barth's insights into this process. This could very well become a paradigm for Jewish-Christian dialogue at the very highest theological level.

The Rabbis presented the three cardinal prohibitions in a definite order: (1) idolatry, (2) sexual immorality, (3) murder. And not only are these three prohibitions seen as binding on the gentiles, they are also seen as the absolute "bottom line" of Judaism as well. They are the cardinal prohibitions to sustain which a Jew is to die a martyr rather than transgress them. All other commandments must be violated to save one's life.[20] Furthermore, both the Rabbis and Paul saw homosexuality as the primary manifestation of sexual immorality.[21] How does it closely follow from idolatry?

If Barth is correct — and I think he is on this main point — Paul's understanding of the prohibition of idolatry is that it is the primary *via*

18. This was the opinion of the sixteenth-century jurist and exegete Rabbi David ibn Abi Zimra in *Responsa Radbaz* (Warsaw, 1882), vol. 6, no. 2211.

19. See B. Sanhedrin 57a.

20. B. Sanhedrin 74a.

21. See David Novak, *The Image of the Non-Jew in Judaism: An Historical and Constructive Study of the Noahide Laws* (Toronto and New York: Edwin Mellen Press, 1983), pp. 212-15.

negativa revelation requires as its precondition for human acceptance of it. For idolatry is the most fundamental manifestation of falsehood in human existence. In the Hebrew mind, the opposite of truth *(emet)* is not error but the lie *(sheqer).*[22] Being true is remaining steadfast *(emunah)* to that which exists prior to one's own thought and action. Lying is actively substituting the product of one's own thought and action for that which exists prior to it. It is the attempt to transcend that which cannot be transcended. Being-true or lying is both theoretical and practical.[23] Truth is not the *co-respondence between* the mind *(noēsis)* and its object *(noēma).* It is not *adaequtio rei ad intellectum,* nor is it even *adaequatio intellectus et rei.* Truth is ordering my existence (including my mind) to that which is always greater than my self, to that than which nothing greater can be conceived.[24] That is why idolatry, not atheism, is the primary sin. Atheism is a theoretical possibility inasmuch as one can adopt an intellectual neutrality, cogently asserting that there is no consistent hierarchy in nature. This can be seen in natural philosophies from Anaxagoras to Einstein.[25] However, atheism is a practical impossibility inasmuch as everyone acts on the basis of some prime authority, an authority that necessarily orders and evaluates all one's acts hierarchically, designating some good and others evil, some less good and some more good, some less evil and others more evil.[26] And when God is not that highest authority, the self and its projections are the lie that rushes in to replace this absent truth.[27] One's highest authority is always one's god. As Paul said, "for the splendor of the immortal God, they have substituted *(ēllaksan)* images in the form of mortal man" (Rom. 1:23). It would seem, then, that ultimacy presupposes the moral intuition of hierarchy before it can be intelligibly predicated of God.

---

22. That is why *sheqer* is often contrasted with *tzedeq* (justice). See, e.g., Ps. 52:5; see also Martin Buber, *Good and Evil* (New York: Charles Scribner's Sons, 1952), pp. 7ff.

23. For the relation between the theoretical and the practical in Jewish thought, see David Novak, "The Role of Dogma in Judaism," *Theology Today* 44, no. 1 (April 1988): 59-61.

24. See Karl Barth, *Anselm: Fides Quaerens Intellectum,* trans. I. W. Robertson (London: SCM, 1960), p. 123.

25. See Ernst Cassirer, *Substance and Function,* trans. W. C. Swabey and M. C. Swabey (New York: Dover, 1953), p. 310; also, Bertrand Russell, *Mysticism and Logic* (Garden City, N.Y.: Doubleday, 1957), pp. 116-17.

26. See G. E. Moore, *Principia Ethica* (Cambridge: Cambridge University Press, 1903), chap. 4.

27. T. S. Eliot, I think, expressed it best in modern times: "If you will not have God (and he is a jealous God), you should pay your respects to Hitler or Stalin" (*The Idea of a Christian Society,* 2d ed. [London: Faber & Faber, 1982], p. 82). See Josh. 24:15; 1 Kings 18:21.

Now we can understand why Paul and the Rabbis saw homosexuality as following from the idolatrous lie and its replacement of truth. The most fundamental human relationship is the transcendent one with God. Idolatry perverts human existence as a whole (the soul) by substituting no gods for the One God. When human existence as a whole has been so spiritually perverted, it follows that there is nothing to prevent the immanent relationship of the whole human self with its body from succumbing to its own perversion as well. After God, we are most intimately related to our own bodies. That is why idolatry leads men to assume the identity of women and women the identity of men. In a homosexual relationship between men, one of them assumes a female role; in a homosexual relationship between women, one of them assumes a male role. Furthermore, even the masculine man in a male homosexual relationship is not relating to a real woman, but rather to his male alter ego. The feminine woman in a female homosexual relationship is not relating to a real man, but rather to her female alter ego. And even if both participants in a male homosexual relationship claim to be wholly masculine one to the other, and even if both the participants in a female homosexual relationship claim to be wholly feminine one to the other, this celebration of absolute masculinity or absolute femininity belies the very biological truth of the essentially intersexual relatedness attested to by the fact that the sexual organs and the organs of procreation are the same.[28]

It is quite interesting to note that Barth is much closer to the rabbinic understanding of the connection between idolatry and homosexuality in his later writing than he is in his earlier writing. Thus, in his *Epistle to the Romans,* he states, "When God has been deprived of His glory, men are also deprived of theirs. Desecrated within their souls, they are also desecrated without in their bodies, for men are one. . . . Everything then becomes Libido; life becomes totally erotic. When the frontier between God and man, the last inexorable barrier and obstacle, is not closed, the barrier between what is normal and what is perverse is opened."[29] It would seem from this passage that Barth, at this point in the development of his thought, regarded sexuality per se — libido — to be demonic if not contained and ordered by an outside power. In this regard, one can see him as part of the long history of Western dualism,

28. See David Novak, "Some Aspects of the Relationship of Sex, Society, and God in Judaism," in *Contemporary Ethical Issues in the Jewish and Christian Traditions,* ed. F. E. Greenspahn (Hoboken, N.J.: KTAV, 1986), pp. 147ff.

29. Barth, *The Epistle to the Romans,* pp. 51, 53.

which has included such diverse thinkers as Plato and Freud. There is no attempt to understand sexuality phenomenologically, that is, to discover within it sources for authentic human existence capable of receiving and appreciating revelation.

However, in the *Church Dogmatics,* Barth does engage in a phenomenology of sexuality, one where he more closely connects homosexuality with idolatry. There he writes, "In *Rom.* 1 Paul connected it with idolatry, with changing the truth of God into a lie, with the adoration of the creature instead of the Creator (v. 25). . . . The real perversion takes place, the original decadence and disintegration begins, when man will not see his partner of the opposite sex and therefore the primal form of fellow-man [*die Urgestalt des Mitmenschen*] . . . but trying to be human in himself as sovereign man or woman. . . . For in this supposed discovery of the genuinely human man and woman give themselves up to the worship of a false god."[30] Here Barth sees authentic sexuality as the origin of the human capacity for relationality. And authentic sexuality is the prime manifestation of the essential lack of autonomy in human life, either masculine, feminine, or a combination of the two.[31]

Sexuality, then, presents a dialectic between self-possession and relatedness. In Barth's words, "Male and female being is the prototype of all I and Thou, of all individuality in which man [*Mensch*] and man differ from yet belong to one another."[32] When human beings attempt to construct their autonomous self-sufficiency collectively, heterosexuality asserts their fundamental differentiation as separate human bodies. And when human beings attempt to construct their autonomous self-sufficiency individually, heterosexuality asserts their fundamental relatedness to the other side of their humanness.

Continuing this line of thought, it is illuminating to look at the rabbinic treatment of the verse "Therefore a man shall leave his father and mother and he shall cleave to his wife; and they shall become one flesh" (Gen. 2:24). "'He shall cleave to his wife' — *cleave* [with her] but not with a male; 'to his wife' — but not the wife of his neighbor. . . . 'They shall become one flesh' — with whom one is capable of becoming one flesh, excluding the various animals with which one cannot become one flesh."[33]

30. Barth, *Church Dogmatics,* authorized English translation (Edinburgh: T&T Clark, 1961), 3.4:166.

31. See also Barth, *Ethics,* ed. D. Braun, trans. G. W. Bromiley (New York: Seabury Press, 1981), p. 181.

32. Barth, *Church Dogmatics,* 3.4:150.

33. B. Sanhedrin, 58a.

Note how authentic sexuality, which is as much a description *of* human nature as it is a prescription *to* it, involves a limited relationality. Looking at these three prohibitions together, we see that sexuality is limited to human life, it is further limited to a specific relationship between men and women, and it is finally limited to a particular relationship (marriage) between a man and a woman. Hence, it is not something limited from without, but its essential phenomenology indicates that its very authenticity itself requires self-limitation. Moreover, this self-limitation, by decreasing its range, thereby increases its intensity and continuity. Sexuality is to be only between humans (contra bestiality); it is to be only between men and women (contra homosexuality); and it is to be only between husband and wife (contra adultery). Finally, it is to be nothing that permanently inhibits or precludes the procreation of new human life, that is, even the heterosexual marital relationship is not to be taken by its participants as a self-sufficient symbiosis.

One can now see the connection between the prohibitions of homosexuality and murder when homosexuality is taken as the prime example of the illusion of absolute human self-possession, either collectively or individually. This comes out in the rabbinic treatment of the scriptural account of the first murder, the story of Cain and Abel. Scripture cryptically states, "Cain said to his brother, Abel . . . and it was while they were in the field that Cain rose up against Abel his brother and killed him" (Gen. 4:8). The question, of course, that immediately presents itself is, Why did Cain kill Abel? The Rabbis, although offering various specific details, all seem to have agreed that the human desire for dominance and mastery over all other humans was at the root of Cain's crime. "What were they quarrelling about? They said, 'come let us divide up the world.' So one took the land and the other took all the movables. One said, 'the land upon which you are standing is mine!' And the other one said, 'those clothes you are wearing are mine!' . . . So 'Cain rose up against Abel' . . . Rabbi Judah said that they were quarrelling over the first woman."[34]

This difference between the interhuman relationship and the human relation to things comes out in Cain's sarcastic reply to God after God questions him about his brother, namely, "Am I my brother's keeper?" (Gen. 4:9). The Hebrew word used is the noun, *shomer,* one who guards or cares for something. Now, as is well known, all Hebrew nouns are hypostatizations of verbs. The verb "to keep" — *shamor* — first appeared in the second creation account when God designated the first humans as those who are to "work

---

34. *Beresheet Rabbah* 22.7.

and keep" *(u-le-shomrah)* the garden (Gen. 2:15).[35] This is parallel to the designation of humans as those who are to "subdue and rule" (Gen. 1:28) the earth and its creatures in the first creation account.[36]

The two accounts complement and qualify each other. Thus, if humans think that they have capricious control over the earth, they are reminded that this control is a responsibility. And, if humans think that they are simply part of the natural order of things, they are reminded that they occupy an exalted position in comparison with all other creatures and even with nature as a whole. With this in mind, we can see why Cain's answer to God is a lie. The very fact that he is not his brother's *shomer* — his keeper or guardian — does not mean that he is not responsible for what he did to him. Quite the contrary, because he is not his brother's keeper but his brother *(aheev)* — his equal — means that he has no authority over his life at all and is, thus, more answerable for anything he might do to him. For whereas he may use other creatures for his own needs, even killing some of them if need be (note Abel's sacrifice of firstlings from his flock in Gen. 4:4), he may not use his brother's life at all. In other words, he is more answerable for his brother's life than for the life of anything beneath him precisely because he does not have authority over it. As the Rabbis pointed out, no human being can say "his blood is redder than someone else's."[37]

Barth is quite insightful in making this fundamental distinction between our relationship with human life as opposed to our relation to nonhuman life. This comes out in the course of a polemic with Albert Schweitzer and his theory of "respect for all life" *(Ehrfurcht vor allem Leben):*

> *Life,* absolutely *alien* life, which cannot be just object, which is thus the likeness of the life of the invisible God and its primary vicar and representative, is the life of our fellowmen. This always places us *primarily,* and this alone places us *strictly,* before the factuality of an alien life that is to be respected for the Creator's sake, before an eye-to-eye claim of this alien life which — no matter how close we may be to the rest of creaturely life — is alone made on the same footing, a claim to be the object of my awe, my piety, and my sympathy.[38]

35. Note *Beresheet Rabbah* 16.5, where "to work and keep" refers to keeping the commandments, namely, the emphasis of responsibility.

36. For the theological significance of the two creation accounts in Genesis 1 and Genesis 2, respectively, see Joseph B. Soloveitchik, *The Lonely Man of Faith* (New York: Doubleday, 1992), pp. 9ff.

37. B. Pesaḥim 25b.

38. Barth, *Ethics,* p. 143.

What we see in looking at how the Rabbis and Paul, especially as interpreted by Barth, constituted the three cardinal sins of idolatry, homosexuality, and murder is the inherent connection between idolatry as the lie
about one's created status, sexual immorality — especially homosexuality
— as the lie about one's relationship with his or her own body, and murder
as the lie about one's relationship with the life of another human body.
Both for the Rabbis and for Paul, the acceptance of these three prohibitions is the necessary human precondition for receiving God's self-
presentation in revelation.

Barth's Philosophical Turn

We have seen that Barth's discussions of the cardinal sins strongly suggest
that he, too, had to accept certain basic normative preconditions for revelation, even though he opposed natural theology and natural law, at least
in its usual Thomistic or secularist versions.[39] Nevertheless, Barth himself
seems to have ruled out even this limited role for a prerevelational philosophy. In his famous 1934 polemic against his fellow Swiss Reformed theologian, Emil Brunner, Barth passionately wrote, "Shall we not have to do
what Roman Catholic theology has always done and ascribe to him a
potentia oboedientalis which he possesses from creation and retains in spite
of sin?"[40] However, significantly enough, Barth admits that even he himself, in his early theological period, entertained similar notions. He states
that "Brunner's theory was very much more interesting in its earlier form,
in accordance with Kierkegaard and Heidegger. . . . I confess that around
1920, and perhaps even later, I might still have succumbed to it."[41]

Finally, quite late in his career, Barth seems to have made the theological closure of his thought complete. In a work summarizing his *magnum
opus,* he wrote in the late 1940s,

39. For a recent critique of Barth for his failure to distinguish between natural theology
as metaphysics and natural law as ethics, namely, that the latter need not be based on the
former, see Oliver O'Donovan, *Resurrection and the Moral Order: An Outline for Evangelical Ethics* (Grand Rapids: Eerdmans, 1986), pp. 86-87.

40. Barth, "No!" in *Natural Theology,* trans. P. Fraenkel (London: Geoffrey Bles, 1946),
p. 82.

41. Along these lines, he even rejects Kierkegaard, whom he recognizes as an important
influence on his earlier thought. See *Natural Theology,* pp. 114-15, 120; also, H. U. von
Balthasar, *The Theology of Karl Barth,* trans. J. Drury (Garden City, N.Y.: Doubleday, 1972), pp.
45-47.

When we approach the truth which the Christian Church confesses in the word "Creator," then everything depends on our realizing that we find ourselves here as well confronted by the mystery of faith, in respect of which knowledge is really solely through God's revelation. The first article of faith in God the Father and His work is not a sort of "forecourt" of the Gentiles, a realm in which Christians and Jews and Gentiles, believers and nonbelievers are beside one another and to some extent stand together in the presence of a reality concerning which there might be some measure of agreement, in describing it as the work of God the Creator.[42]

This decided turn by Barth can be more precisely seen in a work that many consider to be pivotal in the development of his thought, his book on Anselm's proof of the existence of God. I shall try to demonstrate that this turn in his thought is a philosophical one, and that it is based on a wrong use of a key category in Kant.

Anselm had devised a way of dealing with the noetic question of the existence of God, one which has intrigued theologians and philosophers ever since. This is the core of it: "And, indeed, we believe that thou art a being than which nothing greater can be conceived. . . . For, it is one thing for an object to be in the understanding and another to understand that the object exists. . . . And assuredly that, than which nothing greater can be conceived, cannot exist in the understanding alone: then it can be conceived to exist in reality; which is greater."[43]

From this one can see five points. (1) Some things exist only in the understanding (thoughts). (2) Some things exist only in reality, that is, what is outside of thought (unknown entities). (3) Reality is greater than thought. (4) Reality that is also conceived by understanding is greater than reality not conceived by understanding. (5) God must be considered greatest in both thought and reality, that is, reality that is conceived by understanding. If this were not so, then something else could be conceived of as greater than God.

Contrary to Descartes, who seems to have restated Anselm's proof in the ontological argument, Barth asserts that Anselm is not discussing an innate idea in the mind, one that only God could put there. And contrary to Aquinas, who rejects this argument by anticipation, asserting that ideas about God can only be inferences from ordinary experience, Barth

---

42. Barth, *Dogmatics in Outline,* trans. G. T. Thomson (New York: Harper & Row, 1959), p. 50.

43. Anselm, "Proslogion," trans. S. N. Deane, in *St. Anselm: Basic Writings* (LaSalle, Ill.: Open Court Publishing Co., 1962), pp. 53-54 (hereafter, *Basic Writings*).

asserts that Anselm's proof is not even in the same category as inferences about ordinary experience and their inherent limitations.[44] He reads Anselm altogether differently. Anselm's proof, in his version of it, stems from a different sort of experience altogether, one from which one is not to make inferences about its cause inasmuch as its very subject speaks for itself. Inferences here can only be about what this experience entails. He thus states, "It does not say that God is, nor what he is, but rather, in the form of a prohibition that man can understand [*vernommenen Verbotes*] who he is . . . to reach a knowledge of God the revelation of this same God from some other source is clearly assumed."[45]

Revelation is clearly that "other source." Thus, humans only know God in the way that God has chosen to reveal himself to them, that is, in the events Scripture records *(Heilsgeschichte).* Humans do not know God from either their own thoughts or from their own experience of the external world. They do not know God except where God has explicitly presented himself to them. From revelation alone, then, comes the prohibition of thinking of God in any other way than as "that than which nothing greater can be conceived." To think of God otherwise is to commit the sin of idolatry in one's heart, the place where all sin originates. "The fool says in his heart, 'there is no God'" (Ps. 14:1; 53:2).[46] Once revelation has occurred and has been accepted, the prohibition of idolatry can be seen as logically necessary. Concerning this necessary connection between affirmation of God *(Deus sit)* and negation of affirmation of anything else as God *(id quo maius cogitari nequit),* Barth writes, "It simply says that if God should or could be conceived . . . then nothing else may be conceived of as greater than God. . . . The Proof that is to be worked out on the assumption of this designation of God will not be an analytic but a synthetic proposition. In that it corresponds to its object."[47]

Now, if I understand Barth correctly here, he is saying that the proposition "God exists" must be understood in the sense of what Kant designated as an a priori synthetic proposition.[48] His language here is unmistakably Kantian. For Kant, an a priori synthetic proposition is a presupposition that is inferred from experience retroactively.

As an a priori synthetic proposition, Barth sees Anselm's logic as fol-

---

44. See Descartes, *Meditations V:* Saint Thomas Aquinas, *Summa Contra Gentiles,* 1.10-11, and *Summa Theologiae,* 1, q.2, aa.1-3.

45. Barth, *Anselm,* p. 75.

46. See Barth, *Anselm,* pp. 103-4.

47. Barth, *Anselm,* pp. 88-89; see also pp. 152-53.

48. See Kant, *Critique of Pure Reason,* B11ff.

lows: when God reveals himself to us, in order for that revelation to be intelligible, it is *necessary* to presuppose that the God who revealed himself to us is that than which nothing greater can be conceived. It is not that we have an idea of God that subsequent experience validates, in the way that Einstein had a mathematical idea of special relativity in 1905 that was subsequently validated by the solar eclipse of 1919. According to Barth, we would not even have this idea if God had not already revealed himself to us. The presupposition of the idea is only logical (although not analytic); it is not chronological. As such, its meaning can only be grasped retroactively. Any presupposition for revelation is still subsequent to revelation in actual occurrence.

Here is where we can dispute with Barth on philosophical grounds. (Whether his interpretation of Anselm is right or wrong, I will leave to Anselm scholars.) I believe he is misapplying the Kantian category of the a priori synthetic to revelation.

What Kant meant by the a priori synthetic is something that applied to ordinary sense experience, experience that is ubiquitous. One cannot posit an actual time prior to that experience in human consciousness. Therefore, any presupposition *(Voraussetzung)* of this experience could not have possibly taken place before it happened. The presupposition, then, is purely formal and is in no way material.[49] However, revelation is not the same as ordinary sense experience. It is not ubiquitous because it is historical.[50] There was a time before it occurred and there are places where it has not yet occurred. There are, thus, both times and places when and where it has not occurred. "Seek the Lord when and where he may be found [*behimotzo*]; call upon him when and where he is near [*beheyoto qarov*]" (Isa. 55:6). Furthermore, the memory and awareness of these times and places is always the background for revelation. As such, it is necessary to speak of the historical situation outside revelation and what aspects of the experience of it enabled the human recipients of that revelation to be so receptive. Along these lines, the experience of human finitude can lead perceptive human beings to conclude that neither they nor anything they have experienced is that than which nothing greater can be conceived, even though it must always be emphasized that such conclusions can never

---

49. For Kant, the same relation pertains between freedom as the *ratio essendi* of morality and morality as the *ratio cognoscendi* of freedom. Note: "Denn wäre nicht das moralische Gesetz in unserer Vernunft eher deutlich gedacht, so würden wir uns niemals berechtigt halten, so etwas als Freiheit ist . . . , anzunehmen." *Kritik der Praktischen Vernunft,* ed. K. Vorländer (Hamburg: Felix Meiner Verlag, 1929), preface, p. 4 note.

50. See R. G. Collingwood, *The Idea of History* (Oxford: Clarendon Press, 1946), pp. 210ff.

produce revelation or anything like it. For that would be divination, and divination is idolatrous.[51] However, when the conclusions are only negative, we have enough of an opening on the human side for revelation to be possible for it.[52]

That is what the early Barth remembered and what the later Barth forgot. To remember it again requires a greater appreciation of the historicity of revelation and the historicity of its human object than Barth was willing to finally admit.

Barth and Dialogue Today

It would seem, however, that Barth's acceptance of philosophical preconditions for revelation is not only to be found in his *Commentary on Romans* from around 1920; there are also passages in the *Church Dogmatics* where Barth seems to see the prohibition of idolatry and its corollaries as being presupposed by revelation as much as being mandated by it. In other words, Barth — happily, at least for non-Christians who desire to engage in dialogue with his thought — was not able, however hard he tried, to achieve absolute closure in Christian revelation for his theology. Hence, theological dialogue between Jews and Christians, even between rabbinic theologians and Barthian theologians, has enough of a logos for *dia-logue* to emerge from it. The fact that this logos is primarily human rather than divine must never be obscured or minimized. This logos is primarily philosophical. However, revelation is bound by creation before it, and as fellow human creatures open to revelation, we can discover common points of openness to our respective revelations for us to elaborate together. And revelation must itself always be seen as intending the final redemption that is not yet come. That should remind each of us of our own religious insufficiency. Thus, I believe that, in our day, the recognition of the mutual need for dialogue by Jews and Christians is what is needed to dispel our respective temptations to take God's word to each of us as our own total possession, temptations that eclipse the authentic need for the redemption of all humankind and all creation.

51. See Yehezkel Kaufmann, *The Religion of Israel,* abridged and translated by M. Greenberg (Chicago: University of Chicago Press, 1960), pp. 40ff.

52. See Karl Rahner, "Philosophy and Theology," in *A Rahner Reader,* ed. G. A. McCool (London: Darton, Longman & Todd, 1975), pp. 75-76; also, David Novak, "A Theory of Revelation," in *Law and Theology in Judaism,* vol. 2, chap. 1.

Karl Barth on Divine Command: A Jewish Response

The Philosophical Engagement of Barth

Usually one does not include Karl Barth in contemporary Jewish-Christian dialogue. Unlike his Protestant theological contemporaries, Paul Tillich and Reinhold Niebuhr, there is no evidence that during his long theological career Barth had any real contact with Jewish thinkers.[1] The only contemporary Jewish thinker whom he engages, to my knowledge, is Martin Buber, but in his magnum opus, *Church Dogmatics*, Buber is discussed almost *en passant* and with a rather hurried dismissal.[2] Barth's relations with

---

1. For the best current study of Barth on Jews and Judaism, see Katherine Sonderegger, *That Jesus Christ Was Born a Jew: Karl Barth's Doctrine of Israel* (University Park, Pa.: Pennsylvania State University Press, 1992).

2. See *Church Dogmatics* 2/2 [hereafter *CD*], ed. G. W. Bromiley and T. F. Torrance; trans. G. W. Bromiley et al. (Edinburgh: T&T Clark, 1957), p. 698, where he calls Buber a "neo-Pharisaic Jew." In *CD* 1/2 (1956), p. 80, Barth refers to Buber (and H. J. Schoeps and E. B. Cohn, two other Jewish theologians) as those who "are instructive to listen to on our question [the meaning of the Old Testament, which Barth defends against the attempts of Schleiermacher et al. to denigrate its importance for the Church], both in what they say as earnest Jews, and what they cannot say as unconverted Jews." In *CD* 3/2 (1960), pp. 277-78, Barth distinguishes his theological anthropology from that of Buber (and some other non-Christians). See also E. Busch, *Karl Barth,* trans. J. Bowden (Grand Rapids: Eerdmans, 1976), pp. 272, 368-69 for some epistolary connections of Barth to Buber.

This essay previously appeared in the *Scottish Journal of Theology* 54, no. 4 (2001): 463-83. It was subsequently reprinted in *Doing Ethics in a Pluralistic World: Essays in Honour of Roger C. Hutchinson,* ed. P. D. Airhart, M. J. Legge, and G. L. Redcliffe (Waterloo, Ont.: Wilfrid Laurier University Press, 2002), pp. 57-76.

Judaism are seriously complicated, but one gets the impression from reading what he says about Judaism that he is doing typology, engaging a type already created in his mind largely by Paul and those who followed in his path. He does not seem to be dealing with Judaism as a living tradition, indeed a current rival religious option to Christianity. After all, how can one engage Judaism as a living tradition, let alone as a current rival, if one has no serious contact with living Jews during the most productive years of one's thought?[3] For that reason it would seem an engagement of Barth's thought by a contemporary Jewish theologian could only be, at most, an arcane academic exercise having no real Jewish significance.

Nevertheless, there are some very good reasons for a contemporary Jewish engagement of Karl Barth that does have theological significance here and now. First, Barth's theological position is still such a dominating presence in contemporary Christian theology (obviously Protestant, but also Roman Catholic).[4] As such, significant Jewish-Christian dialogue at the highest theological level cannot very well exclude Barth's voice, albeit posthumously. Second, some very important contemporary Barthians have been in close conversation with Jewish thinkers and, as such, they have already shown that their involvement with Jews is quite consistent with, perhaps even urged by, their involvement with Barth.[5] Third, and what might be most important, Barth is very concerned with where Judaism's prime theological emphasis lies: the commandments of God *(mitsvot)*. Moreover, since both Judaism and Christianity find the prime source of those commandments in the Hebrew Bible (for Christians, the "Old Testament"; for Jews, *kitvei ha-qodesh* — "the Sacred Scriptures"), and since many of the commandments that each community finds there are virtually identical, it would be strange if Jews could not learn some significant insights from Barth, a Christian thinker who spent some much of his time, energy, and overwhelming intellect in thinking of the commandments of the biblical

3. Nevertheless, for Barth's opposition to anti-Semitism, both theological and political, throughout his career, see Busch, *Karl Barth,* pp. 234-35, 247-48. For various Jewish engagements of Barth's thought, see the chapter in the present volume entitled "Before Revelation: The Rabbis, Paul, and Karl Barth."

4. For Barth's influence on the increasingly influential work of the Roman Catholic theologian Hans Urs von Balthasar, see his *The Theology of Karl Barth,* trans. J. Drury (Garden City, N.Y.: Doubleday, 1972).

5. For two of Barth's disciples whose interest in Jews and Judaism exceeded that of the master, although very much inspired by his overall thought, see Helmut Gollwitzer (with R. Rendtorff and N. P. Levinson), *Thema: Juden-Christen-Israel* (Stuttgart: Radius Verlag, 1967); and Friedrich W. Marquardt, *Die Entdeckung des Judentums für die christliche Theologie: Israel in Denken Karl Barths* (Munich: Kaiser Verlag, 1967).

God. Hence, following this approach to Barth, contemporary Jewish thinkers might have something significant to say on this very subject to Barth's disciples who are still our conversation partners and, indeed, to any Christians whose Christian faith has been illuminated by Barth.[6] That is especially the case in the area of the commandments we would call "ethics," namely, what the Rabbis called commandments pertaining to what is "between humans themselves" (*bein adam le-havero*).[7]

Finally, the fourth reason is that the common ethical interests of Barth and modern Jewish thinkers have in common their very location in modernity, a major strand of which, since Kant, has seen ethics (in one form or another) as the most important type of thought humans can possibly engage in.[8] For Barth, this has further significance since the one Jewish thinker who did greatly influence him in his youth was the German-Jewish philosopher Hermann Cohen (1842-1918), with whom he studied at the University of Marburg. Cohen was the greatest Kantian of his time, and a thinker whose serious Judaism, which was so obviously integrated with his philosophy — especially his ethics — could not have escaped someone as perceptive as Karl Barth.[9]

For these reasons, then, it might be best not to engage Barth on what he actually said about Judaism, but to engage him on what he said about Judaism's prime concern. Nevertheless, it might be questionable whether that engagement can or should be properly theological, at least in the way Barth saw theology. Barth famously says, "The Law is the form of the Gospel."[10] But how can that theological statement, which epitomizes his approach to ethics, be directly engaged theologically by any Jewish thinker, for whom the Gospel is not the source of his or her religious/ethical life? At this point we would be left with the Christian "yes" and the Jewish

6. See, e.g., the chapter in the present volume entitled "Theology and Philosophy: An Exchange with Robert Jenson." Jenson is one of Barth's most important contemporary students. I don't think my conversations with Robert Jenson over the years would have been as illuminating as they are had it not been for what we both have learned, *mutatis mutandis*, from Karl Barth, who, even when not explicitly present, is always in the background.

7. These commandments are always in a dialectical relation with the commandments that pertain to what is "between humans and God" (*bein adam le-maqom*). See *Mishnah:* Yoma 8.9; Maimonides, *Commentary on the Mishnah:* Peah 1.1.

8. See *CD* 2/2, pp. 515-16.

9. See Busch, *Karl Barth,* pp. 44, 56, 69. For the integration of Judaism and philosophy in Hermann Cohen's person and thought, see Simon Fisher, *Revelatory Positivism? Barth's Earliest Theology and the Marburg School* (Oxford: Oxford University Press, 1988), pp. 80-122.

10. *CD* 2/2, p. 757.

"no," and there would be nothing to mediate any further discussion between Jews and Christians that could possibly overcome this fundamental antinomy. (Lest one simply think of Judaism as the rejection of Christianity, however, the inverse response of yes and no would be the case when a Jew asserts, "The law is the form of the exclusive covenant of God with the Jewish people." Here a Jew would have to say "yes" and a Christian "no.") Conversion by a Jew to Christianity or by a Christian to Judaism would be the only way to get beyond this impasse at this directly theological level. But if this were to happen, there could be no more dialogue between distinctly Jewish Jews and distinctly Christian Christians. One side would have totally capitulated to the other.[11]

In order to keep the dialogue on track and include Barth in it, perhaps one could engage that statement and all it involves and implies philosophically, that is, by employing philosophical reasoning as a mediation through which to translate what is ultimately theological into what is more immediately accessible to those outside of Barth's theological circle. That possibility becomes more evident when one notices that in the German original of the quote above, Barth says *das Gesetz die Gestalt des Evangeliums ist*.[12] That could be translated as "the law is the way the Gospel shows itself," namely, how the Gospel manifests itself in the world. The German word *Gestalt* is much richer in meaning than the English word "form." As such, the phenomenality of the Gospel (which, for Christians, is the New Covenant) is not an object to be observed but a commandment to be obeyed. In that way, a Jew can appreciate, indeed learn from, Barth's phenomenology of some of the same commandments of God Jews also accept, indeed have accepted before Christians have accepted them. That would not require Jewish acceptance of the primary ground of the law for Barth, which is Jesus Christ, for any such acceptance by Jews would make continued Jewish identity impossible for Jews. Barth says about the Word of God, "It is first Gospel and then Law. . . . His grace is also Law."[13] For a Jew, Barth's "and/also" is where he or she can properly enter into a discussion with him.

Whether Barth himself would have approved such a methodological move is doubtful since he usually insisted on all of his statements being

---

11. See the chapter in the present volume entitled "What to Seek and What to Avoid in Jewish-Christian Dialogue." For a longer version of this argument, see the chapter in the present volume entitled "Avoiding Charges of Legalism and Antinomianism in Jewish-Christian Dialogue."

12. *Kirchliche Dogmatik* 2/2 [hereafter *KD*] (Zurich: Evangelischer Verlag, 1948), p. 847.

13. *CD* 2/2, p. 511.

read within the circle of distinctly Christian theology.[14] Nevertheless, whenever one writes something which will inevitably be read by others beyond one's own communal circle, it is also inevitable that some of those others will deconstruct the author's words, bracketing the author's intentions for purposes that the author would probably not endorse. That is because the object of the author's intention is not a project of his or her will but, rather, a datum given to him or her and to others as well, indeed a datum that the author by writing of it must share rather than control. Only the word of God in revelation can claim that it be interpreted according to the author's original intention inasmuch as the very datum of which the word speaks is the creation of the divine author. No human author, however, can make such an absolute claim on his or her readers. Theologians can only dispute among themselves as to what that original intention of revelation is, but they may not propose meanings that in any way bracket the assumption of original intent. That is why a Jew can constructively dispute with Barth philosophically but not strictly theologically. A purely theological dispute between a Jew and a Christian could only result in an impasse. The infamous medieval Jewish-Christian disputations are clear evidence of that impasse.

This essay will address itself critically to two main philosophical questions. One: How does Barth deal with the relation of commandment *(Gebot)* and law *(Gesetz)?* Two: How does Barth deal the problem of keeping God's ethical commandments in essentially secular space? Both of these questions have been dealt with by Jewish thinkers who are Barth's contemporaries, and like all of the great questions Barth addressed or that can be addressed to Barth, these questions are by no means antiquarian. They concern living Jews and living Christians here and now. But the second question is about those who, at least functionally, act in public neither as Jews nor Christians nor as members of any faith based on revelation (like Islam, for example). Indeed, one could very well see this question as the most important one for normative Jewish or normative Christian ethics in the world today, which is politically secular. Politics is the necessary context of ethical action, that is, action that takes place in an interhuman realm.[15]

---

14. See his *Dogmatics in Outline,* trans. G. T. Thompson (New York: Harper, 1959), p. 50.

15. See Alasdair MacIntyre, *After Virtue* (Notre Dame: University of Notre Dame Press, 1981), pp. 23-34.

Commandment and Law

Barth is intent on showing the superiority of ethics over law, and then the superiority of theological ethics over philosophical ethics. Concerning the superiority of ethics over law, Barth engages his Jewish philosophical teacher, Hermann Cohen, when he writes, "Morality may be understood, as in the teaching of H. Cohen, as the immanent power of all legality. . . . But it has never yet occurred to anyone seriously to assert a simple equation of ethics and politics, of ethics and jurisprudence."[16]

But what is the essential difference between law and ethics? The answer is that law *(Gesetz)* is that application of ethics that can be adequately taught, administered, and judged by human political authorities. Thus Barth is not differing from Cohen in the assertion of law being based on ethics. Indeed, if law were not based on ethics, then what is right, which is the concern of law, would not have to be based on what is good, which is the concern of ethics. That being the case, the validity of law could only be based on the power of the human authority who makes the law. Might would then be the only other source of right possible. Surely, that would have been unacceptable to Karl Barth, himself expelled from Germany in 1935 by the demonic Nazi regime, and writing the above words in 1941-42 when Hitler and his minions were trampling the rights of everybody within the range of their political and military power. Thus what Barth seems to be saying is that ethics is the transcendent power of all legality. That is, ethics both grounds law but is not subsumed by law. Indeed, in order for ethics to sufficiently ground law it must have a range of operation outside of law and prior to it. Law should not exhaust ethics.

Barth's qualification of the range of law can be better understood, I think, when one compares his distinctions with the distinction in Jewish theology between "commandment" *(mitsvah)* and "law" *(halakhah)*. In many ways one could say in this context that the content of Jewish religious life (which is all of life) is the *mitsvot* (commandments), and the structure or form or gestalt of that life is the *halakhah*. Thus if one were to look, for example, at the laws of the Sabbath, one would see there intricate structure, but one would never experience the true content which is so structured by the *halakhah* unless one experienced through his or her

16. *CD* 2/2, p. 514. Note Cohen himself in his major work in ethics, *Ethik des reinen Willens*, 5th ed. (Hildesheim and New York: Georg Olms Verlag, 1981), p. 70: "Das Recht des Rechts ist das Naturrrecht oder die Ethik des Rechts." Barth was undoubtedly familiar with the first edition of 1904. According to Fisher (*Revelatory Positivism?* p. 341), Barth purchased his copy of this work for his library in Geneva in June 1910.

own action the sanctity that doing God's Sabbath commandment truly gives.[17] It is the same with ethical commandments, commandments that pertain to interhuman relationships. Here the foundational norm is "You shall love your neighbor as yourself" (Lev. 19:18). That overarching commandment is structured by the *halakhah* in a variety of directions.[18] But the experience of the presence of another human person, whom we are commanded to presently love, can only be experienced by one's own personal deed in the commandment. How one actually sanctifies the Sabbath in his or her own particular circumstances is largely a matter left to how one actually experiences the commandment in his or her own moment. So, also, how one loves his or her neighbor is largely left to how one experiences the commandment and responds to it in his or her own moment. This fact of Judaism is illuminated by Barth's statement that "this command of God is an event [*Ereignis*]."[19] Only an antinomian, which Barth certainly is not, could object to a law that gave structure to the commandments, more by teaching what may not be done to fulfill them than what must be done to fulfill them as commandments and not as humanly imposed rules. Law has only overstepped its covenantal function when it sees itself as identical with, indeed a substitution for, the directly given commandments of God to his people. "And its worship of Me has been a commandment of men [*mitsvat anashim*] learned by rote" (Isa. 29:13).

Barth's understanding of the relation of commandment and law can be fruitfully compared to a Jewish debate in the 1920's between two of Barth's contemporaries, Martin Buber (1878-1965) and Franz Rosenzweig (1886-1929). Both Buber and Rosenzweig attempted to develop a new Jewish theology, which they hoped would go beyond the antinomy between Orthodox and Liberal Judaism in Germany at that time on the question of law and commandment. The antinomy was that the Orthodox seemed to believe the sanctity of the commandments is identical with the authority of the law, thus making the presence of the commanding God fully mediated by normative Jewish tradition. Thus it would seem, for them, the difference between divine authority and human authority is one of degree rather than one of kind. The rabbinical authorities are seemingly

---

17. For the great modern phenomenology of the experience of Sabbath observance, see my late revered teacher, Abraham Joshua Heschel, *The Sabbath*, 2d ed. (Cleveland and New York: Meridian Books, 1952).

18. See *Palestinian Talmud: Nedarim* 9.4/41c, where this commandment is designated by the greatest of the Sages in the Talmud, Rabbi Akibah, to be "the most inclusive commandment [*kelal gadol*] in the Torah." See also Maimonides, *Mishneh Torah: Mourning*, 14.1.

19. *CD* 2/2, p. 548 = *KD* 2/2, p. 608.

held to operate *in loco Dei.* The Liberals, on the other hand, seem to believe that the commandments, even the commandments pertaining to the divine-human relationship, can be reduced to some universally evident ethical principles and norms. The commandments, for them, seem to be *in loco homini.* In both cases, though, the distinction between law and commandment seems to have been elided. For the Orthodox, all law becomes commandment; for the Liberals, all commandment becomes law.

With a striking resemblance to the position of some of the most radical Christian reformers, Martin Buber emphasizes the antinomy between commandment and law:

> What is it that is eternal: the primal phenomenon, present in the here and now, of what we call revelation [*Offenbarung*]? . . . Man receives and what he receives is not a "content" [*Inhalt*] but a presence [*eine Gegenwart*]. . . . I know of nor believe in any revelation that is not its primal phenomenon . . . that which reveals is that which reveals. That which has being is there [*das Seiende ist da*], nothing more.[20]

Buber is not denying the legitimacy of law in the secular (what he calls "I-it") realm. He is not a complete antinomian. But in the truly religious/ethical (what he calls "I-thou") realm he finds no law other than commandments, which are only directed to particular individuals at a particular time and place, whether their object be God or other humans. The commandments themselves have no continued duration or extension. In this realm, the very notion of law is at best irrelevant and at worst a negative hindrance, a blocking out of pure presence. As such, he has totally severed commandment from law, from any legal structure whatsoever. That is why many Jews have taken him to be a religious antinomian.[21] This comes out when Buber says to his friend and colleague, Rosenzweig, "I told you that for me, though man is a law-receiver, God is not a law-giver, and therefore the Law has no universal validity for me, but only a personal one. I accept, therefore, only what I think is being spoken to me."[22]

Franz Rosenzweig answers Buber's religious/ethical antinomianism as follows:

---

20. Buber, *I and Thou,* trans. Walter Kaufmann (New York: Charles Scribner's Sons, 1970), pp. 157-58 = *Ich und Du* (Heidelberg: Verlag Lambert Schneider, 1962), pp. 110-11, 113.

21. See David Novak, *Jewish-Christian Dialogue: A Jewish Justification* (New York: Oxford University Press, 1989), pp. 80-86.

22. Rosenzweig, "The Builders," trans. William Wolf, in Franz Rosenzweig, *On Jewish Learning,* ed. N. N. Glatzer (New York: Schocken Books, 1955), p. 115.

Whatever can and must be done is not yet deed, whatever can and must be commanded is not yet commandment. Law [*Gesetz*] must again become commandment [*Gebot*] which seeks to be transformed into deed at the very moment it is heard. It must regain that living reality [*Heutigkeit*] in which all great Jewish periods have sensed the guarantee for its eternity.[23]

How does Rosenzweig differ from Buber in his constitution of the relation of commandment and law? And how does Barth enhance Rosenzweig's theological position for Jews?

The key to understanding the difference between Buber and Rosenzweig, it seems to me, lies in the difference between their use of singular or plural reference, respectively, in terms of who the object of the commandments of God truly is. Buber speaks of the validity of the commandment being "personal" rather than "universal." Rosenzweig, conversely, speaks of "all great Jewish periods." Thus Rosenzweig speaks of the Jewish *people* as the subject or addressee of the commandment*s* (understanding *Gebot* generically), whereas Buber speaks of *himself* (or any other individual self) as that subject or addressee (understanding *Gebot* particularly). There is a fundamental difference whether one sees the commandment as being addressed to a communal self or an individual self. That difference, in this issue, lies in the continuity and extension of the commandments in time and space. Commandments addressed to a communal self must have a continuity in time and an extension in space in order to have communal intelligibility. A community is continuous in time: it has a history and a destiny. A community is extended in space: it is a universe, a plurality of persons who participate in its present life. Each aspect of basically communal human existence necessarily entails thinking in universals. But a commandment solely addressed to any individual person is exclusively an event *(Ereignis)*, necessarily unconnected to any other event; it is what is unique *(eigentlich)*.

Despite Barth's insistence that the commandment of God is an event, it is an event experienced by a communal self and, as such, it has communal significance. On this key point Barth would, it seems, agree with Rosenzweig (a Jewish thinker of whom, to my knowledge, Barth was unaware).[24] Thus he writes:

23. Rosenzweig, "The Builders," p. 85.

24. For Rosenzweig's recognition of the early Barth, see N. N. Glatzer, *Franz Rosenzweig,* 2d ed. (New York: Schocken Books, 1961), p. 278. There Rosenzweig concentrates on Barth's early notion of God as *ganz Anders,* famously expressed in his 1919 commentary on the Epis-

The question must actually be: What ought *we* to do? [*was sollen wir tun?*] and not what *I* ought to do? The former does not exclude the latter. Indeed, it can seriously be put only if it really includes the latter. . . . The one absolute thing which is the object of God's command . . . is declared to us, [it] is not something that I am and have alone, but only in the community and solidarity, perhaps of all men. . . . Even the claim which is addressed to me is not as a so-called personality or individual or special case, but as a responsible partner [*verantwortliche Genosse*] in the divine covenant.[25]

The question, though, is whether Barth (or Rosenzweig) adequately dealt with the communal character of the commandments of God. That leads us to the question of the manifestation of the commandments as law, which to be sure is not an assertion that the commandments of God are derived from some prior universal manifestation of the being of God.

The Lawful Community

Barth is rightly concerned that the commandments of God not be taken as specific conclusions of more general premises. It is a point he emphasizes many times. For example:

The Law of God [*das Gebot Gottes*] cannot be compared with any human law. For it is not merely a general rule but also a specific prescription [*Vorschrift*] and norm for each individual case. At one and the same time it is both the law and the Judge who applies it.[26]

In order not to fall into the trap of seeing the divine commandment subsumed under some prior universal, it would seem that Barth has to see the community of faith, that is, the community whose task it is to be responsive to and responsible for (both implied in Barth's preferred German term: *verantwortlich*) the commandments of God, as being consti-

tle to the Romans. Rosenzweig contrasts that with the nearness of God emphasized by the eleventh-century Jewish theologian/poet Judah Halevi. But I suspect that Rosenzweig would have resonated much more favorably to Barth's later theology, which also emphasizes the nearness of God. Along these lines, see Randi Rashkover, "Covenantal Ethics in Theologies of Revelation: A Comparison of Franz Rosenzweig and Karl Barth," Ph.D. dissertation, University of Virginia, 1999.

25. *CD* 2/2, p. 655 = *KD* 2/2, p. 729.
26. *CD* 2/2, p. 663 = *KD* 2/2, p. 739.

tuted by those who have heard the commandment of God addressed to themselves. For Christians, that suggests the image of the disciples becoming a community *after* they have heard Jesus' call to them to obey God's commandment to follow him. However, is that how the covenanted community comes into existence? Is the community the subsequent association of like-minded believers? Is the community constituted a posteriori, that is, after the fact of the plural hearing of the commandment of God? Does the community have any a priori status and function? These philosophical questions have profound implications for the way Jewish ethics and Christian ethics can be practiced, especially in a context that has become increasingly secular. Furthermore, it raises the philosophical question of whether secularity (which need not be confused with modern attempts to make it atheistic per se) does not lie in the background of the revelation-receiving community as well.

We must now ask: Does the commandment of God itself create the community *of* those who hear it, or does the commandment of God come directly *to* a community who is already lawfully constituted by transcendent criteria of justice not of its own making? If the former, that is, the community is made de novo *by* the direct commandment of God, then there is no human precondition necessary so that the commandment of God might be intelligible, let alone desirable, to its human hearers. If the latter, though, then one must discover just what these human preconditions are and why they are necessary *for* the human acceptance of the commandment itself. Moreover, in order to comply with Barth's rightful concern that the commandment of God not be derived *from* something prior to it, one must show just how this human precondition operates *for* the commandment of God. That operation has logical and chronological priority in human experience, but it does not have ontological priority. The commandment per se cannot be derived from anything other than God's revealed will. The precondition is not an existential ground. The commandment of God is *in* the world, not *of* it. It is a ground clearing not the grounding factor.[27]

If Barth is right in his preclusion of even any precondition for (let alone grounds of) God's commandment, then one might ask: How could one know what a commandment is if one never had any experience of a commandment *before* the event of revelation? The rabbinic principle "The Torah speaks through human language [*ke-lashon benei adam*]" is

---

27. See David Novak, *Natural Law in Judaism* (Cambridge: Cambridge University Press, 1998), pp. 142-48.

helpful here.[28] Full revelation of God's word occurs within a human history already in progress, a history that language not only describes but actually comprises. Revelation is not synonymous with the creation of humankind and its communities. As such, full revelation comes to a people already organized by its concerns for the persons in its care, however rudimentary that order is. Without that connection to creation and its order, specifically the creation of humans as political beings, one runs the risk of the Gnostic (for Christians, the Marcionite) rupture between revelation and creation. Revelation comes *to* and *for* us *in* the world; it is not meant to remove us *from* the world. Finally, revelation promises redemption *(ge'ulah)*, which will come *into* the world but not take us *out of* the world.

At this level, there is no antinomy between commandment *(Gebot)* and law *(Gesetz)*. Instead, we can understand law as the gestalt of commandment. The difference between the two, then, is not between commandment and law but, rather, between direct and indirect commandments of God. And each one of these commandments, both direct (what has been called "special revelation") and indirect (what has been called "general revelation"), comes with its own gestalt, its own law.[29] And, we experience indirect revelation before we experience direct revelation.[30]

We first experience God's commandment in the claims our fellow human presences make upon us. The reason we are bound to respond to these claims is because we gradually see the uniqueness of human existence as reflecting an innate relationship with, what is at this level, *the divine*.[31] The human "other" mediates the presence of the divine "Other," anticipating Him — but never able to force it — as it were. That is why we ourselves relate to that human other differently than we do to any of our other co-creatures, which (not who) are the products of divine making *of* them, not divine speech *to and with* them as is the case with humans only.

---

28. See Maimonides, *Guide of the Perplexed,* 1.26; also, 2.40.

29. Cf. John Calvin, *Institutes of the Christian Religion,* 1.2.1-3; 1.3.1. I disagree with Calvin et al. that our intuition of God is a causal inference. Instead, it is a phenomenological trace of the divine behind human presence. Cf. Emmanuel Levinas, *Of God Who Comes to Mind,* trans. B. Bergo (Stanford, Calif.: Stanford University Press, 1998), p. 75.

30. Barth himself makes this distinction between what is direct and indirect in theologically justified ethics. See *CD* 2/2, pp. 541-42.

31. In Scripture, it seems that the universal recognition of prime divine authority is designated *elohim* ("God," but perhaps better translated "divinity") in distinction from YHWH ("Lord"). See, e.g., Gen. 20:11; Exod. 1:17; cf. Exod. 3:13-14; 5:2. As *elohim* God need not be experienced as person.

Law is the way a human community coordinates and adjudicates the claims made by one human person upon another, claims made by many human persons upon one human person, and claims made by one human person upon many human persons.[32] Natural law, or the "orders of creation," or cosmic justice *(mishpat),* comprises those standards deemed necessary for any human community to claim the moral allegiance of human persons who are the image of God. Natural law governs whom we need to be with. It prepares us for God's covenantal entrance into our community that transforms it without destroying it.

Our desire for the human others in all their variety, which is the basis of all ethical motivation, reveals to us our ultimate desire to hear the word of God. Our desire for that direct presence of God must first be mediated by our desire for the always indirect presence of humans. That is because when the presence of God comes to us, it comes to *us* as communal creatures, *already* aware of our communal nature and, thus, *ready* for the covenant that we hope will come *to* us, but which can never be conjured up *by* us. God's presence, then, speaks to us in a language *we* have been speaking among ourselves, even though its content is a novum. God's word comes to the community, who is always becoming his people, to do good for them. Some of that good they already comprehend; more of it they are ready to apprehend, thereafter. It is through our desire for human presence that we can best appreciate how revelation shows us that God too desires that human presence, indeed that God, both before us and after us, desires that same community. "For the Lord's portion is his people . . . he found them in a desert land . . . keeping them as the pupil [*k'ishon*] of his eye" (Deut. 32:9-10).

Of course, it is true that the demands of the other, whether human or divine, rightly make their claims upon us even when we are not ready for them, even when we don't like them. Nevertheless, in order for those claims to be properly fulfilled by us, we have to learn to love them. Learning to love them means discovering our primal desire for God, the desire which is more often repressed into unconsciousness than any other. Indeed, without the recovery of that desire, we could only come to hate the commandments and thus inevitably defy them. And all love is desire; all love is erotic in one way or another.[33] In this way, we are com-

---

32. See David Novak, *Covenantal Rights: A Study in Jewish Political Theory* (Princeton: Princeton University Press, 2000), pp. 3-25.

33. One could certainly say that in the Hebrew Scriptures all love (*ahavah, hesheq,* etc.) is eros. See esp. Deut. 7:7-9. The famous thesis of the Lutheran theologian Anders Nygren in

manded to love God and our neighbor, commandments whose immediate source and immediate object could be seen to be identical. This is unlike the other commandments where the source of the commandment (God) addresses Himself to the subject of the commandment (humans) to act upon the object of the commandment (for example, unleavened bread to be eaten on Passover).[34]

To be sure, the covenanted community takes on its unique identity *because of* the direct commandments of God. The content of these commandments is unique because, in one way or another, it celebrates what God has done for-with-and-through His people in their singular history together. In this sense, Passover is the paradigm for all other such commandments. Nevertheless, the gestalt or law of these commandments is often very similar to the gestalt or law of what has transpired between humans themselves before revelation. That is why commandments where God is the direct object of our action, prayer being the best example, whose preferred (although not exclusive) locus is during communal worship, always have an immediate relation to ethical/communal concerns. Thus God rejects the prayers of unrepentant murderers, thieves, and adulterers. "Even when you pray in excess, I do not listen; your hands are full of blood" (Isa. 1:15). And, just as the ethical commandments of God have historical/legal precedents in human attempts to honor the transcendent intention of human personal existence, so do the cultic commandments of God have historical/legal precedents in human gropings toward a direct relationship with God, one that can only come from God Himself.

Without the assertion of these human preconditions, it is hard to explain why the gestalt of God's commandments frequently looks so much like the gestalt of human institutions that are open to the coming of the ultimate end of their desire, and that this similarity is not accidental. Thus the gestalt of the direct commandments of God has already been

---

his *Agape and Eros,* trans. P. S. Watson (Chicago: University of Chicago Press, 1982), who sees eros as "egocentric" (p. 722), built on "the foundation of self-love" (p. 723), and being "after the pattern of human, acquisitive love" (p. 723), is mistaken about eros phenomenologically. Instead, true eros is ecstatically self-giving, so much so that the true lover allows himself or herself to be radically affected by his or her beloved. That is why God, as the exemplar of all eros (see Exod. 34:6; *Babylonian Talmud:* Shabbat 133b re Exod. 15:2), allows us to love him wholeheartedly and erotically in response (see Deut. 6:5; *Mishnah:* Berakhot 9.5). That is why in both Jewish and Christian traditional exegesis, the mutual love between God and His people is best expressed in the palpably erotic imagery of the Song of Songs. True eros is not lust, which inevitably turns into violence (see 2 Sam. 13:1-19; Novak, *Natural Law in Judaism,* pp. 36-39).

34. See Maimonides, *Mishneh Torah:* Benedictions, 11.2, and Karo, *Kesef Mishneh* thereon.

prepared for it by the gestalt of the indirect commandments of God. These indirect, mediated commandments are experienced in the human claims that always come first in our personal history, which is concretely communal and only abstractly individual. That is why Jewish or Christian theology need not and should not reject true historical scholarship of our respective histories, whether cultic or ethical. Such enquiry helps us better appreciate the necessarily human gestalt of the commandments of God. Jews and Christians need only reject the type of historicist reductionism that assumes revelation is impossible. Here is where critical philosophy, especially analytic philosophy, can serve a useful theological purpose.

Divine Commandments and Ethical Discourse

The practical problem raised by Barth's theory of divine commandments is that it does not seem to be able to adequately address the changed political context of most of our ethical action brought about by modernity, which is a political context that seems irreversible and which many, including many Jews and Christians, think ought to be irreversible. The fact is that today, indeed by now yesterday and probably tomorrow, most of our ethical action is necessarily conducted in secular space. Thus even if I as a believing Jew am convinced that protecting human life from wanton destruction is directly commanded to me by God, I cannot argue for that commandment, which I believe is addressed to all humans along with me and my fellow Jews, I cannot argue for public policies to implement that commandment qua commandment (*mitsvah* or *Gebot*). That is due to the fact that not everyone in the society in which I responsibly participate — turning into the state of which I am a loyal and law-abiding citizen — is a Jewish believer, or a Christian or Muslim believer with whom I can share an acceptance of some basic divine commandments that function ethically, that is, which are addressed to interhuman situations. In other words, in the secular, democratic society where most of my interpersonal relationships (except those that are most intimate, like those in my family and synagogue) are conducted and where I frequently want to be a public advocate, there I cannot speak of the claims of *my* commanding God except as my *private* motivation. Publicly, I can only speak of divine wisdom manifest in human nature.[35] That is because membership in that society cannot, indeed should not, be based on ac-

---

35. See Novak, *Natural Law in Judaism,* pp. 16-26.

ceptance of historical revelation, which is the only possible source of the direct commandments of God.

Now there are some Jews and some Christians who attempt to retreat into sectarian enclaves, where they can live more consistently and continually according to the direct commandments of God to their respective traditional communities. Such retreats should be respected, but one can still very much doubt their wisdom. Because of growing national and international economic interdependence, economic survival requires more and more participation in the secular realm, whether desirable or even only necessary. That cannot help but have a growing effect on even the most sectarian enclaves. And because of that reality, which is beyond the control of any community to reverse, religious believers — Jews, Christians, or Muslims — need to be able to argue for ethical positions that are consistent with the divine commandments they have accepted, but which cannot be deduced from them. Maximally, that means that religious believers can make some positive contributions to the democratic societies that have, in many cases, provided them with a haven from religious persecution. Minimally, that means that religious believers need to be participants in the moral discourse of their democratic societies so that they can effectively oppose public policies that would make observance of the commandments of God more difficult and in some cases impossible, and so they can support public policies that make the observance of the commandments easier by providing more public space for their observance.

Barth and Jewish advocates of ethics limited to only what can be deduced from divine commandments would seem to have no answer to the secular need of the religious believers described above. Nevertheless, since most of these Jews and Christians are not sectarians — not Hasidim or Amish — they cannot in good faith avoid at least an attempt to deal with the problem. And, even if Barth does not have an answer for us, can we find any hints in his work for those of us who do not want to avoid this secular, this philosophical need?

Almost *en passant*, Barth recognizes some value in a nontheological ethics, which he calls "an ethics whose self-reflection, self-understanding and self-responsibility were from the outset overshadowed, determined and guided by a prior, even if more or less inexplicit, knowledge of the word of God."[36] Despite some hyperbole here, it would seem that such an ethics is "determined" by the word of God not as a premise determines its

36. CD 2/2, p. 541.

conclusion but, maybe, like a desire is determined if and when its object appears to it, and that can be a desire which is more often than not yet to be self-conscious. Barth continues his speculation on this matter:

> An ethics of this kind would renounce all claim to try to speak a final word in solution of the problem of right conduct . . . without being guilty of that apotheosis in the background, without asserting that there is an ultimate reality either from or within the human self as such. . . . It would be an ethics that knew the limits of humanity, and would not therefore treat humanity as an absolute but would for that reason do justice to it. . . . Indirectly, it too would call man away from himself.[37]

In reading a passage such as this, I wonder why Barth had such antipathy to the idea of natural law. Couldn't one see natural law minimally as a few basic negative principles that delimit the pretensions of human will — collective then individual — in claiming absolute authority for itself? And couldn't one see natural law minimally as a few basic positive principles that advocate the justice of certain essential human claims? Couldn't one call this type of law or justice *(dikē* or *Recht)* "natural" insofar as nature *(physis)* functions as both limit *(peras)* and goal *(telos)?*[38] Couldn't natural law be seen as the necessary delimitation of the human subject for the sake of the human object? And, couldn't one see this very enhancement of the human subject qua person as the necessary precondition for the acceptance of revelation as that grace which recognizes and validates the ultimate dignity of the human person in community, which is to be capable of being addressed by God in revelation?

I think Barth had a blind spot regarding natural law. That is evident in how he seems to see only two natural law alternatives: the "neo-Protestantism" of Wilhelm Herrmann, and the Aristotelianism of Thomas Aquinas and his disciples.[39] The theology of the Marburg theologian, Herrmann, is the attempt to see Christianity, especially Christian ethics, on a Kantian basis, which means, in the end, to place revelation on a rational basis. Now it should not be forgotten that Herrmann's chief dialogue partner in his years at Marburg was Hermann Cohen. In fact, one can see much more of an influence of Cohen's Kantian rationalism on Hermann than

---

37. *CD* 2/2, p. 541.

38. For the original philosophical use of these important terms, see Aristotle, *Metaphysics,* 1022a14.

39. See *CD* 2/2, pp. 520-28, 543-51.

vice-versa.[40] For Barth, I would speculate, that meant that if there was to be a natural law theory, it had to be done à la Kant-Cohen-Herrmann, and that would mean ultimately reducing revelation to reason and thereby making it lose its absolute primacy. This would explain his famous "Nein!" to the attempt of his fellow Swiss Reformed theologian, Emil Brunner (truth be told, a much less impressive theologian than Herrmann), to propose an ethic that recognized "orders of creation," which is a Protestant synonym of natural law.[41] As for Thomistic natural law theory, Barth recognized its greater theological integrity than that of neo-Protestantism, but it is still a theology that seems to be unable to place divine command at the foundation of all theology, the queen of the sciences. Thomistic natural law theory seems founded upon a metaphysics that Barth is convinced is incompatible with Christianity.[42] In some important ways, I wish Barth had been more of a Calvinist in his treatment of law.[43] As such, he might have been able to make better use of the natural law type thinking of some other modern Calvinists.[44] Finally, I might add, reflecting on my own community, that there are Jewish opponents of natural law who employ an almost identical logic to that of Barth in rejecting any Jewish natural law theory.[45] In other words,

40. For Cohen's influence on Herrmann, see Fisher, *Revelatory Positivism?* pp. 124-26, 153-63. For Herrmann's uneasiness with that influence, however, see ibid., pp. 133-40.

41. See *Natural Theology: Comprising "Nature and Grace" by Emil Brunner, and the Reply "No" by Karl Barth,* trans. P. Fraenkel (London: G. Bles, 1946).

42. See *CD* 2/2, p. 528.

43. For Barth in the context of Lutheran-Calvinist debates about law, see J. van Dijk, *Die Grundlegung der Ethik in der Theologie Karl Barths* (Munich: Manz Verlag, 1966), pp. 262-63nn.95-99.

44. Even though he was certainly not in Karl Barth's theological league, it is still useful, along these lines of enquiry, to look at the work of the Dutch Calvinist theologian/statesman Abraham Kuyper. See *Abraham Kuyper,* ed. J. D. Bratt (Grand Rapids: Eerdmans, 1998). I think that Reinhold Niebuhr, who certainly was in Barth's theological league, has a theological anthropology, upon which he bases his political theory, closer to that of Calvin than that of Barth. See his *Nature and Destiny of Man,* vol. 1 (New York: Charles Scribner's Sons, 1941), pp. 158-59. Indeed, despite Niebuhr's criticisms of natural law theory as represented by the Roman Catholic moral theology of his day (*Nature and Destiny of Man,* pp. 278-97), his own critiques of the pretensions of human culture and politics can now be seen as akin to the minimalist natural law theory being suggested here. For a comparison of Barth and Niebuhr, favorable to Niebuhr as having a more politically adequate theological position, see Will Herberg's introductory essay, "The Social Philosophy of Karl Barth," in *Karl Barth, Community, State, and Church,* ed. Will Herberg (Garden City, N.Y.: Doubleday, 1960), pp. 55-67.

45. See Marvin Fox, "Maimonides and Aquinas on Natural Law," in *Interpreting Maimonides* (Chicago and London: University of Chicago Press, 1990), pp. 24-51. Cf. David Novak, *Jewish Social Ethics* (New York: Oxford University Press, 1992), pp. 25-29.

my philosophical difference with Barth is one I also have with some of my fellow Jewish thinkers, and some of his fellow Christian thinkers have this disagreement with Barth. So, there are Jews who would agree with Barth, not me, and Christians who would agree with me, not Barth.[46]

Nevertheless, I think if Barth had attempted to rethink the idea of natural law along theological lines, and had not assumed that it had already been exhausted by theories he found theologically dangerous, he might have very well been able to do with the idea of natural law some of the things he was able to do with other traditional ideas he was able to masterfully rework and redirect.[47] If Barth had done that, he would have employed philosophy more effectively in his theology, and his theological ethics would have been able to be entered more authentically into current ethical discussions that have no choice but to be held in essentially secular space. Nevertheless, some of us who have learned from Barth — both Christians and Jews — can employ many of his extraordinary insights and formulations in directions that, for whatever reason, he himself did not care to go. Along those lines, Barth's magnificent discussion of divine command can very much help us remain modest in the claims we make for a natural law theory, be it Christian or Jewish. For Barth the idea of natural law said too little; we who respect him and have learned from him should not let it say too much.[48]

---

46. See Stanley Hauerwas, "Christian Ethics in Jewish Terms: A Response to David Novak," in *Christianity in Jewish Terms,* ed. Tikva Frymer-Kensky, Peter Ochs, David Novak, Michael Signer, and David Sandmel (Boulder, Colo.: Westview Press, 2000), pp. 135-40.

47. Barth accepted the idea that there is a law of God pertaining to universal human nature, but he denied that this commandment could be known universally, except by direct divine revelation. For Barth, there only seems to be specific revelation, which, without a reference to general revelation, becomes singularly exclusive revelation. See his *Ethics,* ed. D. Braun, trans. G. W. Bromiley (New York: Seabury Press, 1981), pp. 209-10.

48. See Novak, *Natural Law in Judaism,* pp. 174-78.

What Does Edith Stein Mean for Jews?

The recent canonization of Edith Stein as Saint Teresa Benedicta of the Cross by the Roman Catholic Church poses a number of very serious challenges to living Jews, we who are still members of the people of whom Edith Stein believed she too had remained a member even unto her death with us in the gas chamber of Auschwitz. These are challenges thoughtful Jews cannot avoid. How could we not be concerned with the life and death of one of our own at the time when we all could have died, even though in life she chose to live apart from us? How could we not be concerned with the life and death of one of our own, who has been granted the highest posthumous honor possible by a community of hundreds of millions of people with whom we live, converse, even suffer in the world, often quite closely?

However, any Jew who discusses the whole case of Edith Stein, especially with a group of Catholics, seems to be at an essential disadvantage. When a Catholic speaks of Saint Teresa Benedicta of the Cross, he or she is speaking with the public authorization, the *magisterium* of the Church herself. Conversely, when a Jew speaks of Edith Stein, he or she is speaking what seems to be only an individual opinion. Does that mean, therefore, a Jew like myself here today, not speaking with the institutional authority of my community, is coming to the case purely subjectively, with nothing grounding him? No. That is because I must present my opinion as a valid *Jewish* opinion, one that is consistent with the normative thrust of the

This paper was originally delivered at the Symposium on Edith Stein, held by the Lumen Christi Institute of the University of Chicago and Loyola University, Chicago, 9 April 1999. A shorter version of it appeared under the title "Edith Stein, Apostate Saint," in *First Things* 96 (1999): 15-17.

Jewish tradition itself and what is not just the opinion of someone like myself or Edith Stein or anyone else who happens to have been born of a Jewish mother. And this truth criterion applies even to Jewish remarks made to a non-Jewish audience since a Jew must always speak to his or her fellow Jews first when speaking of Judaism, even when that speech seems to be more immediately addressed to the outside world. My freedom of opinion, then, must be answerable to authentic Jewish authority, even if not to a political institution. Like anything human, my freedom is finite.

Looking at it now from your side, our methodological difference might be less than it seems at first glance. Does not even the *magisterium* of the Church need to be interpreted by individual Catholics themselves? Is this not the role of *conscience* in Catholic moral theology? Catholic teaching still requires its meaning to be freely chosen by individual opinion, which then is publicly judged by communal authorities to be either right or wrong, sooner or later. Thus the balance of authority and freedom is a difference of degree rather than one of kind between Judaism and Catholicism. In Catholicism, authority is more institutionalized; in Judaism, it is less so. In Judaism one could say it is more a matter of informal agreement, what Catholics might call *consensus fidelium.* So despite this difference of degree regarding authority, in this case or any one like it, a faithful Jew cannot have *any* opinion, and a faithful Catholic is not initially bound to only *one* opinion. In both our traditions, authority requires freedom for the sake of the interpreting subject; freedom requires authority for the sake of the interpreted object. It is important to say all of this at the outset, so that this situation of Jewish-Catholic dialogue we are in here and now has enough of an even playing field to enable us to talk to each other and with each other, not past each other, or worse, at each other. So now it could be said that we do have enough freedom in the foreground to make this a truly personal interaction, and enough authority in the background to make this an interaction of persons truly situated in communities with cosmic orientation in this world and beyond. Our finitude is free, and our freedom is finite. That alone befits creatures who are also the image of God. That alone befits communities covenanted with God.

Hopefully, we are oriented enough by now in our communicative speech situation (the importance of which has been made with great insight by the contemporary German philosopher Jürgen Habermas) to properly raise the question: What does Edith Stein mean for Jews? Edith Stein was, arguably, the most significant Jewish convert to Christianity of the twentieth century — theologically speaking, that is. It might be best to begin with an analysis of some of the meanings that have been offered by Jews in cases of Jewish converts to Christianity. In general, Jewish tradition regards such persons as apostates *(meshumadim),* who have removed themselves from the assembly of Israel *(keneset yisrael)* in a radical way, even if they still consider themselves personally part of the body of the Jewish people. That general judgment stands even if the apostate is a person of extraordinary intellectual and moral virtues like Edith Stein. Our feelings in such cases, however great or small the person before us is, range from anger to sorrow. We cannot very well be indifferent. But feelings are not enough. Instead, they must either lead us to or be derived from genuine knowledge in order to be justified. Genuine knowledge either leads to insightful feeling or shows us how initial feelings were mistaken. Feeling without knowledge is self-indulgent; knowledge without feeling is impersonal.

Here that knowledge consists of the meaning of the case before us and the truth of the Torah above us. The rabbinic principle "be deliberate in judgment" *(metunim ba-din)* must be our method in looking at the case. Each case must be understood in terms of its own phenomenology, which, indeed, is the very philosophical method Edith Stein mastered, and which was such an important element in the most momentous existential decision she ever made: her conversion. It is what Edith Stein's teacher Edmund Husserl called the *Wesenschau,* namely, *how* to look at *what* (or *who)* appears before us. Our method for looking to the Torah, moreover, must be conditioned by the case before us. Since Edith Stein was a philosopher at all times, including her religious life, we need to look to the Torah philosophically in her case just as we need to look at her philosophically. Understanding and judgment need to participate in knowledge in a way similar enough so that they can be correlated coherently. Based on these two connected criteria, I find most of the Jewish reactions to the case of Edith Stein wanting, even though she is, no doubt, one who left the assembly of Israel — that is, as we Jews see it. The usual Jewish reactions to the case of Edith Stein are wanting not because they are keenly felt, but because their feeling is not based on real knowledge nor do they lead to real knowledge. They are either wrong about Edith Stein or wrong about the Torah or wrong about both, specifically if not in general. It is important, though, to go through them now in order to arrive, hopefully, at something more intelligent later.

Since the Holocaust is ubiquitous in moral and religious discourse these days, it seems to be the easiest entry into the question of Edith

Stein, who was murdered in Auschwitz, and who probably would not have been canonized were it not for the way her life ended there. Spokespersons for certain Jewish organizations, themselves undistinguished theologically or philosophically, have been quick to castigate the Church for canonizing Edith Stein. In their eyes, it is the Church's attempt to remake the Holocaust into a Christian event, to hijack it, as it were. Their argument goes something like this. Edith Stein was murdered in Auschwitz *solely because* she was a Jew. Her being a Catholic, even a Carmelite nun, had nothing to do with it. She would have been murdered just the same whether she practiced Judaism, Catholicism, or no religion at all. The Nazis were intent on murdering anyone born a Jew. Their animus was racial. The religious convictions of their Jewish victims were of no concern to them. Edith Stein's Catholicism was, then, accidental to the circumstances of her death.

This calls into question whether Edith Stein was really a martyr. After all, *martyr* means someone who bears witness of God *(martyrein)*. That seems to presuppose the freedom of choice not to be a martyr, that is, the real option to become what one's persecutor demands one become. And that is only the case when there is a forced conversion from one religious or ideological commitment to another, which is a matter of one's identity that can be freely affirmed or denied. But one cannot affirm or deny one's own birth. It is totally involuntary. Edith Stein and all the rest of the six million Jewish victims of the Nazis died because of their involuntary birth, not because of their voluntary faith. Therefore, the Church is accused of using its traditional category of martyrdom to make Edith Stein a Catholic Holocaust martyr instead of a Jewish Holocaust victim. And, implied in this argument, often mentioned in an angry manner, is that the traditional anti-Judaism of the Church itself was a major component in the very ideology whose adherents murdered Edith Stein the Jew. The implication here is that guilt rather than canonical celebration is what truly becomes the Church in this case, first guilt for the Jewish-Christian victims, and then guilt for all the Jewish victims.

Elsewhere I have argued against this simplistic reduction of Nazism to Christian theology, even Christian theology when it has been most anti-Jewish. That Christian anti-Judaism was a contributing factor to Nazi ideology is surely admitted by most fair-minded Christians after the Holocaust. However, it was not the sufficient condition of that ideology at all. Nazism is not applied Christianity. Nazism is, rather, modern racism in extremis, which is the idolatry of the folk, the false gods of *Blut und Boden*. Idolatry is always a temptation, even to worshipers of the one true God.

Nazism has been implicitly anti-Christian from the start, becoming explicitly anti-Christian sooner or later. That point is evidenced by the Nazi murder of many gentile Christians for their Christian faith, which when sincere often involved risking their lives to save Jewish and other victims of the program of mass murder. In fact, to set the record straight, Edith Stein's deportation, first to Westerboerk in the Netherlands and then to Auschwitz in Poland, was part of the Nazi response to the pastoral letter of the Dutch bishops in 1942, in which the bishops protested the inhuman treatment of "the Jews of the Netherlands," which explicitly meant *all* the Dutch Jews and not just those few who had converted to Christianity. That very much included Edith Stein, who left Germany in 1938 for the then safer location of the Carmelite convent of Echt in the Netherlands.

Furthermore, to assert that somehow or other the Holocaust "belongs" to the Jews, even belongs to the Jews exclusively, is simply not true. The only people to whom the Holocaust *belongs* are the Nazi murderers. They alone are responsible for it by their own freely chosen deeds. Those who supported them are responsible for their own contributions to that evil, whether more or less direct. Those who sympathized with the Nazi murderers are responsible for their distorted hearts. No one else is responsible, except all of us, Jews and gentiles, who are responsible to learn enough to be able to intelligently fight against any mass murder and the conditions which serve its horrific purposes. But to assign any inherited guilt is itself racist ideology.

On the other hand, if belonging means to have a right to something, then mourning the victims of the Holocaust is the right of every community of survivors. We Jews have a right to mourn our Jewish victims, whoever they were, just as you Christians have a right to mourn your Christian victims, whoever they were, even if they were Jews like Edith Stein who chose to become like you. Nobody deserved to be murdered in Auschwitz. All the victims were innocent. Every death there was tragic. And mourning any such tragedy is always a particular exercise, recognizing the irrevocable loss of one's own. One cannot mourn strangers; one can only *empathize* (the concept of which Edith Stein so carefully analyzed in her dissertation) about their plight. Christian mourning is only objectionable when it loses sight of the fact that Jews were the chief victims of the Holocaust. But Jewish mourning is also objectionable when it loses sight of the fact that there were other victims too, including those who were both Jewish and Christian: Jewish by birth and Christian by conviction. The sympathy of mourning for our own should not exclude empathy for the mourning of others.

As for any judgment of the Holocaust by universal morality to the world at large, which can only be international, that can only be made on the grounds that the Holocaust was a crime against humanity, and it is, therefore, the responsibility of all humankind to defeat this evil when it is still alive and condemn it forever thereafter. There is no monopoly of remembrance of either the murdered or the murderers. May God compensate the innocent and avenge their deaths from the hands of the guilty, be it in this world or in the world-to-come. And there is no monopoly of human judgment both to condemn the murderers in life and in death and to comfort the survivors in life and to commemorate the victims in death. Thus it would be perverse of the Church or any other community not to mourn her own dead in her own way, and not to utter moral judgment for humanity to all humankind. Should the Church forget Edith Stein and all those like her any more than she should forget those in her midst who chose evil and rejected good? I think not.

What follows from or precedes this kind of Jewish reaction, in its misguided attempt to claim the Holocaust for ourselves alone, is to make Jews, for all intents and purposes, a species apart from humankind. But was that not the logic of the murderers themselves? Such a move precludes Jews from making any universal moral judgment in the world or from being the object of such moral judgment. Even our mourning becomes an example of special pleading. Indeed, it makes our agony seem so fantastic so as to play right into the hands of those who deny the Holocaust altogether, insisting it is a Jewish hoax, designed to make gentiles feel guilty and thus beholden. The Torah, not the Holocaust, is the "inheritance [*morashah*] of the congregation of Jacob" (Deut. 33:4). If the Holocaust has to lose some of its "uniqueness" in order to allow for multinational mourning and international moral judgment, so be it. Only God and God's Torah and God's people are unique *(ehad)*. The Holocaust can be said to be only the first example of a category of events in the world that are directed against God with and through His people.

Finally, the argument from the Holocaust also misunderstands the essence of martyrdom, which is not an originally Christian idea, but one that Christians learned from Judaism. Martyrdom, bearing witness of God to the world, is what Jews call *qiddush ha-Shem,* "the sanctification of the divine name." It is a commandment; therefore, it is a matter of free choice. Yet that free choice can be of two kinds. One, it can be the choice whether to die or not. That was the choice of Rabbi Akibah, who chose to teach the Torah in public rather than be a living accomplice to the Roman attempt to kill the soul of the Jews by outlawing the public teaching of the

Torah. In doing that, he knew very well he would soon be killed. Rabbi Akibah saw his freely chosen death as the highest form of loving God with "all your soul" (Deut. 6:5). Two, that free choice can be the choice not whether to die but how to die. Thus on one's deathbed a Jew is supposed to commend his or her spirit back to God who gave it, and to see his or her death as an act of reconciliation with God. "May my death be atonement [*kapparah*] for all my sins." This is also an act of sanctification of the divine name, even though one's death there is inevitable and not a matter of his or her own free choice. So I would say that any Jew who was murdered in Auschwitz, who at the moment of death accepted being a Jew, one of the elect of God, and was able to die with the affirmation of the uniqueness of God and the uniqueness of Israel His people asserted by the *shema* on his or her lips, such a person is definitely a martyr. And since we refuse to believe that any Jew in his or her heart of hearts would not be grateful to God for the election, despite our humanly unbearable suffering in this world, when we Jews mourn the dead of the Holocaust, we refer to all of them, religious or irreligious or even antireligious in life, as *qedoshim*, as "saints."

I fail to see how the Church, who regards herself to be a covenanted community, could possibly take a view much different — *mutatis mutandis*. So, we Jews had better understand the Jewish origins of the idea of martyrdom and its Jewish interpretation very well before we criticize its enunciation by another community that derives its own identity out of Judaism. Just as we have no monopoly on the Holocaust, we have no monopoly on martyrdom. To belittle the Christian understanding of martyrdom is to belittle the Jewish understanding of martyrdom. What is Judaism without martyrdom? "You are my witnesses [*edei*], says the Lord, My servant whom I have chosen, that you know and be faithful to Me" (Isa. 43:10). The fact that Edith Stein does not bear witness to me as a Jew does not in any way make her claim to be a martyr and the Church's confirmation of that claim in her canonization disingenuous. It is only those who have no understanding of martyrdom per se, thinking it foreign when it is really domestic, who find the idea unintelligible. Thus a faithful and knowledgeable Jew can understand Christian martyrdom by *analogia entis*, a Thomistic term Edith Stein might have very well thought to be the root of the empathy she studied so carefully even in the days she lived as a philosopher without faith.

So far we have seen that Jews cannot accuse the Church of any duplicity or deceit in seeing Edith Stein to be a Holocaust martyr. What, then, are our reasons for not being able to celebrate with you the life and death of Saint Teresa Benedicta of the Cross? The Holocaust should not be one of them. Why would most of us have had to distance ourselves from her in life as did her pious Jewish mother, and why would most of us have joined that segment of her family who chose not to attend her beatification in Cologne several years ago by Pope John Paul II? Here again, though, the usual Jewish answers to this question are inadequate, not in many other cases, but in the case of Edith Stein. These other cases are often quite similar to one another, even though each should be judged separately and distinctly. But Edith Stein comes across as a person who is almost *sui generis*, in a class by herself. In fact, she might be the most uniquely problematic Jew for us since Saul of Tarsus.

We must never forget that Edith Stein was a *modern* Jewish convert to Christianity. Jews are experienced with several types of modern Jewish converts. We shall soon see that Edith Stein corresponds to none of these types, however. Nevertheless, it is helpful to examine these types so that we can more accurately view her by the sharper focus which contrast offers.

In the Middle Ages, when European nations were defined as Christian nations, European Jews were not citizens of those nations that were republics, nor were they the individual subjects of Christian monarchs. Instead, they were members of a foreign community, one whose presence was tolerated in Christendom by various local agreements. Therefore, medieval Jews could plausibly assume that Jewish converts to Christianity in their age could very well have a political motive for their conversion. To become a Christian was to move from the margins of political power to the center of it. The same could be said about moving from the margins of economic power to the center of it. Political power and economic power are closely interrelated. Indeed, this was one Jewish response to the claim of Christian triumphalism that the political power of Christendom in contrast to the political impotence of Jewry was a sign of God's acceptance of the Church and His rejection of the Jewish people. Jews had to remind Christians not to confuse the power of Caesar and the power of God. (This Jewish judgment of the motivation of Jewish converts is very much like the assumption in the Talmud that Jews were suspicious of converts to Judaism during the days of King David and King Solomon because these converts could very well have converted out of political and economic motives rather than sincerely religious ones.)

In the modern period, when nations became secular nation-states, political requirements of religion were gradually eliminated. Thus Jews no longer had to become Christians to gain the full political franchise. Nev-

ertheless, the cultures of the European nation-states still had enough vestiges of Christianity in them to make being a Christian culturally advantageous. Thus in the nineteenth and early twentieth centuries, almost
every West European or North American Jew knew some other Jew who
became a Christian for what obviously seemed to be reasons of social or
professional advancement. The best example of this, when looking at
Edith Stein, was her teacher Edmund Husserl. Despite her report of
Husserl's apparent profession of true Christian faith just before he died as
an outcast in his own university in 1938, during his successful academic
career no such piety was evident. Most Jews probably assumed that
Husserl (and a number of others like him) was convinced that it was
better to be a famous German Protestant professor of philosophy than an
obscure Bohemian Jew. (Indeed, it is to the moral credit of the great neo-
Kantian philosopher Hermann Cohen that he was the first unconverted
Jew to achieve a regular professorship in philosophy in a German university, at a time when philosophy had a good deal more cultural import
than it does now.) Along these lines, some of the most delicious Jewish
jokes of this period make fun of those who would sell their Jewish birth-
right for a mess of gentile cultural pottage. Such converts are morally odious because their practice is deceitful.

Jews had ready answers for such converts from Judaism since we have
not been fooled by their poorly disguised cultural ambitions. But Edith
Stein hardly fits this type. One does not become a cloistered nun to "make
it" in the world. Furthermore, such modern converts are usually ashamed
of their Jewish origins, even trying to obscure them whenever possible.
From everything I have read by Edith Stein or about her, she was quite
proud of her Jewish origins and had love and respect for her fellow Jews,
beginning but not ending with her own very Jewish family. I mention all
of this because Edith Stein converted in 1922, almost ten years before she
entered the Carmelite order. Thus her conversion could have been seen as
a way of advancing her academic career. But if that were the case, a conversion to Lutheranism, not Catholicism, would have been more useful in
the world of German philosophy at that time. In some important ways,
Catholics were as intellectually marginal as were Jews in the atmosphere
of *Kulturprotestantismus* of pre-Hitler German academic life. No, Edith
Stein did not display in any way the moral vice of hypocritical ambition.
To use the rabbinic phrase, she did not use her faith as a spade to dig with.
This is the first type of convert Edith Stein does not fit.

The second assumption of modern Jews (and even pre-modern Jews) is
that Jews who convert to Christianity are irrational. Some of this goes

back to the late medieval Jewish-Christian polemics. Then, Jews, basing themselves mostly on the Aristotelian philosophy respected by Jewish, Christian, and Muslim thinkers, attempted to portray Christianity as a less rational religion than Judaism is. (Along these lines, Jewish and Muslim anti-Christian polemics were almost identical.) Thus the Incarnation is seen as more irrational than the Sinai revelation. However, these polemics were ofttimes quite inaccurate since for defensive reasons they had to play down Jewish doctrines that were just as irrational by Aristotelian criteria. Similarly, nineteenth-century Jewish polemic, basing itself on Kantian rationalism, had to pretend that the Jewish mystical tradition, Kabbalah, did not exist when, in fact, it was the predominant form of Jewish theology for over five centuries and still has had living adherents in modern times. (When writing Jewish theology, Hermann Cohen had to pretend that the mystical and the mythical were problems only for Christianity, Judaism having already overcome them.)

In modern times, the rejection of Christianity as irrational is just as easily turned against Judaism itself. That is because a prime assumption of much of modernity is that all religion is irrational, so any religion is irrational. One could argue, along Freudian lines, for example, that religious passion is a form of neurosis, something rational people should outgrow. I remember often being told this when I was an undergraduate at the University of Chicago around 1960, and I made some important Christian friends because of it when I found out that this anti-religious animosity does not confine itself to anti-Judaism. The fact is, that by any criterion of self-sufficient human rationality, which is the criterion of modern rationalism, Jews are just as irrational as Christians and vice versa. Furthermore, if modern rationalism claims to be universal and self-sufficient, not particular and contingent, then it seems easier to universalize a cosmic Christ than it has been to universalize an earthly Jewish people. Nevertheless, when Christians have said to me that Christianity is more universal than Judaism is, I retort: What kind of universal God decides to become incarnate in the body of an obscure Jewish carpenter from a backwater district like Galilee? Buddhism is much more universal than either Judaism or Christianity, which might explain its attraction in post-Jewish and post-Christian spiritual quests. The fact is that both Judaism and Christianity can only appear to the modern world to be hopelessly parochial. Edith Stein's cloister and the proverbial "four cubits of the Law [*halakhah*]" are both quite limited and limiting by any modern universal criterion. Surely, they will be so until the end. The most a Jew or a Christian can do — and here I think of the wonderful encyclical of Pope

John Paul II, *Fides et Ratio* — is to show how reason (universally projected) can prepare one for revelation, and how reason can be used with integrity to understand revelation. But revelation cannot be reduced to reason without doing violence to both.

Some Jews have gone even further than accusing Jewish converts to Christianity of irrationality; they have assumed they are mentally unbalanced. Here the charge of psychological pathology is necessarily connected to the modern prejudice that religious passion itself is pathological. Of course, it is true there are people whose desire for a change of religious identity is connected to psychic disturbance. We have all seen converts who either move from religion to religion to religion, or who look to faith as compensation for their depression. Any responsible pastor or rabbi knows whom to give theological counsel and whom to recommend for psychotherapy. The desire for God is not identical with the desire for the love of a mother or a father one feels robbed of from childhood. Christianity does not have any monopoly on occasionally attracting such disturbed people, who certainly need our compassion before our theology.

Again, from everything I have read by Edith Stein and about Edith Stein, I see no such pathology in her life. She impresses me as she impressed all who knew her in person as a remarkably integrated personality, quite capable of ordinary human pleasures and desires. Indeed, only such a strong personality could have possibly sustained her focused pilgrimage, which was the teleological thrust of her whole life unto death. To assume pathology in her case is tantamount to assuming that anyone attracted to Christianity suffers from psychic disturbance. But most people are more reasonable than that, and are thus suspicious of those who assume that everyone of whom they disapprove or with whom they disagree is crazy. Edith Stein is much too challenging to be so easily dismissed. Reason and experience would indicate that this type of radical psychological reduction is wrong about Edith Stein and wrong about Christianity — indeed, wrong about Judaism and Islam, which are also religions of revelation.

Nevertheless, Jews have seen a more subtle pathology at work in the lives of some Jewish converts to Christianity. That is the pathology of self-hate *(Selbsthass)*. There are cases of Jews converting to Christianity because they hated being Jews. In most cases, this pathology is the internalization of cultural attitudes that regard others as being humanly inferior, if not actually subhuman *(Untermenschen)*. Such self-hate might even be seen in the question of one of Edith Stein's Jewish friends, who at the beginning of the Nazi regime in 1933 wanted to know "why does Hitler hate us so?"

This question can, of course, be a question about what in Hitler's inner experience *(Erlebnis)* led to his hatred of the Jews. That is important if it helped his potential victims predict what Hitler was likely to do. The question is about the motives of Adolf Hitler himself. (After Hitler's death, one wonders, though, whether he is worthy of such attention, attention that always flirts with fascination.) But the question could mean: What is it about *us* that makes Hitler (and all the Jew-haters) hate us so? Here the question is about the experienced object *(Erfahrung)* of Hitler's hate. What is so *hateful* about the Jews? This strongly implies that the Jews deserve hatred and that we Jews ought to become un-Jewish to avoid it. Today we rightly call this "blaming the victim."

When this is done by the victims to themselves, it is self-hate. It is a disease that frequently results in suicide. Edith Stein was concerned about the high suicide rate of German Jews (some of whom were in her own family) even before the Nazi period, recognizing how the loss of Jewish faith was a contributing factor. And it is no accident that the highest cause of death among German Jews from 1933 to 1939, even before the mass killings began, was suicide. One can certainly say, as many psychoanalysts could show, that self-hate is internalized hate whose origin lies in a desired other. Finally, such self-hate is evident in some Jews who converted to Christianity during or after the Holocaust because they hated what their Jewish identity had brought upon them or could bring upon their children. The case of the Jewish parents of former U.S. Secretary of State Madeleine Albright, who hid their Jewish origins even from their own daughter, seems to be a case in point.

Once again, I see no self-hate at all in Edith Stein's case. Quite the contrary: among other things, she tried to arrange for an audience with Pope Pius XI to implore him to do something about the persecution of the Jews. I have never seen one word of scorn or contempt about Judaism in what Edith Stein wrote or what was written about her. She also offered great comfort and help to Jewish family and friends trying to endure the Nazi terror. A martyr who saw her being a Jew as lying at the core of her martyrdom cannot be seen as self-hating — that is, unless one sees no difference between martyrdom and suicide, a confusion a loyal Jew or a loyal Christian must belie. Moreover, one of Edith Stein's closest Jewish friends recalled with gratitude how her firm decision to remain a Jew in religion was respected by Edith, who never tried to proselytize her firmly Jewish friends in any way.

Finally, the last charge I can think of in Edith Stein's case is that she does not seem to have made a thorough enough investigation of Jewish theology before adopting Christian theology. She admits that the Judaism of her German-Jewish home had already lost the deep immersion in the classical Jewish sources that still characterized many Polish-Jewish homes in her time. The piety of her home was more *gemütlich* than *gebildet*, more customary than educated. (Several years ago at a conference in France, I had a conversation with an elderly Israeli woman, originally from Breslau, who knew the Stein family quite well, and who confirmed Edith's picture of the character of their Jewishness.) One wonders why she did not pursue the intensive retrieval of the Jewish tradition of her contemporary, Jewish philosopher Franz Rosenzweig. Rosenzweig, who almost converted to Christianity himself for the purest of motives, reversed his near decision after what can only be seen as an epiphany on Yom Kippur in a Berlin synagogue in 1913. Edith Stein mentions discussions about philosophy in Breslau with the Jewish philosopher Julius Guttmann: he the neo-Kantian and she the phenomenologist. (Julius Guttmann, who taught in Jewish institutions, first in Germany and later in Israel, was a Jewish thinker and not just a philosopher who happened to be a Jew.) But did she and he ever discuss what it means to be a Jew; what Jewish faith means? It seems they did not. (Her lack of very deep Jewish knowledge is even mentioned by her Carmelite biographer, Sister Waltraud Herbstrith.) Nevertheless, I feel as though Edith Stein was so directed toward a type of religious life only to be found in a Catholic convent that greater Jewish knowledge would not have made any real difference. Her very quest seems to have been a Christian one even before she fully knew it. Conversion is a matter of free choice, to be sure, but Edith Stein's conversion seems to have been inevitable, at least looking at it retrospectively.

The easiest way out of this conundrum about Edith Stein is to accept the liberal assumption that one's religious convictions are a matter of individual choice and that everyone must respect the choice of everyone else to believe whatever they want and practice any religion or no religion they want. Accordingly, Edith Stein had a *right* to become a Catholic, even to change her name to Sister Teresa Benedicta of the Cross, just as the Catholic priest Father Kenneth Cox had a *right* to become a Jew, even to change his name to Abraham Carmel. At the political level, which is our involvement in civil society, most Jews and most Catholics have accepted the liberal idea of religious freedom. Some of us see it as a necessary part of the social contract that enables us to participate in civil society. Others of us see it actually being in the best interest of faith itself, which is endangered when coerced. At the pragmatic level, some of us have always realized that our religious communities are probably better off without people who somehow or other have found a spiritual home elsewhere and do not want to be with us anymore. We do not want our communities to be places of incarceration for political prisoners. That is how we have to talk or how we ought to talk in the public square. It is not disingenuous, just partial — indeed, secondary — to our primary commitments. But it is only disingenuous to those who think that the secular public realm must not recognize the prior communal commitments of its participants. Hence, it is only disingenuous to intolerant secularists, whose illiberality becomes more and more evident in the great public debates of our time. Not having any understanding of Judaism or Christianity, someone like Edith Stein must appear to them to be extraterrestrial.

Most of the most fruitful dialogue between Jews and Catholics (and other Christians as well) has been conducted with the issues of the public realm as the topic of our discussions. Here Jews and Catholics have discovered significant common ground to discuss in theory and apply in practice. These topics are issues of public morality where, despite some unconvincing denials, there is indeed a Judeo-Christian morality, one where Judaism is not just proto-Christianity and where Christianity is not just universalized Judaism. I think of my own involvement with Catholics in pro-life activities for many years now. And that commonality certainly extends to questions of religious liberty in our democratic societies. I think of the new cooperation emerging now between Jews and Catholics in the province of Ontario (where I now live in Canada) concerning the right of parents to receive some state support for the education of their children in schools where the religion of their choice is a major part of the curriculum. Obviously, those who do not want to be publicly coerced cannot advocate any public coercion in good faith.

Nevertheless, the discovery of such commonality, as necessary and desirable as it is, should not overlook the fact that at the deepest level of our existence, Jews and Christians are not only making different communal claims, we are making *rival* communal claims. The best way to God, the one that ought not be changed for something less, is *either* by the Torah and the Jewish tradition *or* by Christ and the Church. The choice is unavoidable. One cannot accept Christ and still be part of the normative Jewish community; one cannot practice the Law and still be part of the Church normatively. To assume otherwise is to perform the logical fallacy of the excluded middle (namely, A = not-A). Quite early in our common history — indeed, almost simultaneously — Jewish authorities ruled against the practice of Christianity by Jews as the Church ruled against the practice of Judaism by Christians ("judaization") — even by Christians born as Jews. Hopefully, our acceptance of the liberal order of civil society in good faith has enabled us to make these rival communal claims *civilly,* without fear of political reprisal. But that should not make us slide into the superficiality of civil religion or the disorientation of religious syncretism. It is in this context that Jews and Christians have to speak to each other without the commonality that the mediation of the secular public realm has provided for us of late. And here is where we are speaking to each other, most importantly, about Edith Stein.

To look at Judaism and Christianity as covenantal religions is to see that the relationship with God of the individual Jew and the individual Christian is always within *covenanted community.* Even when physically alone, as was Edith Stein in her nun's cell, one is still part of the faith community existentially. Catholics can understand that very well since you, unlike many Protestants, know the Church is not a society into which like-minded persons associate in order to subsequently share in common what they have already experienced as individual believers. In the covenant, one hears the voice of God and responds to it only when already within the community. The communal *where* one hears the voice of God is the necessary condition of *how* one hears it and *what* it concretely says to one. There is no universal revelation until the end of history (which for you is the Second Coming and for us is the Final Redemption: *ge'ulah shelemah*). In the case of converts, that presence in the community is a potentiality waiting to be actualized by the prescribed rites of conversion. Converts are reborn, which is the term used both in the New Testament *(anagenēsis)* and in the Talmud *(ke-qatan she-nolad)*. In the case of those literally born into the covenant, birth actualizes what is taken to be the intending potential of the faithful parents. (Thus, even though it is said *Christianos non nascitur sed fiat* — "A Christian is not born, but made" — since almost all Christians practice infant baptism, and since for Catholics anyway baptism is indelible, most of you were as much born into the Church as I was born into the Jewish people.) That is why the key Jewish and Christian doctrine of identity is election. God chooses His people, which in some ways is like parents choosing to co-create their child. A child can be grateful to the parents and love them for *their* choice, or a child can be ungrateful to the parents and hate them for *their* choice. But the child does not choose his or her parents. That is the case in the natural order; all the more so is it the case in the covenantal order. God chooses us; we do not choose God, at least originally. That election is either by natural birth or by the rebirth of conversion, which is very much like adoption. We only can confirm or deny the elected community into which, as one former Christian philosopher put it, we have "been thrown."

Based on these covenantal assumptions, it logically follows that what Judaism and Christianity assert, liberals can only regard as an unfair asymmetry: One can check into the covenant, but one cannot check out of it. A convert is "born again," which also means that he or she has always been in the community retroactively. An apostate, conversely, does not quit the community existentially; he or she is only absent without leave. The community can bar an apostate from the privileges of its religious life (like *excommunication,* which bars a sinful Catholic from receiving the sacraments, but not from the Church herself, however, just as Jewish *herem,* the ban of ostracism, does not make any Jew no longer a Jew). Nevertheless, such exclusion is a temporary measure designed to encourage proper penance so one can be readmitted to the active life of the community in a way in which one is not a danger to oneself or to others in the community. The exclusion is the religious equivalent of quarantine. That is why we regard Edith Stein as a Jewish apostate, but always a Jew nonetheless. And she agreed with us about her Jewish identity; it is about her apostasy that she obviously had a different opinion from ours. We cannot avoid the question of apostasy because it brings us face to face with the rival truth claims our two communities make: to ourselves, to each other, and to the world. These rival truth claims can be understood in two ways.

We could say either *extra ecclesiam nulla salus* ("outside the Church, no salvation") or *extra populum Ioudaeorum nulla salus* ("outside the Jewish people, no salvation"). For Christians of this mind-set, all non-Christians — including Jews, maybe especially Jews — are totally cut off from God. (One thinks of the famous or infamous remark made some twenty years ago by the president of the Southern Baptist Convention: "God does not hear the prayers of the Jews.") For Jews of this mind-set (who do exist, despite liberal Jewish efforts to pretend they do not), all non-Jews — including Christians, maybe especially Christians — are idolaters. Needless to say, idolatry in a biblically based religion is being totally cut off from God.

However, such a position has been rejected by many Jews and Christians, and not just in recent, "more tolerant" times, especially when dealing with each other. Because of our historical connections, most importantly our agreement on the exact text of the Hebrew Bible and that it is the intact word of God for both of us, Christians are for Jews different from all other non-Jews, and Jews are for Christians different from all other non-Christians. But this should not lead us into the type of relativism that would have religious faith suppress the question of truth and turn religious experience — that is, the reception of revelation — into a question of *meaning* alone. As Hegel insightfully pointed out, "meaning" *(Meinung)* comes from *mein,* with all the limitations thereto. (That was a criticism Edith Stein's fellow philosopher, Martin Heidegger, directed against the phenomenology of their teacher Edmund Husserl, a point Edith qua Sister Teresa Bendicta of the Cross would have to agree with, it seems. It was also a theological point that Karl Barth made devastatingly against the liberal theology of Schleiermacher and his disciples.) Faith, yours and mine, should not be taken as a subjective affirmation *(Erlebnis)* of oneself (however idealized). It is, rather, an objective confirmation of what is other than (but not alien to) oneself *(Erfahrung).*

One can very well see Judaism and Christianity as presenting themselves as the fullest truth of God's relationship with the world possible rather than the only truth available in the world. Consistent with this view, one can recognize more limited forms of truth elsewhere. Confirmation of the covenant need not lead to a feeling of having a monopoly on God. As the prophet Amos put it to the overly proud people of Israel, "Are you not for Me like the Ethiopians?" (Amos 9:7). Morally, that enables us to live in peace with other people in good faith and to have genuine respect for them and their traditions. That should begin with those people just across our own borders: for Jews they are Christians; for Christians they are Jews. That is what I have derived from the theologies of two of our great medieval sages, Judah Halevi and Moses Maimonides, and more recently from my late revered teacher, Abraham Joshua Heschel (whose effect on Catholics, I might add, was nothing short of revolutionary). That is what you have derived from Thomas Aquinas's theology of the "Old Law" and, most recently, from the *Nostra Aetate* document of Vatican Council II.

This approach, common in form but different in substance for us, might be summarized in the talmudic principle "One is to rise, not descend, in holiness" *(ma'alin ba-qodesh ve-lo moridin).* Let me set up four possible situations and suggest the Jewish answer I would have to provide in each of them if asked. Your substantive answer would have to be different from mine in two of the four situations, but I think your logic would have to be the same as mine in all of them. The four situations are: (1) a pagan wanting to convert to Christianity instead of Judaism; (2) a pagan wanting to convert to Judaism instead of Christianity; (3) a Christian wanting to convert to Judaism; (4) a Jew wanting to convert to Christianity. By "pagan," I mean someone who neither by bodily birth nor by the rebirth of conversion has ever been a Jew or a Christian. (Most Jews would have to see Muslims as different from other non-Jews too by virtue of our common monotheism, but the Muslim relationship to Judaism need not concern us in the case of Edith Stein. In her world, there were only Jews, Christians, and pagans.)

Following our argument so far, first I would have to say to a pagan wanting to convert to Christianity instead of Judaism, "This is a good choice inasmuch as Christianity is a valid gentile relationship with the Lord God, maker of heaven and earth, elector of Israel, giver of the Torah, and redeemer of the world." Second, to a pagan wanting to convert to Judaism instead of Christianity, I would have to say, "You have made the best choice possible in your quest to have a full relationship with the Lord God, maker of heaven and earth, elector of Israel, giver of the Torah, and redeemer of the world."

Third, to a Christian wanting to convert to Judaism (someone like Abraham Carmel, formerly Father Kenneth Cox, mentioned above), I would have to say, "You have made the best choice [as in the case of the pagan wanting to convert to Judaism], and Christianity has been an excellent preparation for that decision, having introduced you, however partially, to the Lord God of Israel." That answer might very well surprise many people who know that Judaism does not engage in proselytizing. That is true, and there are historical, political, and even moral reasons for that restraint. But I say "restraint" because Judaism never ceased to accept converts *(gerim)*, even when it was politically dangerous to do so. And as Maimonides clearly pointed out in his treatment of the laws pertaining to conversion, the converts are to be told that their decision to become part of the Jewish people is a decision to truly fulfill human nature, whose teleological thrust is to know God. Following this logic, Maimonides considered Christians to be prime candidates for conversion to Judaism because of their introduction to the Lord God of Israel in their study of Scripture — Hebrew Scripture, that is. (Muslims seem to be the next prime candidates because of their monotheism.)

The fourth option, the Jew wanting to convert to Christianity, is, of course, the option of Edith Stein. In fact, it is especially Edith Stein since we have seen her motives in conversion were theological to the core, with no violations of ordinary morality by hypocrisy or racial shame. In attempting to understand the profundity of her decision, I would like to quote an important statement of my fellow speaker, Professor Alasdair MacIntyre, a philosopher from whom I have learned much for almost twenty years, and with whom I am honored to be associated in this symposium. In his 1988 book *Whose Justice? Which Rationality?* Professor MacIntyre wrote:

> Yet the achievement of the understanding of one tradition by the adherents of another may have as its sequel a number of different types of outcome . . . in certain rare but crucial types of cases . . . to understand may lead to a judgment that by the standards of one's own tradition the standpoint of the other tradition offers superior resources for understanding the problems and issues which confront one's own tradition.[1]

Now Professor MacIntyre is speaking in the context of his theory of how the Thomistic tradition superseded the Augustinian tradition. The context is, then, an essentially intramural issue of Catholic theology. However, this same logic applies to a much bigger issue, namely, the relationship of Judaism and Christianity. That is, this is precisely what Christians have said to Jews: Christianity solves the problems of Judaism better than Judaism can do without Christianity because Christianity provides the savior to whom Judaism has always looked. Edith Stein, therefore, considered herself not a runaway from Judaism (however rudimentary her own Judaism was) but, rather, a Jew whose Judaism brought her into the Church. Her logic was clearly supersessionist. How could it have been otherwise?

Supersessionism is the subject of deep theological debate today. Many Jews have seen it as the core of Christian anti-Judaism. Many Christians are embarrassed by it, seeing it as part of the anti-Judaism that was so easily appropriated by modern anti-Semitism. Nevertheless, Christian supersessionism need not denigrate Judaism. It can look to the Jewish origins of Christianity happily and still learn of those origins from living Jews, those whom Pope John Paul II likes to call "our elder brothers." And Christian supersessionism can still affirm that God has not annulled His everlasting covenant with the Jewish people, neither past nor present nor future. But Jews cannot expect any more than that from Christians, and Christians cannot expect any more than that from yourselves. If Christianity does not regard itself as going beyond Judaism, why should Christians not become Jews? It is always a ready possibility. Where else could you possibly find the Lord God of Israel? And, conversely, any Jew who believes Christianity supersedes Judaism can only become a Christian in good faith — like Edith Stein.

---

1. MacIntyre, *Whose Justice? Which Rationality?* (Notre Dame: University of Notre Dame Press, 1988), p. 370.

Faith *(emunah)* is the human existential response to God's revealed grace *(gillui Shekhinah)*. One's experience of that grace realizes whatever possibilities that person brings up with him or her to that revelation. *Where* that revelation fundamentally occurs is *the* existential question.

Our fruitful conversations of late have had to largely bracket *the* existential question confronting us for good worldly reasons. It is, nevertheless, the crucial question that leaves us both at an impasse. All attempts to get beyond this theological impasse, be they political, exegetical, or philosophical, have been failures. We usually have to bracket *the* existential question, but it surrounds everything we have to say to each other and do with each other nonetheless. After all, it is *the* question of truth *(emet),* and truth is what we are both all about. To bracket this question is quite different from either suppressing it altogether or reducing all discussion to it.

At this theological level, which is the most profound aspect of our understanding of ourselves and each other, Edith Stein is a great manifestation of our impasse. She cannot be invoked as a bridge in dialogue between Jews and Catholics because in this world one cannot be both a faithful Jew and a faithful Catholic in tandem. These necessarily communal identities are mutually exclusive here and now. Moreover, one cannot expect the approval of the covenanted community one has left, be that pilgrim Edith Stein on her way to the Church or Father Kenneth Cox on his way to the Jewish people. As with Abraham our father, our answer to God's call always involves leaving some earlier home in one way or another, and that home does not and cannot provide one with a farewell. (That is what I think Kierkegaard meant by the "teleological suspension of the ethical," understanding "the ethical" as *ethos,* what is *heimlich,* what is familiar and comfortable.)

We do have much to say to each other and much to do with each other in this world. But our more important task of waiting for God is one we must do by ourselves apart. That is why the agenda of dialogue must be kept separate from the agenda of conversion. Dialogue is more about this world; conversion is more about the world-to-come. That can be frustrating, but that is what it means to wait for the kingdom of God without premature flight from this world. Until that time, it is not for us to judge matters of identity, except in the most mundane cases involving communal rights and penalties. Because of that, we Jews can only *empathize* that you Catholics have found yet another saint, another exemplary holy life, even if that life is one we have lost. We can *feel for you,* but we cannot *feel with you,* which is *sympathy* (what Edith Stein would have called *Mitgefühl*).

At this deepest level we are still strangers to each other. It seems that we shall have to remain strangers to each other until God judges us all in the end in a world where we all hope to be the lasting friends of God and thus lasting friends of each other. May that day come speedily, even in our own lifetime on earth!

Jewish-Christian Relations in a Secular Age

The topic that was announced, "Jewish-Christian Relations in a Secular Age," is still my overarching topic. However, when one deals with a relationship between two communities, especially the relationship between the Jewish people and the Catholic Church, a relationship that has been so complex and one that has lasted now almost two millennia, it is important to be aware of just where that relationship stands at the point in history where we now find ourselves situated. And since we negotiated the topic of this lecture today some months ago, something very significant has happened in the course of Jewish-Christian relations, and especially in Jewish-Catholic relations. This past March, just about two months ago, a public statement was issued by the Vatican, "The Catholic Church and the Holocaust," authored by Cardinal Edward Cassidy, the president of the Vatican's Commission for Religious Relations, and introduced by Pope John Paul II himself.[1] The document itself is one that has received wide publicity and has already stirred up a good deal of controversy. So, I think that it would be quite useful in terms of my being here and you being here for me to give a Jewish reaction to what I consider to be the overall thrust of this important document, to express agreement with most of it, but also to point out in a forthright manner what I take to be some problems within it. To ignore this document in favor of the more general

1. All quotes from this document are from the version of it in *First Things*, no. 83 (May 1998): 39-43.

This was the 1998 Swig Lecture presented at the Swig Judaic Studies Program at the University of San Francisco. A revised version of it appeared subsequently in *First Things* 89 (January 1999): 20-25.

talk I had originally planned would pass up an opportunity for true dialogue that simply should not be missed. Nevertheless, this new subtopic is still within the range of the overall topic announced inasmuch as anything that happens in our age, even between religious communities, even within religious communities themselves, happens within an age that is not religious but very much secular.

Speaking of history, let me tell you at what point in history I came to be interested in Jewish-Catholic relations. History is best appreciated and gains ethical significance when one's own personal story is connected with the larger story of the community and communities in which he or she lives and works.

I came to Jewish-Catholic relations at a pivotal time in my own life history and at a much more pivotal time in the relationship between the Jewish people and the Catholic Church. In my own case, I feel privileged that this was during my youth, when I was unformed enough to be able to give Jewish-Christian relations a prominent place in my life's work as a Jewish scholar and thinker. In the early 1960s, 1963 to be exact, while studying for the rabbinate at the Jewish Theological Seminary in New York, I became the student — indeed, the close disciple — of a man who to the mind of many was the most important Jewish theologian to work in America, my late revered teacher, Abraham Joshua Heschel. At that time, Professor Heschel was engaged in serious discussions with the leadership of the Catholic Church at the highest levels, especially with the late Cardinal Augustin Bea, in preparation for Vatican Council II, which in 1965 issued a landmark statement *Nostra Aetate* ("In Our Time") about its view of Judaism and the Jewish people, a document that is undoubtedly the most significant statement of the Church regarding the Jews in modern times, perhaps ever.[2] I remember how hopeful my teacher was for this new attitude that was emerging in the Church then, and the tremendous chance he was taking in becoming the chief Jewish advisor to the Church in this whole enterprise. And not only was he taking a chance, but Cardinal Bea and Pope Paul VI were also taking a chance, and for similar reasons. Professor Heschel was taking a chance because of the harsh criticism to which he was subjected by some other prominent Jewish scholars — quite unfairly, I think — for assuming that a new relationship was even possible with the Catholic Church.[3] That criticism

2. See *The Documents of Vatican II,* ed. W. M. Abbott, S.J. (London: Geoffrey Chapman, 1966), pp. 660-68.

3. See, e.g., Joseph B. Soloveitchik, "Confrontation," *Tradition* (1964): 26. Cf. David Novak, *Jewish-Christian Dialogue: A Jewish Justification* (New York: Oxford University Press, 1989), pp. 3-9.

sometimes took the form of verbal abuse, both private and public. And the leaders of the Church took a chance because there were elements in the Church, powerful elements, who argued that since the Jewish people had rejected Jesus of Nazareth as the Christ, what kind of positive relationship could there be with such a people? Yet there was enough momentum on both sides of this great divide to take the chance on developing a new relationship as something important, something good, and perhaps even something holy in the world, especially in a secular age.

We are all the beneficiaries of those chances taken over thirty years ago. In the wake of what happened "in our time," conversations between Jews and Catholics are now in progress, including conversations conducted at the highest levels of philosophical and theological discourse. Anyone who has watched what has happened from then until now cannot help but marvel at how far we have moved from suspicion to a level much deeper than simply that of goodwill and tolerance. But in terms of this new relationship, there has always been a dark cloud hanging over it. And that has been that the Jewish people in particular and the whole Western world in general still very much live in the shadow of the Holocaust, the systematic program of mass extermination that resulted in the murder of six million Jews, and many others too, but which was directed against the Jewish people most particularly and vehemently. The question must thus be raised, on both sides: Just what role did the Catholic Church play in this historical drama in whose shadow we all still live? Until we engage in the most soul-searching discussion of this question, we may very well be at an impasse in this new relationship, which many — but by no means all — of us celebrate. This recent statement of the Vatican is certainly a major step in that direction.

But what was the reaction to this statement when it was issued? For the most part, with a few exceptions, the reaction of most of the Jewish leaders, at least those who have access to the media, was a negative one. Thus the *New York Times,* which although not an "official" Jewish publication certainly reflects — indeed influences — a certain type of American Jewish opinion, in a recent editorial basically branded the Vatican statement a whitewash, a rationalization of the conduct of the Church during the period of the Holocaust. The Anti-Defamation League of B'nai B'rith, which does have an official Jewish status of sorts, also issued a reaction to the Vatican statement, expressing much the same disappointment. Now it should be pointed out that this view is not unanimous in the Jewish community. So, Rabbi James Rudin, who heads the department of the American Jewish Committee that deals with Jewish-Christian relations, issued a much more positive and hopeful response. However, Rudin's reaction seems to be a minority voice, at least so far.

What is the reason for this Jewish criticism? After all, the statement did condemn the Holocaust, it did condemn anti-Semitism, and it even spoke of "the sinful behavior" of certain Christians, certain members of the Church.[4] So, why should there be this kind of negative reaction? Shouldn't Jews be happy to hear all of this from the Church? Isn't this an important way of putting the Holocaust in the kind of perspective that enables us to get on with our lives, precisely not by forgetting but by remembering, which is itself for the sake of a painfully honest reconciliation? Hence, we must ask just what was all of this disappointment all about? As an attempt to answer this basic question, I would like to briefly explore with you today why I think this disappointment is largely mistaken, and why it is not only a misunderstanding of Catholic theology but also of Jewish theology as well. These reactions, then, were not only uncharitable, they were also unjust. For they do not reflect any attempt to try to understand how Catholic theology operates (and the statement was very much theological and not just political in the usual sense) and how its operation is in many ways quite similar to the way Jewish theology operates.

The line in the statement that seems to have elicited the most negative Jewish response is actually a quote from none other than Pope John Paul II, from a speech he made on 31 October 1997 in Rome. "In the Christian world — I do not say on the part of the Church as such — erroneous and unjust interpretations of the New Testament regarding the Jewish people and their alleged culpability have circulated for too long, engendering feelings of hostility toward this people."[5] And this negative reaction to a statement of John Paul II, of all people, is itself ironic inasmuch as there has been no other pope in modern times, perhaps in all history, who has done more to develop rapprochement with the Jewish people and Judaism. And that is not accidental. Karol Wojtyla as a philosopher and a theologian has been deeply interested in the connection between Judaism and the teaching of the Catholic Church for most of his life. Furthermore, Karol Wojtyla has been intimately related to Jews all of his life, beginning with his childhood in Poland, where Jews were among his closest associates. The Pope speaks Yiddish, and I know that for a fact because in 1985,

---

4. See sec. I, p. 39a.

5. Sec. II, p. 40b, quoting from the speech to the Symposium on the Roots of Anti-Judaism on 31 October 1997.

when twelve of us had a private audience with him during a conference to celebrate the twentieth anniversary of *Nostra Aetate,* I briefly spoke with him in Yiddish. And in the face of much opposition, it is during this papacy that the Vatican has established formal diplomatic relations with the State of Israel. So, it would seem that Jews have had nothing but good from this pope. Why, then, has there been such consternation over this one sentence in the Vatican statement quoting John Paul II — indeed, tying the whole document to it?

The criticism all seems to be about the fact that the Pope did not apologize for *the Church per se.* Where is the apology? Those who have now criticized the Church — and especially the Pope — have placed all their hopes on the utterance of an official apology by the Church "as such." But the Church seems to have separated herself as an institution from her condemnation of the behavior of those of her sons and daughters who cooperated with and endorsed the Nazi program of persecution and murder of the Jews. Of course, we must understand just what the Pope meant by "the Church as such." If we can reach some understanding of what that really means, then I think we can arrive at another perspective on this statement, and it can be a Jewish perspective properly informed by an understanding of the Jewish tradition. In truth, Jewish statements that are not informed by our own tradition are not really Jewish in any essential sense, but simply express the views of a group of people who *happen* to be Jews. None of the negative reactions I have seen to date is informed by the Jewish tradition, even though I do not rule out the possibility that an authentically Jewish negative response could be so formulated.

When a Catholic speaks of "the Church," let alone when the occupant of the Throne of Peter speaks of "the Church," he can mean one of two things. On the one hand, the Church is undoubtedly a collection of fallible human beings. The Church is made up of her members, the parts of her body, so to speak. At this level, it is certainly recognized that these fallible human members of the Church can do either good or evil as is their free human choice to do. However, on the other hand, when the Pope speaks of the Church "as such," he is not speaking about a fallible collection of human beings; instead, he is speaking about what the Church understands as her *magisterium,* her teaching authority, an authority Catholics see as expressing God's will, beginning with Scripture and extending into the ongoing development of Church doctrine. So, at one level the Church is a human association in the world, but at another level the Church is *mater et magistra* — "mother and teacher" of her members. Understanding the Church at either of these levels, however, one can see why an "apology" is inappropriate. Thus, a little later on, we will examine the word the document did use, which is a word of far more theological significance than "apology" ever was or ever will be.

Let us first take the Church as a group of human beings, which is certainly the easier thing for a non-Catholic like myself to do. Now just *who* would apologize to *whom*? If one takes a Catholic who actually participated in the Nazi atrocities against the Jews, how could such a person possibly apologize? How do you apologize to someone in whose murder you were a participant? In order to apologize, you have to make your apology to someone who is capable of accepting your apology. But those who were murdered are hardly in a position to absolve anyone else. And who am I as a Jew who was only a potential victim of Nazi murder (for if Hitler had been successful, I who was born in 1941 would also be dead) to forgive someone who asks my forgiveness for what he or she did to Jews now dead? How can I exonerate somebody for what he or she did to somebody else? Wouldn't that be what Christians call "cheap grace"? And there is a parallel to this in the Jewish tradition, and it is important to call it to mind because we can only understand someone else's tradition by analogy to our own. Thus, when the Sanhedrin functioned in ancient Israel and had the power of capital punishment, a criminal about to be executed for murder had the right to confess his or her crime and assert that the death to be undergone is to be "atonement for all my sins."[6] This was seen as one's reconciliation with God in the world-to-come, but it was not, nevertheless, in any way a means of exonerating the criminal from the punishment he or she deserves in this world. And along these lines, I am reminded of the report that when Hans Frank (who had been the Nazi governor of Poland, where the largest number of atrocities took place) was about to be executed after having been sentenced to death at Nuremberg in 1946, he said that a thousand deaths would not atone for the crimes he committed. But that is between Hans Frank and God. We who have survived have no right to forgive him for what he did; we have no right to accept any apologies from him or from anyone like him. And, on the other hand, if an apology is made by people who did not commit any such crimes, either directly or even indirectly, and who do not at all even sympathize with the murders, then what would they be apologizing for?

The Jewish tradition on this point is quite clear: We do not believe in inherited guilt. Indeed, when the Church declared in *Nostra Aetate* in 1965 that she no longer regarded the Jews as collectively guilty of "deicide,"

6. *Mishnah:* Sanhedrin 6.2 re Joshua 7:25.

that is, the murder of Jesus as the son of God, she was making a point she now holds in common with the Jewish moral tradition.[7] Each person is only responsible for his or her own sins. Even the Christian doctrine of "original sin" does not mean that humans are punished for the sin of the first human pair but, rather, that humans seem to inevitably copy the sin of the first human pair. Thus the Talmud asks about how God can in all justice "visit the sins of the fathers on the sons" (Exod. 20:5). It answers that children are only punished for their parents' sins when they themselves willingly identify with them and repeat them by their own free choice.[8] So, justice, whether human or divine, must recognize as did the prophet Ezekiel that "the person who sins shall die" (Ezek. 18:20) — alone. Thus at either of these levels of humanly applicable justice, an apology makes no sense. At either level, an apology could only be empty rhetoric.

But what about the second notion of the Church, namely, *the Church as such*? This refers to the *magisterium,* the teaching authority of the Church. Now the teaching authority of the Church does not refer to what we usually mean by "teaching," that is, imparting information, like what is given by a professor in a university lecture to a class of passive note-takers, whose only responsibility is to pass an examination or write a term paper in order to "pass" the course and thus get it behind them. *Magisterium,* for which the Hebrew equivalent would be *hora'ah,* from whose same root the word *Torah* comes, means teaching that calls upon the one taught to do something or believe something which is essential for the very existence of that person within the community for whom that teaching is authoritative.[9] When the Church is understood *as such,* then the Church cannot possibly apologize based on her own theological assumptions. For if the Church at this level were to apologize, that would presuppose a criterion of truth and right that is higher than the revelation upon which the Church bases her authority, the revelation that the Church claims as her own. In other words, the Church cannot criticize herself based on criteria external to her own revelation and tradition because the Church not only claims what she teaches is true — even more so she claims that what she teaches is the truth per se, namely, the ultimate criterion whereby everything else is either true or false, right or wrong. So, for example, the great encyclical of Pope John Paul II is called *Veritatis Splendor,* "the splendor of truth." That is the way the Church presents herself in and to the world.

---

7. See *The Documents of Vatican II,* p. 666.
8. *Babylonian Talmud* (hereafter "B."): Berakhot 7a.
9. See *Mishnah: Avot* 1.16.

Now, of course, self-presentation of oneself as *the* truth is highly offensive to people of a largely secular mentality. That is much of the modern charge against all religion. Religions seem to arrogate to themselves divine authority. They seem to hold themselves above judgment by "impartial" criteria. And this lies at the heart of much of the criticism of the "authoritarian" character of the Catholic Church. But I must tell you that on this score, Judaism is no different. Even though Judaism and Catholicism make some very different claims, some of which are not only different but mutually exclusive, the logic of the way the Jewish tradition makes her claims and the way the *magisterium* of the Church makes her claims is virtually identical. Thus when Jews thank God for giving us the Torah — that is, not only the Five Books of Moses but the whole authoritative tradition of the Jewish people throughout history — we speak of *torat emet,* which means not just "true teaching" but that "the Torah is *the* truth." The Jewish tradition presents herself as the greatest revelation of God's truth that can be known in the world. That is why we call ourselves "the chosen people." It is not that we choose ourselves. It means that we have been elected by God and given the Torah. The law of heaven has now come down to earth to a singular community entrusted with its teaching.[10] That does not mean we should not share this truth with other people, and that does not mean this truth has nothing in common with other sources of truth. That is why we do not reject science; we do not reject the proper findings of human reason. But a Jew who is committed to the Torah as the word of God cannot in good faith criticize anything taught within the Jewish tradition based on external criteria.[11] Thus the criticism of liberal Judaisms by traditionalists like myself is that they have all in one way or another attempted to judge Judaism based on criteria that can only be regarded as higher than Judaism herself, and that is simply contrary to the way the tradition has ever defined herself in the past. And how could a tradition that admits of external justification require her members to die as martyrs rather than exchange her for any other identity in their lives, as does Judaism (and Catholicism)?[12]

However, if that is the situation both for Jews and for Catholics, does that mean religious traditions like Judaism and Catholicism are incapable of any critical development? Does that mean they cannot in effect ever

---

10. Thus the great ninth-century Jewish theologian Saadiah Gaon stated that the Jews are only a people because of the Torah (*Book of Beliefs and Opinions,* 3.7).

11. See *Palestinian Talmud:* Peah 1.1/15b re Deut. 32:47.

12. See B. Sanhedrin 74a.

change their minds? No, religious traditions are in a constant state of development and renewed self-understanding. But the criteria of development, the standards for change, are based upon what is within. That is, if we discover that something we may have taught in the past now appears not to be God's will, or even contrary to God's will, then we have to discover again what are the fundamental principles of our own revelation and tradition and reinterpret our teaching so that we do not lead our people astray again. Thus the rabbinic principle that "the Sages be careful in their words" means that even correct teaching, when not properly formulated, can lead people to conclusions that are really unwarranted by the tradition when properly interpreted and understood.[13] They can lead to "erroneous and unjust interpretations"; in fact, these are the very words the Pope used when speaking in a self-critical mode about Catholic teaching, words we have seen are repeated in the document we are now analyzing.

This charge that the Pope could not criticize the Church *as such* is true but mistaken. Of course, the Pope cannot criticize the Church the way an uncommitted outsider might criticize her. The Church, like the Jewish tradition upon which she is largely patterned, can only look inward for guidance. The only criticism, then, that could be made either by an insider or a sympathetic outsider is if either the Jewish tradition or the Church as such refused to engage in any self-criticism at all. But, clearly, if that were the stance of the Church under this pontificate of John Paul II, a document like "The Catholic Church and the Holocaust," and even more so *Nostra Aetate,* could have never been written. That is how the Pope, when he spoke in the synagogue in Rome (by his own unprecedented invitation, I might add), condemned anti-Semitism "at any time from any source," which means that when anti-Semitism has come out of Church teaching, those who so taught it are to be considered in error by the internal criteria of the teaching authority of the Church per se.[14]

Much the same is the case with reappraisals of morally charged issues within the Jewish tradition, which enables Jews who know our tradition and the way it operates to appreciate something quite analogous in another tradition. A good example of this type of reappraisal is the way Jews have been dealing with the whole question of the role of women in Judaism. Now such reappraisal is false to the whole internal integrity of the Jewish tradition if it simply assumes that *because* the role of women *has*

13. See *The Fathers According to Rabbi Nathan,* chap. 5, trans. J. Goldin (New Haven: Yale University Press, 1955), p. 39.

14. See sec. IV, p. 42b at n. 18.

changed so radically in the surrounding society and culture, *therefore it ought to change* in Judaism accordingly. One must look into the tradition herself for sources — and there are such sources — for a process of careful and responsible reinterpretation.[15] That is not to say that religious traditions are not, to a certain extent, influenced by what is happening in the surrounding culture, even a culture largely indifferent, perhaps even hostile to these traditions. How could it be otherwise? Are not religious traditions and the faith communities that sustain them *in the world?* Nevertheless, those external influences can only stimulate thinkers within a tradition to be sensitive to some issues more than others, issues for which there are already sources within the tradition herself.[16] These influences are part of the human judgment even religious teachers must exercise, but they are not in any way sources of authority themselves from which moral conclusions can be drawn.

This analogy between Jewish and Catholic moral logic is not to say that the issue of the Holocaust for the Church and the issue of women for Judaism (and for the Church as well) have the same moral gravity. I have simply made this analogy to illustrate how much of the logic employed in the criticism of the Church on this issue could be similarly employed against Judaism. Of course, it might well be true that many of the Jewish critics of the Vatican statement on the Holocaust think Judaism can and should be subjected to the same type of criticism they have leveled against the Church. But if that is so, I find it rather disingenuous that such critics would label their criticism in any way "Jewish," unless, that is, they regard the Jews as nothing but a contemporary political interest group, having no tradition from which to draw authority to make any kind of authentic Jewish critique at all.

When one sees how moral logic within religious traditions like Judaism and Catholicism operates, then it is possible to understand why it is not an apology that is called for. Apologies are cheap. It seems that everyone is apologizing for just about everything in the past these days. No, this is not an apology, nor should it be an apology, either. Instead, it is a process of the most profound introspection. As such, we Jews can appreciate the way the Church, and especially the Pope as its current leader, are grappling with this issue in the way we Jews ourselves have to grapple with this and similar issues. Indeed, as regards this issue of the Holocaust, as

15. See David Novak, *Halakhah in a Theological Dimension* (Chico, Calif.: Scholars Press, 1985), pp. 61-71.

16. See *Mishnah: Avot* 5.22.

much current Holocaust scholarship is showing, we Jews also have great moral questions of our own to confront and judge.

If, then, the Church, either as an association of fallible human beings or as a community claiming authority from the revelation of God, could not and should not utter an "apology," what should it be doing? Well, the statement says it is "an act of repentance." And then, *mirabile dictu,* in parenthesis we see the Hebrew word for "repentance": *teshuvah.*[17] Here the Church has quite consciously and deliberately chosen a central term straight out of the Jewish theological tradition. Why an act of repentance, an act of *teshuvah?* It is because, as the statement then says, "as members of the Church, we are linked to the sins as well as the merits of all her children." This means what we might very well take it to be: a certain kind of collective responsibility. Of course, in a literal moral sense, I am not responsible for somebody else's sins, and so a Catholic today who is horrified by Nazism and all it stood for and all it wrought in the world is certainly not responsible for what Hitler did, even though Hitler was baptized a Catholic. It is not that person's responsibility by any moral logic I know of. However, the religious tradition, be it the Catholic Church or the ongoing tradition of the Jewish people, is "covenantal," that is, for both, the relationship with God is primarily a communal affair. It is not primarily a relationship between an individual person and God, as many seem to think is the essence of any religion, especially in a secular age when many would like to confine religion to the realm of individual privacy. That is because human beings are essentially communal creatures. If we are to be related to God in the fullness of our humanity, then it has to be in the context of a community. In the covenant, a particular community is elected by God for a unique relationship with God. Traditional Jews can recognize this point quite readily. For example, virtually all Jewish prayer is uttered by plural subjects — "we," not "I." And that is the case even when a Jew is unable to pray with a congregation. He or she is always part of the congregation, even when unable to be physically part of them.[18]

In a covenantal religion, the ties are not only between the community and God. For these very ties with God undergird the ties between the members of the community herself. As such, these human ties within the community are themselves much more intense and long lasting than the ties we experience in our largely secular society and culture. Thus in an ordi-

17. Sec. V, p. 43a.
18. See B. Rosh Hashanah 34b-35a.

nary society, we are obligated to practice justice, and a certain degree of compassion as well. But the interhuman relations in an ordinary, secular society are quite "thin" when compared with the much "thicker" ties within a covenanted community.[19] Thus in a covenanted community, even though one is not morally responsible for the sins of fellow members of the community, there still is an *existential* sense of collective sorrow and shame when another member of the community — even those as estranged from the community as many of the Nazis were — commits a sin, especially a sin having great public consequences. In talmudic teaching, one says, "Every Jew is responsible for every other Jew" *(kol yisra'el arevim zeh ba-zeh)*.[20] That is what it means to be part of a covenanted community. So, I remember how my grandmother would occasionally read in the newspaper that some Jew or other had committed a crime — someone she didn't even know or know of personally — and she would express her sense of sorrow and shame at what they had done. She felt that what they had done personally affected her, even if by standards of ordinary morality her reaction would have to be judged irrational. And in the same way, by contrast, she would take pride when some Jew or other — also someone she didn't know or know of personally — did something that had benefitted others. And, although my grandmother was not a learned woman, she was reflecting by a kind of folk wisdom about what the Rabbis called *qiddush ha-shem* ("the sanctification of God") or *hillul ha-shem* ("the profanation of God"), that is, when Jews do good in the world, it reflects well on God, who elects them for the covenant; and when Jews do evil in the world, it reflects badly on God similarly.[21] With this in mind, we Jews can see how the Church, who after all learned about covenant from us, is engaged in the covenantal act of repentance, of *teshuvah*.

As regards the Holocaust, the Church feels sorrow and shame about those of her members who did not respond properly to the moral outrage that Nazism surely was, or even only sympathized with what was being done to the victims of Nazi persecution and mass murder. And here we do see a powerful moral component at work, for although a covenant is more than just a moral relationship between humans, it certainly takes much from human universal morality (what is called "natural law") as well as contributing to it.[22] And that sorrow and shame is not just because of a

19. For this "thick" and "thin" distinction between cultures, see Clifford Geertz, *The Interpretation of Cultures* (New York: Basic Books, 1973), pp. 5ff.

20. B. Shevuot 39a-b re Lev. 26:37; Sanhedrin 44a.

21. See *Palestinian Talmud: Baba Metsia* 2.4/8c.

22. See Thomas Aquinas, *Summa Theologiae* 2/1, q. 94, a. 4 ad obj. 1.

kind of guilt by association with Nazis and Nazi sympathizers who happen to have been Catholics or of Catholic origin; it seems to be sorrow and shame that perhaps the teaching authority of the Church did not do enough to influence such persons to resist the evil to which they so horribly succumbed. In other words, perhaps the Church did not do a good enough job of teaching what the Pope has called "the principles of Christianity" to many of her sons and daughters.[23] This sorrow and shame has led the Church to condemn racism and anti-Semitism.

The Church has thus learned from her mistakes, and she seems to be doing this by an ongoing process of introspection. Isn't that more prolonged and more painful than any mere apology? For an apology under these circumstances would either be a once-and-for-all way of getting the Holocaust "out of the way," or it would be an act of moral suicide. That is because no religious community can judge itself by someone else's standards and still exercise its existential claims upon its own faithful. A covenanted community engages in *teshuvah,* which literally means "return." Those responsible for teaching the tradition must constantly be returning to her true, revealed sources, always discovering that they could have interpreted them better and made their principles more intelligible and more effective.

However, to expect an apology rather than *teshuvah* is to call for something quite cheap when there is the possibility of doing something much more precious. It calls for something ephemeral when there is the possibility of something more permanent. An apology is an event; *teshuvah* is a process. An apology gets us "over" the past, putting it permanently behind us; returning is always on the horizon. Thus we Jews pray daily — three times daily, to be exact — for God to enable us to return to God and to forgive us our sins that have been a barrier between God and us. To be a member of a covenanted community means to acknowledge the sins of all our fellow members. This is an awesome covenantal responsibility; it is certainly beyond the demands of any ordinary morality. Indeed, one can only bear such responsibility when he or she believes that the community has been elected by God and is the object of God's special, supernatural concern. What all of this shows, I hope, is that only Jews who are theologically sensitive can appreciate what the Church is trying to do in this statement. Furthermore, it does not in any way diminish the fact that Jews have a different, even contradictory, view than that of Catholics as to *how* God makes contact with us and *what* that contact consists of. Actually, by

23. Sec. IV, p. 42b.

properly understanding what we have in common with Catholics, we are better able to understand what makes us different from one another. To assume we have nothing in common is as erroneous and spiritually dangerous as to assume that there is nothing that separates us from each other.

From all of what I have tried to say so far, you can see that I am very much sympathetic to the Vatican statement. I appreciate its significance, not only because it is immediately beneficial to Jews, but even more importantly because it is part of a larger process of the Church's coming to grips in a way she has never come to grips before with her Jewish origins and with her co-existence with the Jewish people until the end of history. But, by way of conclusion, I must state, in a spirit of friendly response, what I find lacking in the statement. This critical response is not a moral one, and it is not a theological one, either. That should be evident from all that has been previously said in this lecture. Rather, my critique here is rhetorical. On one point in particular, I think the statement tries to say too much and thus does not say it well.

The statement raises the whole issue of the behavior of Christians who did resist the Nazis policies, especially the Nazi policies against the Jews. Thus it cites the 1937 encyclical of Pope Pius XI, *Mit brennender Sorge* ("With Burning Concern"), which condemned Nazi racism quite explicitly. And this was an encyclical, an official statement of Church teaching, unusually written in German rather than the usual Latin, which seems to be a way of making its point directly to the Nazi powers in Germany then. Also, it seems quite likely that the actual author of this encyclical was Eugenio Cardinal Pacelli, the Vatican secretary of state, who was to become Pope Pius XII two years later, in 1939. Nevertheless, this Vatican statement raises the complex historical question of the entire role of Pope Pius XII during the Holocaust, especially in its discussion about the actual conduct of his papacy in that incredibly difficult time. It raises this issue in order to defend the whole record of Pius XII.[24]

There is a tremendous historical debate about Pius XII. On the one hand, it is well known that Pius XII did save a number of Jewish lives and encouraged others who were doing likewise. But, on the other hand, ever since Rolf Hochuth's 1963 play *The Deputy*, which builds on the plausible assumption that the Pope did know about the mass extermination of the Jews from 1942 on, the question has been raised with increasing frequency:

---

24. See sec. IV, p. 42a, n. 16.

Why didn't the Pope condemn what the Nazis were doing to the Jews? But on that whole question, we might say "the jury is still out." If we assume that the Pope did know what was happening — and for argument's sake, let us assume that, as the Vatican document itself seems to assume — then the question is whether the Pope's public silence was an act of moral cowardice or an act of moral prudence. Concerning moral cowardice, it has been said that the Pope did not want to upset the Nazis under whose control he was living in occupied Italy (and Vatican City), and also that he had always been more concerned with the danger of Communism, with its very explicit anti-Christianity and anti-Catholicism particularly, than he had been concerned with Nazism. After all, wasn't it the Pope when he was Cardinal Pacelli, the Vatican secretary of state, who had negotiated the concordat of 1933 with the new Nazi regime in Germany, an act that gave this questionable new regime much international respectability? And wasn't the Pope a good deal less reticent in condemning the evil of Communism than he was in condemning the evil of Nazism, which is evidenced by the fact that after the war he excommunicated any Catholic who even voted for Communist candidates, something he did not do to any Catholic supporters of Nazism?

Concerning the assumption of moral prudence on his part at that time, it could be said that he reasonably feared that he might be killed by the Nazis if he so spoke, or that certainly many other Catholics, especially Catholic clergy who would be taken as his agents, would be killed. Because moral judgment in this case still requires much more historical inquiry, one can hardly be very conclusive about either alternative in this most complicated case. And the case is further complicated by the fact that we are dealing here with a moral judgment, which, if unfavorable, would be condemning Pius XII for a sin of omission — a sin of omission rather than a sin of commission. For no one could say that the Pope actually spoke or acted positively on behalf of the Nazi regime (as did some bishops), and certainly not on behalf of the crimes of the Nazis.

As anyone can readily see, it is far more difficult to fix blame on somebody for what he or she could have done but did not do than it is to affix blame on somebody for what he or she should not have done but did do. The reason for this distinction is because what has not been done, like any negative, is potentially infinite, whereas what has been done is actually finite. Needless to say, it is easier to get a hold on what is finite than on what is infinite. Of course, that does not mean we cannot condemn sins of omission. Surely, we would morally condemn somebody who would, as Scripture puts it, "stand idly by the blood of your neighbor" (Lev. 19:16).[25] However, once the proximity of the one being condemned to the victim of harm is not literal physical proximity, then the cogency of any condemnation becomes more and more vague. Furthermore, at least according to Jewish morality, one cannot be condemned for not gravely risking his or her own life for the sake of the life of another.[26]

Hopefully, the historians will be able to tell us enough so that we will be able to decide whether Pius XII was blameworthy, praiseworthy, or somewhere in between. That cannot be done now. So, for that reason, and for the sake of presenting an undiluted theological-moral statement, the Vatican document would have been stronger and less open to the wrong kind of criticism from those usually hostile to anything Catholic if it had simply not raised an issue it cannot possibly adequately deal with here, or anywhere else so far.

Finally, though, I think we need to look at one more statement from the document in order to better appreciate what it means for Jews. It says, "The Nazi regime was determined to exterminate the very existence of the Jewish people, a people called to witness to the one God and the law of the covenant."[27] No Jewish statement could have better enunciated any more precisely just what the purpose of the existence of the Jewish people is in the world. Jews are committed to survival. Much of our language, uttered both to ourselves and to others, is the language of survival. Surely, that is quite understandable considering what the Jewish people have suffered, especially in this century. But survival for Jews is not enough. Jews always have to understand *for what* — better, *for whom* — we are surviving. (Assimilationists of various stripes have concluded that there is no good reason for Jewish survival, and that only as human beings in general should individual Jews survive.) And perhaps that for which the Jews are to survive is the true source of the Nazi venom against the Jewish people. That a statement issued by the Catholic Church recognizes the chosenness of the Jewish people, the vocation of the Jewish people, is nothing short of what we Jews call *qiddush ha-shem,* "the sanctification of the name of God."[28] If this is now what the Church, from the top down, as it were, recognizes as the reason for the survival and ongoing strength of the Jewish people, which is a reason we Jews ourselves ought to recognize

25. See B. Sanhedrin 73a.

26. See B. Baba Metsia 62a re Lev. 25:36.

27. Sec. IV, p. 41a.

28. See David Novak, *The Election of Israel: The Idea of the Chosen People* (Cambridge: Cambridge University Press, 1995), pp. 1-5.

because this is what the Torah has always taught us, then despite certain reservations about how appropriate the exercise in posthumous moral exoneration is, we Jews have to see this document as making a most positive contribution to the always complex relationship between the Jewish people and the Catholic Church. It is a document Jews can and should accept because its theological thrust and conclusions have a resonance in our own theology and law. It is by no means the last word — nothing is in this world — but its integrity and wisdom should not be missed because of moral and political antagonism stemming from those having less integrity and less wisdom.

The Moral Crisis of the West:
The Judeo-Christian Response

To speak of Jewish-Christian relations at the present time requires one to immediately recognize how different these relations are in this more secular period of the history of Western civilization than they were in earlier, more religious periods of that history. Jewish-Christian relations today are certainly different in character from the way they were during much of the past two millennia, when "Western civilization" was very much a "Christian" civilization. Throughout this very long, earlier period of history, Jews related to Christians as the masters of the world in which we were continually struggling to survive and maintain our communal life.

Christians related to Jews as a community in their midst whom they could not absorb and would not totally eliminate. But hardly anyone would assume anymore that the former political hegemony called "Christendom" is still politically or even culturally dominant in the Western world today.

Now there are some Christians who do long for the return of Christendom. Needless to say, almost no Jews would join them in any such longing, however unsure some of us might be about modernity. Almost no Jews would long for the return of the world of medieval Europe.[1] Despite

---

1. Nevertheless, one must take notice of the recent impressive argument for "Christendom" made by the Anglican theologian Oliver O'Donovan in *The Desire of the Nations: Rediscovering the Roots of Political Theology* (Cambridge: Cambridge University Press, 1996). Even though he eschews religious compulsion (p. 220), his is still a vision of "a state that [gives]

This essay was originally delivered as the Malcolm Hay of Seaton Memorial Lecture at the University of Aberdeen, Scotland, on 16 February 1999. It appeared subsequently in the *Scottish Journal of Theology* 53 (2000): 1-21.

all its dangers, virtually all Jews today have opted for modernity, whether as a desideratum or only as a necessity, for better or for worse, like it or not. Most Western Catholics, Protestants, and Orthodox seem to be of the same opinion. Thus "secular age" is synonymous with "modernity," which one can certainly distinguish from the earlier ages of the Jewish-Christian relationship, both in their common ancient origins and in their subsequent medieval divergences. One could well say that for the vast majority of Jews and Christians today, this *secular* age is very much *our* age too, and it is not just that of self-proclaimed "secularists" (more about whom we shall discuss later).

Since all human relationships do have a history, historical reflection must be part of our analysis from beginning to end. Malcolm Hay himself was a historian. Yet I do not think historical reflection is the primary task of the Malcolm Hay of Seaton Memorial Lecture. History *per se* is a descriptive enterprise. Nevertheless, considering Malcolm Hay's public career, something more normative is called for: not only what has been, but what ought to be. Indeed, from what I know of his most distinguished life, even his scholarly research as a historian of the Jewish-Christian relationship was motivated by clear moral interest throughout. The expression of that type of moral interest is what I take to be the charge of this lecture. A morally indifferent historical analysis would not pay Malcolm Hay the posthumous honor he so richly deserves.[2] Thus the question this lecture addresses should be morally conceived.

Furthermore, in my view (and it is by no means unique to me), moral questions and political questions are two sides of the same coin. That is, morality always involves my life with other persons, hence it is political; and politics involves how I am to act with these other persons, hence it is moral. On this point I have been most deeply influenced by the contemporary philosopher Professor Alasdair MacIntyre, who like Malcolm Hay is himself a Catholic.[3] To be sure, much of this lecture will deal with our

---

entrenched, constitutional encouragement to Christian mission not afforded to other religious beliefs, and [expects] of its office-holders deference to these arrangements as to constitutional law" (p. 224). For some other issues of greater commonality in the Jewish-Christian relationship raised by this book, see David Novak, "Response to *The Desire of the Nations*," *Studies in Christian Ethics* 11 (1998): 62-68.

2. Along these lines, see Hans-Georg Gadamer, *Truth and Method*, trans. G. Barden and J. Cumming (New York: Seabury Press, 1982), pp. 274-78.

3. See *After Virtue* (Notre Dame: University of Notre Dame Press, 1981), pp. 139, 201; *Whose Justice? Which Rationality?* (Notre Dame: University of Notre Dame Press, 1988), pp. 126-41.

common history. But that reflection will be for the sake of discovering a moral trajectory, requiring moral judgment in the present and moral projection into the future.

The moral-political question before us could be formulated as follows: How ought our different religious communities deal with each other in the still strange secular world into which both of us have been thrown, a world neither of us controls?

The first thing to notice after asking this question is that our mutual marginality gives us a more even playing field for Jewish-Christian relations than, perhaps, we have ever had before. Moreover, unlike the time early in Jewish-Christian history, when Jews and Christians were individually marginal in civil society, today, however marginal our historical traditions are in civil society, as fully enfranchised citizens we are both full participants in the political life of the societies in which we now live. For that reason, significant discourse *between* Jews and Christians is just as much mediated by the secular realm as is discourse between Jews or Christians and *anyone* else beyond the confines of our own traditional communities. We are both not only *in* the world but also very much *of* the world. Conversely, I think that when Jews and Christians attempt to speak to each other today in an exclusively theological way, bracketing the secular culture in which our moral and political problems arise, we can only revert to medieval-type disputations or engage in merely informative or "interesting" comparative religion. So, despite its dangers for us, the secularity of the world enables us to speak to each other and act with each other in some new and, hopefully, more fruitful ways. That seems to be very much due to secularity being our common problem and challenge.

One new and more fruitful way we can speak to each other and act with each other is to construct effective philosophical arguments for the sake of our mutual survival and benefit in the secular world. I call these arguments "philosophical" because they are to be made in secular public space. They do not pre-suppose revelation. Here the language of theology, the language rooted in revelation that we speak within our own communities, is unintelligible. The most we can look to our theologies for in this case is that they authorize our adoption of philosophy as our second, more generally understood, language. Philosophy is the most conceptually precise language of the world.[4]

An additional new and even more fruitful way we can speak to each

---

4. See David Novak, *Natural Law in Judaism* (Cambridge: Cambridge University Press, 1998), pp. 16-26.

other and act with each other is to construct philosophical arguments that are more than just for the sake of our mutual self-interest. Instead, this type of philosophical argument should be for the sake of the common good of the secular world in which *we and all others* live — at least for the time being. Along these lines, especially, it is valid to speak of a Jewish or a Christian *public* philosophy. To be sure, our own theologies should be taken by Jews and Christians to be more internally significant than philosophy. They are our primary languages. Our own theologies are never to be forgotten or minimized even when we "do philosophy." Yet a strong case can be made that in the secular world we now find ourselves in, our best common effort might come from our mutual construction of some persuasive public philosophy. In order to do that, though, we must locate exactly where it should most properly enter worldly discourse, and why it is best constructed in common between Jews and Christians rather than each community doing it separately in isolation from the other.

In terms of the location of such a public philosophy, we first need to affirm the value of its being within Western civilization. By "Western civilization" I mean those nations of Europe and the "New World" who recognize a common history and who affirm four main political institutions: (1) the due process of law, (2) majority legislative rule, (3) human rights, and (4) free-enterprise economy. But after the Holocaust, the value of "our" civilization is not self-evident, neither for Christians nor for Jews. A moral argument must be made as to why a Christian or a Jew should remain part of this civilization and be committed enough to its survival and growth to want to construct a public philosophy for it.

To Christians, the value of Western civilization is not self-evident since Christianity proved to be largely ineffective in preventing the Nazi Holocaust, which, of course, took place within European societies whose majorities were at least nominally Christian. It is not, as some have assumed, that Nazism automatically follows from Christianity.[5] Nazism is paganism, a paganism that would have eventually eliminated Christianity within its domain as it nearly eliminated Judaism there had it lasted longer than twelve and one half years.[6] Yet Nazism could never have accomplished what it did in that brief, horrible period had Christianity exerted

5. See Eliezer Berkovits, *Faith after the Holocaust* (New York: KTAV, 1973), pp. 25, 36; and more recently and famously, Daniel Jonah Goldhagen, *Hitler's Willing Executioners: Ordinary Germans and the Holocaust* (New York: Knopf, 1996), pp. 41-43, 49-53, for this common view.

6. See Emil L. Fackenheim, *Encounters between Judaism and Modern Philosophy* (New York: Basic Books, 1973), pp. 192-95.

its moral teaching with full conviction and vigor, and had traditional Christian anti-Judaism been repudiated before it could be so easily exploited by the Nazis. Malcolm Hay showed that most powerfully in his great book, *The Foot of Pride.*[7]

Nevertheless, Western civilization did in the end defeat Nazism, and that defeat came largely at the hands of European and North American Christians, drawing upon Christian sources of morality for their inspiration. Along these lines, I think of the poignant film of President Roosevelt and Prime Minister Churchill taken on board a ship in the mid-Atlantic during the dark days of 1940, when it seemed that Hitler and his followers could very likely destroy our entire civilization. The scene which sticks most in my memory is their leading the British and American crews on board in singing "Onward, Christian Soldiers." Without the final victory of those mostly Christian soldiers, our Western civilization would have been killed, along with all the Jews in it. Christians need to understand wherefrom, as Churchill put it about the people of wartime Britain, "it was their finest hour." Indeed, those Christians who today have become anti-Western, opposed to what they call "Euro-centrism," are so radically denying their own history that it is quite doubtful how long they can maintain a consistent Christian identity. Christians should not be so guilt-stricken that they cut themselves off from indispensable traditional sources for their own moral renewal.

Many Jews today, who are still understandably searching for any explanation of what happened to us during the Holocaust, are quick to notice the contribution of traditional Christian anti-Judaism to modern anti-Semitic ideology. Because of this, some Jews have judged Western civilization to be a Christian civilization to be eschewed. Yet Jews are less likely to be aware of Christianity's contribution to making the Nazi project a failure in the end, since that positive contribution is less evident than the negative one. But is that not a significant contributing factor to the choice of the overwhelming majority of Jews today, both in the State of Israel and in the Diaspora, to continue living in the West? Is that not at least a tacit Jewish confirmation of the value of Western civilization?

One can see that in the way Jews have rejected the only alternative to Western civilization to have been available to us: Communism. That rejection was not easy. For during the 1930s, when the Western democracies

7. This was originally published by Beacon Press, Boston, in 1950, and again in 1960 under the title *Europe and the Jews,* and lastly published under the title *Thy Brother's Blood: The Roots of Christian Anti-Semitism,* by Hart Publishing Co., New York, in 1975.

seemed to be economically and politically in a state of decay, the Communism of the Soviet Union under Stalin seemed to some historically sensitive Jews to provide the only bulwark against the final victory of Hitler. Moreover, especially in Eastern Europe, where most of the extermination of the six million Jewish victims took place, the Soviet troops at the last minute, as it were, prevented the Final Solution from becoming truly final. Ask any Jew who survived Auschwitz about his or her grateful memories of their Russian liberators (who were a good deal more vengeful in their treatment of the Nazis tormentors than the British and American troops who liberated Buchenwald, for example). And, in the infant days of the State of Israel in 1948 and 1949, the Soviet Union provided vital military and diplomatic aid to the precarious existence of the newly re-established Jewish state. Yet, Communism, especially from Lenin on, has been an explicit enemy of Western civilization by its opposition to the religious origins and the four characterizing political institutions of our civilization just mentioned.

So, what prevented most Jews from ever becoming Communists in the first place, and what motivated even most Jewish Communists to eventually leave the party in disgust? Two reasons. First, Communism from Lenin on was intent on destroying Jewish religion and culture. Like some other forms of tyranny under which Jews have had to live from time to time, Communism required total assimilation with its attendant loss of Jewish identity, often using Jewish Communists to do the dirty work with particular ferociousness. That is the only option Communism has ever offered the Jews (unlike the Nazis, though, who were unique in offering the Jews no living option at all). Second, as Stalin demonstrated in the 1939 non-aggression pact with Hitler, Communism could only be trusted to do whatever it thought best for its own self-interest. It could offer no moral guarantees to Jews or anyone else since all morality is only a dispensable means in the service of its one totalitarian end, which has been nothing less than world domination. And that proved to be the case once more when the Soviet Union quickly turned against the State of Israel, when that proved more useful for its own *realpolitik*. Thus, in rejecting the temptation of Communism, the vast majority of Jews — with some understandable ambivalence, to be sure — have opted to remain participants in Western civilization, despite its being as imperfect as any human reality is, nonetheless. The acceptance by the West of the right of the State of Israel to exist — indeed, the right of the Jewish people to exist, by contrast to Communist policies — can be seen as a moral commitment on the part of the West to one of its constituent peoples.

Obviously, the choice of the West has been made by all those Jews who live in the democracies of Europe and the Americas. Less obviously, though, it has also been the choice of the Jews who live in the State of Israel, which is a nation that has showed over and over again that it considers itself part of the West as opposed to the former Soviet bloc or the non-Western nations who used to be called the "Third World." The development of this pro-Western public stance is of philosophical significance when made by Christians and when made by Jews, especially by Jews, for whom it has been a harder choice. But this choice must be emphasized when various European and North American critics of the value of Western civilization judge it to be illegitimate, often invoking the Holocaust as proof of the moral bankruptcy of the West. Nevertheless, virtually no Westerner who rejects the moral value of the West thereby chooses to live in a non-Western society. Indeed, no Westerner could survive such a rejection of his or her own civilization except in a Western-type democracy. Does that not cast suspicion on the moral integrity of those who make this type of wholesale rejection of the civilization in which they live? For it must not be forgotten that all moral choices presuppose the affirmation of a certain type of political order and culture. Jews in the Diaspora affirm that cultural-political order more within the larger non-Jewish societies in which they live. Jews in the State of Israel affirm that cultural-political order more within their international dealings as a clearly Western nation. As the Talmud puts it, "Do not cast stones into a well from which you have drunk."[8]

Having determined the general normative location of the construction of a public philosophy by Jews and Christians to be firmly within Western civilization, we must now find a more precise location therein in order for that philosophy to become truly relevant to current moral discourse and most politically effective. A public philosophy must be formulated in response to a real moral crisis in the civilization in which it desires to speak. It must be *engagé,* as some of the post–Second World War Parisian philosophers liked to say. In the West, of course, there is always some kind of moral crisis or other, but yesterday's moral crisis is frequently different from today's. From the 1920s through the mid-1980s, a period one could designate as prewar, wartime, and postwar or cold war, the main moral crisis of the West should be located in the struggle between democracy and totalitarian ideologies and regimes: fascist or communist. The task of the West was to see this struggle between democracy

---

8. *Babylonian Talmud* (hereafter "B."): Baba Kama 92b.

and those who have seen themselves in revolution against its "bourgeois" character as a battle of ideas, with the adherents of democracy having to convince the world that its ideas are more rationally persuasive than the ideas of the totalitarian alternatives. This, of course, has meant that such adherents of democracy have first had to be themselves convinced of what they desired for all human societies ultimately, and for all Western societies more immediately.

In the case of Christians, the choice against Communism was the easier one since Communism has always been so explicitly anti-Christian. Fascism, on the other hand, at least on the surface, often tried to seduce Christians by its own anti-communist stand and by its own selective use of historic Christian anti-Judaism. Christians have, therefore, had to see through such seductive pretensions and recognize Fascism as the pagan menace to Christianity that it truly is. That recognition has brought many Christians to a new sense of solidarity with the Jews.

In the case of Jews, the choice against Fascism was the easier one since, after the domination of Fascism by Hitler, the destruction of the Jews became its overriding concern. Most people, certainly most Jews, are not suicidal. Communism, on the other hand, at least on the surface, often tried to seduce Jews into thinking that the problem of anti-Semitism would be solved with the destruction of "bourgeois capitalism." Jews have, therefore, had to see through such pretensions and recognize that the elimination of anti-Semitism is too expensive if that requires the elimination of the Jews as a distinct people. Added to that has been the fact that the anti-Semitism of the Communists became almost as virulent as Nazi anti-Semitism, and for the same racist reasons. Indeed, it was no accident that just before his death in 1953, Stalin was preparing a Russian pogrom against the Jews that could have even rivaled the German Holocaust in terms of numbers. Jews only had to look at what his regime had already done to many Christians to be convinced of the seriousness of his intentions and his ability to put them into practice.

Nevertheless, despite the threat that Fascism and Communism have presented to Jews and Christians, both together and separately, the long struggle against both of these ideologies did not produce much of a Jewish public philosophy or a Christian public philosophy or, all the more so, a Judeo-Christian public philosophy. Why not?

One could say that the threat these totalitarian ideologies presented to the Western political institutions of the due process of law, majority legislative rule, individual human rights, and free-enterprise economy was so explicit that opposition to them could be explicated on more immediate secular grounds. Secular grounds, being more minimal than religious grounds, are always more readily at hand. Indeed, frequently during this period of history, secularists were more politically astute in recognizing the danger of totalitarianism than were Jews and Christians. Even before their ideas could be put into practice, all one had to do was read the writings of Hitler or Lenin or Stalin or their ideologues to get the horrifying preview of what would surely come with their final political success. One had to argue against their truth claims, but one could not dismiss their meaning as incoherent. Thus ridicule or satire, with its sense of the absurd, is an inadequate means for dealing with these serious ideologies. They meant what they said and said what they meant. Secular reason exposed these political dangers, and did so in a way that religious people could easily accept. Aside from those few religious Jews and Christians who regard democracy itself to be a threat to their view of polity (which is usually based on a romantic view of some "Golden Age" in the past), it has not been hard to bracket the question of religion or non-religion when defending due process of law, majority legislative rule, human rights, and free-enterprise economy.

Today, we are faced with a new set of moral and political problems, and the approach that worked so well during most of this century, for Jews and Christians and secularists together, does not work anymore. That is due to the fact that our moral and political problems are no longer primarily with the ideologies of nations that have the power to destroy our civilization and who have indicated that such is their intention. Instead, these problems are due to internal moral and political differences, differences between people who in general do not dispute the value of due process of law, majority legislative rule, human rights, and free-enterprise economy, institutions our civilization has held to be indispensable for its political life. Thus we can no longer direct our moral and political passions to fighting external enemies, something that usually entails a repression of serious internal, philosophical differences. Because of this, we are now seeing a return of the repressed in the moral and political realm. And what has been long repressed is that Jews and Christians approach some key, internal moral and political questions very differently than do the secularists.

By "secularists" I do not mean those who distinguish between religious and secular domains. That distinction is something most Jews and Christians today have fully acknowledged in good faith. Jews and Christians can accept the legitimacy of a secular realm because biblical revelation itself recognizes the independent integrity of creation and its order. All cosmic space is not sacred.[9] By "secularists" I mean, rather, those people who see the total public sufficiency of the secular realm. At best, they would so privatize religions that religious become sects: neither of the world nor even in it. At worst, they would see no place at all for religions in any democratic polity. Needless to say, Judaism and Christianity as covenantal religions, which are essentially political entities, are mortally threatened (collectively even if not individually) by such secularism, for it would deny them their worldly place.

This ontological dispute over worldliness, whether one has a legitimate place in the order of things or not, translates into a number of moral and political differences. On such issues as determining the beginning and the end of human personhood, the relations of men and women, the relations of adults and children, and the relations of persons and society, on these and other issues we are seeing a deepening division between Jews and Christians — that is, Jews and Christians who are still faithful to their normative traditions — on the one hand, and secularists on the other. I cannot specify these issues here and now, much less present arguments for what is to be done regarding them. I can only deal with the prior procedural question for Jews and Christians, which is this: Just how are we to present our moral and political philosophies in a public realm that is still secular, but not yet secularist? For in any realm governed by a doctrinaire secularism, as is the case in some of the media and in some of our universities, religiously inspired public philosophies are excluded in one way or another.[10]

But wherever there is an opening for us into the secular world, we must enter it with integrity and wisdom. Two forms of such a religiously inspired — in our case, "Judeo-Christian" — philosophical presentation, however, seem to be inappropriate and ineffective, and thus without cogency and without wisdom. We must describe them in order to avoid them. As the Talmud puts it, "From the negative, infer the positive."[11]

The first such erroneous approach is to simply reiterate in public the classical moral teaching of one's own tradition. In the United States, for

9. Thus both Jews and Christians recognize the authority of human law, even when promulgated by non-Jews or non-Christians, as long as it does not directly contradict the law of God. See B. Baba Batra 54b and parallels; Thomas Aquinas, *Summa Theologiae* 2/1, q. 95, a. 2 and q. 96, a. 4.

10. See Stephen L. Carter, *The Culture of Disbelief* (New York: Basic Books, 1993), pp. 44-66, 105-23.

11. B. Nedarim 11a.

example, one occasionally sees religious persons with their Bibles in hand, insisting that their public stance is God's will and that they can do nothing less than proclaim it to the world at large, who they claim must follow them. But such action is inappropriate because it assumes that the whole world accepts the revelation vouchsafed to and interpreted by one's own religious community through its specific tradition. Yet, in their eyes, if the world does not yet accept such authority, it should. That, of course, is proselytism. Even though most democracies permit proselytization as a legitimate exercise of freedom of religion, one cannot use the discussion of issues of politics and morality as an occasion for proselytization and expect to get any kind of public hearing. Indeed, moral and political questions can hardly wait for the type of theological unanimity required within a religious community. This approach, then, commits the category error of confusing philosophy with theology.

This approach is, moreover, ineffective. In the absence of moral persuasion, such dogmatic religious approaches to moral and political questions frequently become authoritarian. That is, they often attempt to manipulate a secular political system in such a way as to get it to enforce their point of view. The political maneuvering of the religious parties in the State of Israel is an example of such authoritarianism. For even though the Jewish tradition dropped the proselytization of gentiles from its agenda long ago, Jews faithful to traditional beliefs and practices are supposed to get other more religiously lax Jews back into the traditional fold. For some, if persuasion doesn't work (when, that is, it is even tried), coercion is advocated and practiced. In Israel, such coercion is exercised by the exaggerated political power of the religious parties that comes with their being necessary for any coalition government so far to maintain a working majority in parliament. The secular governments have had to make more and more concessions to the religious parties in return for their pivotal votes. And a major part of those concessions has been to cede more and more control of public morality to the religious parties and their rabbinical leaders. All of this is ineffective, sooner or later, because it creates more public animosity toward religion than attraction to it. In fact, it offers a convenient generalization for the secularist enemies of religion. For they sometimes argue that what some of the religious do all of the religious would really like to do, which is, as is often said in the United States, to "ram *their* religious morality down everyone else's throat." The enemies of religion would like nothing better than to portray religiously inspired public philosophy as antithetical to democracy. But, as a famous scenario in the Talmud concludes, even God Himself could not force the people of Israel to truly accept His Torah at Mount Sinai. Even God had to persuade His people before His Torah could effectively govern them.[12]

The second approach, which is also both inappropriate and ineffective, is to simply abdicate any religious voice in the area of morality and politics, and to remain content with "spiritual" matters of belief, ritual, and what could be termed "private" morality, which is usually the cultivation of "inner" attitudes. This approach is inappropriate because it is essentially other-worldly.

Now, of course, Judaism and Christianity are "other-worldly" inasmuch as each tradition affirms that beyond this world there is a world-to-come, and that this world is but its antechamber. The world-to-come is when and where humankind and all creation along with it will finally become reconciled with God, which Judaism and Christianity affirm is the end of all creaturely striving. As our common Scripture puts it: "Everything called by My name and which I have created for My glory, so I have formed it and made it" (Isa. 43:7).[13] Yet that common affirmation lies at the heart of what specifically separates Judaism and Christianity from each other, namely, *who* brings us to that world-to-come and *how* we are to anticipate that world-to-come here and now. As Isaiah continues the passage just quoted:

> All the nations will be gathered together, assembled as peoples. Who among them will tell us this, who will let us hear about the first things? Let them put forth their testimonies and be justified, and they [the nations] will hear and say that is the truth [*emet*]. You are My witnesses, says the Lord, My servant whom I have chosen, that you may know and have faith in Me, and understand that I am He before Whom no one has been formed and after Me no one will ever be. (Isa. 43:9-10)

Witness is quite different from political coercion or even from moral persuasion.

For Christians, it is Jesus who brings this world to the world-to-come, and the celebration of his life, death, and resurrection are how Christians anticipate that future. For Jews, observance of the commandments of the Torah is how we anticipate the world-to-come, and we wait for an as-of-now unknown redeemer who will bring this world to it. Even though a

---

12. B. Shabbat 88a. See David Novak, *Jewish Social Ethics* (New York: Oxford University Press, 1992), pp. 27-29.

13. See *Mishnah:* Avot 6.11.

good deal of mutual theological tolerance is possible, we should not ignore the necessary paradox in the relationship between Jews and Christians, precisely because our respective messianic claims are in essential conflict. Here and now, anyway, they cannot both be true. Nevertheless, we can still live together, even fruitfully live together, when we affirm that our differing visions of the kingdom of God and our differing anticipations of it will only be resolved by God in the end. And that *end* will not be the result of one community conquering the other, culturally, politically, or morally. Thus we dare not forget that our different anticipations of that end cannot be the basis of our common action together in the world here and now.

Nevertheless, to leave the matter at this "spiritual" level is to abdicate the moral and political role that Judaism and Christianity must play in the world. Our very waiting for the end of all history should inspire, not depress, our moral-political action in and for the world. To leave the world, so to speak, to purely secular criteria of meaning and practice means that Judaism and Christianity bring nothing to the world except a way of quietly enduring on the sidelines of the world until its appointed end. For some Jews and Christians of this other-worldly outlook, sectarian withdrawal from the realm of public morality or politics is the practical outcome of such conviction. For more Jews and Christians of this other-worldly outlook, who do not care to remove themselves from this public world and its attractions, religion's public function becomes one of endorsing or blessing the secular powers that be. Accordingly, such religious people become like the court prophets and the priests of the royal sanctuary in ancient Israel, whom the true prophets denounced for their refusal to teach God's worldly justice in their eagerness to endorse the injustices of their powerful patrons in return for being put on a kind of pedestal.[14]

Moreover, such unworldliness is often not even other-worldly but merely inward self-indulgence. It cultivates private feelings and is thus devoid of any truth claims at all. Just as moral claims are public, so are the truth claims behind them political. Today, much liberal religion has become a form of popular psychology, having lost its own interest in public questions of truth and justice by ceding them to secularist criteria. It is a form of group therapy, designed to help us feel good about ourselves in a world that increasingly makes us feel bad about ourselves. It is a therapy designed to save us from the world by merely providing us with hiding places within it. But such hiding is hardly effective, even if the world itself,

14. See Amos 7:10-17.

from time to time, lets us escape its public claims upon us. Knowing where to find us, so to speak, the world can pursue us again just as easily as it can let us alone for a while. Accordingly, such anti-public religion is as much a threat to modern Judaism and Christianity as Gnosticism was to ancient Judaism and Christianity, with its offers of secret knowledge born of its ultimate despair of this world ever being redeemed. Such unworldliness, in whatever form, is simply not good for Judaism *or* Christianity apart from each other; all the more so, how can it be good for Judaism *and* Christianity together? It not only does not produce a public philosophy; it is a great impediment to the formulation of one.

So, as I hope we can now see, the task of Judaism and Christianity in our formulation of a public philosophy is not to speak with the authority of theology, or to speak with the unworldliness of sectarianism, or to speak with the inwardness of psychology. Because of the easy prevalence of these kinds of speech, it has been very tempting for Jews and Christians to use them and think they are offering a public philosophy to the world. By learning to avoid these real mistakes, however, we are in a better position to formulate a more appropriate and more effective public philosophy for the sake of morality and politics, and to be convinced why it is necessary that we do this together and not apart.

Of the four defining political characteristics of Western civilization mentioned here several times, the most intense moral discussions of late have been about issues of human rights. Now in this area of public discussion, there are two opposing views over the connection of the religious traditions of Judaism and Christianity to the institution of human rights in Western civilization. For those who see these (or any) religious traditions as being essentially "authoritarian," the achievement of a strong sense of human rights has been in spite of Judaism and Christianity, not because of them. Human rights are seen as coming out of the French Revolution, the revolution that destroyed the *ancien régime,* whose legitimizing institution was the Church. And it was also the French Revolution that destroyed the internal autonomy of the historic Jewish communities (*qehillot*) and thereby delivered individual Jews from the control of communal authorities to full personal liberty and equality in secular nation-states.[15]

The problem with this view is, first of all, its faulty history. The fact is

---

15. See Jacob Katz, *Tradition and Crisis: Jewish Society at the End of the Middle Ages* (New York: Schocken Books, 1971), pp. 79-111.

that the extreme secularism of the French Revolution did not provide a secure foundation for the very human rights it so loudly proclaimed. The ideology of the revolution could not prevent the reign of terror under Robespierre or the despotism of Napoleon. And in both cases, the continued communal loyalties of both Christians and Jews were seen as threats to the social identity of the newly invented nation-state, which no longer required confirmation from an older, more transcendently directed communal order. (The Russian Revolution of 1917 and the German Revolution of 1933 continued this nihilism with even greater vehemence and wherewithal.) Rather, it was the more modest "revolutions" (perhaps, better, "reforms") of Britain in 1688 and of the United States in 1776 that have provided a far more enduring political order that has been consistent (with occasional glaring lapses, to be sure) in their protection and expansion of human rights. And, it should be emphasized, both of these polities reaffirmed their connection to earlier traditions of law and equity, such as English Common Law, including the Bible as one of its roots.[16] Also, it is no accident that in these more "traditional" societies, even the corporate rights of the older religious communities have been more consistently respected, for example, by recognizing that they are not beholden to the state in the way that secularly formed corporations are in matters such as taxation. Of especial interest to Jews and Christians, looking for the way to formulate a public philosophy together, is the fact that the biblical roots so confirmed are those in the Scripture common to us both: the Hebrew Bible, or *Kitvei ha-Qodesh,* or the Old Testament — three names for one and the same book.

---

16. Note Blackstone, *Commentaries on the Laws of England,* vol. 1, introduction, sec. 2 (reprint, Chicago: University of Chicago Press, 1979), pp. 42-43: "The doctrines thus delivered we call the revealed or divine law, and they are to be found in the holy scriptures. These precepts, when revealed, are found upon comparison to be really a part of the original law of nature, as they tend in all their consequences to man's felicity. . . . Upon these two foundations, the law of nature and the law of revelation, depend all human laws; that is to say, no human laws should be suffered to contradict these. . . . Human laws are only declaratory of, and act in subordination to, the former. To instance in the case of murder: this is expressly forbidden by the divine, and demonstrably by the natural law; and from these prohibitions arises the true unlawfulness of this crime. Those human laws, that annex a punishment to it, do not at all increase its moral guilt, or superadd any fresh obligation *in foro conscientiae* to abstain from its perpetration. Nay, if any human law should allow or enjoin us to commit it, we are bound to transgress that human law, or else we must offend both the natural and divine." For the recognition of precedent from English common law in United States law, see K. L. Hall, W. M. Wiecek, and P. Finkelman, *American Legal History,* 2d ed. (Oxford and New York: Oxford University Press, 1996), p. 24.

The importance of this unanimity cannot be overestimated. For it is based on the fact that the differences between Judaism and Christianity are theological, not moral. By this distinction I do not mean to suggest the secularist notion that there is no need for theology in the formulation of morals. For Jews and Christians, morality is law, and all law is rooted in God's will. Nevertheless, whereas theology *per se* is based on God's *particular* revelation to a *particular* community, great theologians, both Jewish and Christian, have argued that when it comes to basic moral laws, they can be discerned as God's will by *universal* human reason understanding the claims of human *nature per se*.[17] This is what philosophers have called "natural law."

To many Christians, the moral teaching of the Old Testament is still binding in the New Covenant that Christianity affirms and proclaims as the Gospel, whereas the "ritual" teaching is only of particular Jewish validity. The validity of the Hebrew moral teaching *(torah)* is because it comes from *general* revelation, discernable by universal human reason even before it is specifically confirmed by the revelation at Sinai. The validity of the ritual teaching (what Christians have called "sacraments," and what Jews have called *isura*), conversely, is because it comes from *particular* revelation to unique, covenanted communities called "Israel" and/or "the Church."[18] It is not as the founder of modern, secular natural law theory, the sixteenth-century Dutch jurist Hugo Grotius, said, namely, that natural law is valid *etiamsi daremus non esse Deum* ("even if we say there is no God"). That would only be true for such thinly disguised atheists as Hobbes, Rousseau, and Kant. Instead, Jews and Christians can only, more modestly, say that natural law is valid *etiamsi daremus non esse revelatio* ("even when there is no revelation").[19] From a Jewish perspective, the very validity of Christianity as an object of our respect and empathy is because of its acceptance of the moral teaching of the Hebrew Bible, including its ultimate theological underpinnings. That is how our theologies enable us to construct a Judeo-Christian public philosophy with integrity.

Because of these parallel theological developments in Judaism and

---

17. See Maimonides, *Mishneh Torah*: Melakhim, 8.11–9.1; Nahmanides, *Commentary on the Torah*: Gen. 6:2, 13; Thomas Aquinas, *Summa Theologiae* 2/I, q. 94, a. 4 ad 1; John Calvin, *Institutes of the Christian Religion*, 2.7.10 and 4.20.16.

18. Thus it is recognized in B. Ketubot 40a and parallels that the reasoning pertaining to civil matters *(mammona)* is to be distinguished from the more purely theological reasoning connected with ritual law.

19. Grotius, *De Jure Belli ac Pacis,* prol. 11 (reprint, Cambridge: Cambridge University Press, 1953), p. xlvi. For further elaboration of this point, see 1.10, pp. 12-13.

Christianity, it is not only accurate to speak of a "Judeo-Christian morality," it is a most worthy enterprise.[20] This Judeo-Christian morality is not just a Christian morality since it is that aspect of Christian normative teaching which Christianity has taken from Judaism without taking Judaism up into itself. Judaism is still alive and well to continue to be engaged with Christianity both in theory and in practice. Indeed, this morality is not true to its Judaic part when Christians look upon Judaism as a historical precedent only. Moreover, it is also not just what could be thought of as a "Jewish morality for the gentiles too." For Jews should not present this moral teaching to Christians or to any other gentile community as an extension of Jewish authority but, rather, as a teaching accessible to every intelligent seeker of justice in the world. This morality is like what Maimonides taught about idolatry: it is not false because the Torah prohibits it; rather, the Torah prohibits it because it is false.[21] Its essential prohibition is the commandment "From falsehood [me-dvar sheqer] one should keep distant" (Exod. 23:7), which is one of those norms about which the Talmud said, "If it had not been written, it should have been written."[22] It is *the* rational commandment *per se*. (Paul made much the same point in the beginning of the Epistle to the Romans.[23])

But how does this morality differ from the morality presented by the various secularisms of modernity? And why should it try to persuade the secular world which is neither Jewish nor Christian, and whose members need more evidence than simply noticing that some Jews and some Christians are now getting along much better together both in word and in deed than they have in the past? What is attractive about Judeo-Christian morality is the anthropology, the idea of human nature, which underlies it from both its Jewish and its Christian visions.

All secularist moralities have to emphasize some feature or other of human nature like rationality or freedom and then use it as the principled background of the various moral norms each one advocates. But since one cannot see one's whole self but only a part of oneself, such a humanly subjective anthropology misses the full reality of humanness. It then misses the full reality of humankind, for when one sees only part of human nature, one always loses those members of humankind who are deficient in their possession of that designated feature of humanness so privi-

20. See Richard John Neuhaus, *The Naked Public Square* (Grand Rapids: Eerdmans, 1984), p. 261.

21. *Commentary on the Mishnah:* Avodah Zarah 4.7.

22. B. Yoma 67b re Lev. 18:4.

23. Rom. 1:18–2:16.

leged. Thus, when rationality is emphasized, we have a human quality which some possess more than others, and some do not possess at all. The same is the case when freedom is emphasized. It is not that rationality and freedom are not desirable human attributes; it is that humanness cannot be reduced to them alone. As such, the morality informed by such limited anthropological perspectives either explicitly eliminates some segment or other of humankind from the status of full personhood with its attendant human rights claims, or has no cogent objection when such exclusion from the realm of human rights is made by others.

Conversely, Judaism and Christianity affirm that humans, individually as persons and communally as humankind, are created in the image of God. There are a number of interpretations of that doctrine, but the one I find most attractive here and now is the one that sees the image of God (the *tselem elohim* or *imago Dei*) as human existence being the object of unique divine interest, so much so that God has regarded human beings as worthy enough for God to directly speak to them — to us. And that speech is what my late revered teacher, Abraham Joshua Heschel, called "God's anthropology, not man's theology."[24] In revelation, God presents to us the most complete image of our humanness that we can possibly bear in this world. God knows us completely, precisely because such complete knowledge can only come from the true objectivity of transcendence. The greatest transcendence is the creator transcending his own creation and all the creatures therein. Indeed, the very presentation of that image by a verbal revelation is its very essence. Thus here, as the late University of Toronto thinker Marshall McLuhan used to say most famously, "The medium is the message."[25] Judaism and Christianity (and Islam, whose quite recent presence in the West makes it a much more nascent dialogue partner as of now) are religions of revelation. And it is the moral affirmation of the dignity, the worthiness, of every human person and all human communities that revelation in and for our world presupposes.[26]

Nevertheless, does this mean that in order to be persuaded by Judeo-Christian moral teaching, those who are not believers have to accept the theology behind it? No. What I would recall for them is the talmudic principle about cases of doubt involving human life: when in doubt, take the

---

24. Heschel, *God in Search of Man: A Philosophy of Judaism* (New York: Farrar, Straus & Cudahy, 1955), p. 412.

25. McLuhan, *Understanding Media* (Cambridge, Mass.: MIT, 1994), pp. 7-21.

26. For the ontology behind this assertion, see David Novak, *Jewish-Christian Dialogue: A Jewish Justification* (New York: Oxford University Press, 1989), pp. 129-38.

most humane option available *(safeq nefashot le-haqel)*.[27] Or, recall the talmudic principle that when human dignity *(kevod ha-beriyot)* is in doubt, even a revealed law of God may be suspended.[28] In other words, give the most humane option the benefit of the doubt. Even if you cannot ever believe or cannot yet believe the Judeo-Christian theory of humanness/humankind, it is certainly more inclusive than the secularist alternatives. Thus moral persuasion only requires this theory be entertained as a plausible hypothesis; it need not be accepted as transcendent truth in advance, nor need it even be a means for eventual conversion in order to be morally effective. It is a matter of human possibility, not a potential Judaism or Christianity. It thus appeals to the main moral concern of secular society today: greater inclusiveness in the human community with greater rights protection for it.

Finally, the pursuit of justice always requires the greatest possible inspiration to be found. Those who speak and practice the Judeo-Christian morality in the world, but with lives lived within a covenant far greater than mere morality, will find their most effective voice together in the world when they properly address themselves to the perpetual moral choice of the world: to choose between life and death.[29] Here and now we must encourage the world to choose life and respect it in all its dimensions.

27. B. Yoma 83a and parallels.
28. B. Berakhot 19b and parallels.
29. See Jon. 3:4-10; cf. Deut. 30:15, 19.

Jews, Christians, and Civil Society

No one, save a prophet, could have predicted the radical change in the relationship between Jews and Christians since Western civilization narrowly escaped physical and moral annihilation in the Second World War. Having narrowly escaped physical annihilation, Jews have had to look at the world surrounding us anew. There some of us have discovered Christians facing us on the immediate horizon in a new and favorable way. Having narrowly escaped moral annihilation, Christians have also had to look at the surrounding world anew. There some Christians have discovered Jews on the immediate horizon in a new and favorable way. This mutual discovery of each other in new ways can be located on three levels.

First, mutual discovery has occurred on the theological level. Through sound historical scholarship, more Christians than ever before have learned how close Christianity has always been to its Judaic roots. The current Christian retrieval of Christianity's true origins has looked not only to the Hebrew Bible but also to the Second Temple Judaism out of which Judaism until this very day has been emerging. That is why Judaism can no longer be dismissed as an historical relic, as mere proto-Christianity. Through the very same type of scholarship, Jews have discovered that Christianity is not a one-time deviation from Judaism. Rather, Christianity has been developing in a trajectory continually parallel to that of Judaism. Jews need to see how much Christianity has had to be

This essay is based on the fifteenth annual Erasmus Lecture of the Institute on Religion and Public Life, which was delivered on 26 November 2001 in New York City. It appeared subsequently in *First Things* 120 (February 2002): 26-33.

similar to Judaism in order to continually differ from it. From this some Jews have learned that we can discuss the Torah with Christians in a way we cannot discuss it with any other gentile people. Thus Jews and Christians today have found a way to talk to and with each other that is mutually affirming and that need no longer be either offensive or defensive, as interaction so often was in the theological disputations of the Middle Ages and the ideological polemics of earlier modernity.

Second, mutual discovery has occurred on the political level. Until quite recently, the political relationship of Jews and Christians in modernity had been almost totally hostile and suspicious. Jews had been seen by many Christians as being in the vanguard of the atheistic trajectory of modernity. Truth be told, some of the most prominent atheistic theorists have been Jews, and some of the most effective public atheism has been promoted by certain Jewish organizations. By "public" or de facto atheism, I mean public policies that advocate "don't ask, don't tell" when it comes to mentioning God in political discourse — even when used by a religiously observant Jew running for the office of Vice President of the United States. Because of this sad fact, Jews have been seen by many Christians as leading the attempt to keep religion — which for the vast majority of Americans is some form of Christianity — out of the public square. Indeed, many Christians have assumed that Judaism itself is identical with the modern progressive ideal that requires the public square to include only those "naked" Christians who have divested themselves of anything Christian at all. What most Christians do not realize, however, is that the public atheism of some prominent Jews, individually or collectively, has been even more injurious to Judaism than it has been to Christianity, inasmuch as naked Jews are still more vulnerable to public disappearance than are naked Christians.

Christians, on the other hand, have been seen by many Jews as resisting an ideal of modern progress that promises political and cultural equality to the Jews. To be sure, there are Christians who still long for the pre-modern world they think they once controlled — a world in which Jews were inevitably political outsiders and cultural pariahs. Nevertheless, many Christians now realize that the notion that Christianity truly controlled pre-modern European and American civil society is in many ways a romantic fantasy. Moreover, many Christians have come to the conclusion that, even where such religious control of civil society did in fact obtain, it was as disastrous for Christian witness of the Kingdom of God as it was for justice in civil society. Thus George Weigel, when speaking of the political theory and practice of Pope John Paul II, has forcefully stated that "the 'Constantinian arrangement' has been quietly buried."[1] Indeed, more and more Christians now do not regard modern political secularity as something to be overcome, but rather as another new challenge to Christian survival and witness in a still unredeemed world.

It is now less common than it once was for Jews to eagerly embrace the secularist ideologies of modernity. That embrace too was a romantic fantasy — in this case about an ideal, utopian future. Fewer Jews today see the earthly Messiah in modern political secularity. In its place is a more sober and less enthusiastic relation to the modern secular political situation — neither overly negative nor overly positive. Many of us, both Jews and Christians, want the public square to be pluralistic, which is neither partisan nor naked. Theoretically, at least, this has led to the discovery of some important new political commonalities between Christians and Jews. These political commonalities should not only be noted, but encouraged. The political playing field between us is more level than it has ever been before.

We have reached a point in history, at least in North America, when Jews and Christians can recognize each other as each other's closest neighbor rather than our most threatening enemy. The power of contemporary secularism, with its enmity against religion, has forced this recognition on both of us. There is nothing like a new common enemy to force us out of old isolations. Those who still affirm that "the earth is the Lord's" (Ps. 24:1) are becoming more and more aware that we are "strangers on earth" (Ps. 119:19).

The theological and political encounter between Jews and Christians has only just begun, but it promises to provide each of our communities with innumerable opportunities for original and fruitful discussion. Yet each topic — theology and politics — carries with it so many burdens that I wonder whether it is wise to separate them in our thinking.

The shortcoming of purely theological discourse between us, even when it is informed by sound historical scholarship, is that in the end it has to conclude that our great difference is greater than all of our commonalities. Our difference, of course, concerns Jesus. Truth be told, it is precisely when we both eschew the kind of rhetoric that assumes the other can be argued into our own faith position — be that argument exegetical, historical, or philosophical — that the difference actually becomes more pronounced. Eschewing polemical confrontations in theology means that we can live better together *in spite of* our overriding theo-

---

1. Weigel, "Papacy and Power," *First Things* 110 (February 2001): 20.

logical difference. But after all is said and done in theological dialogue between us, theology remains a conceptualization of the language of revelation and the worship it commands, and our central institutions of worship necessarily exclude each other. Jews cannot and should not receive communion in church; Christians cannot and should not be called to the public reading of the Torah in the synagogue. That divide outweighs even the most genuine experiences of dialogical intimacy.

The shortcoming of purely political discourse between Christians and Jews arises from the fact that it is largely built upon the perception of a common enemy. For a long time now we have confronted the militant secularism that permeates so much of the culture, and which now enjoys great political power. By *secularism* I mean the ideological matrix that regards human-made law not only as necessary for modern life — a point which Jews and Christians who have not retreated to sectarian enclaves can readily accept — but also as sufficient for human fulfillment. It is the modern embrace of the view of the ancient sophists that "man is the measure of all things."

This belief in secularism as a value goes far beyond the acceptance of the fact of modern *secularity*. All modern secularity requires is that our public norms and the arguments for them not presuppose common acceptance of Jewish or Christian revelation, even if these public norms are consistent with a particular community's revelation and the authoritative teachings it derives from that revelation. Thus Jews and Christians can only make public moral arguments that are based on ideas of the general human condition rather than on the singular experience of God speaking directly to one's traditional community. But it is ideological secularism, not the affirmation of secularity per se, that largely defines the culture of the universities, the media, the foundations, and the courts — that is, the most powerful elite culture in our society. It is what inspires them all. This culture, which is often quite self-consciously the heir of the Enlightenment, regards both Judaism and Christianity as obstacles in its quest for radical egalitarianism, which is as old as the temptation of Adam and Eve by the serpent that they too can become "like God" (Gen. 3:5) and thus replace God altogether. We can live in peace with secularity; we cannot live in peace with secularism as an ideal commanding its own realization in history.

Furthermore, recent terrible atrocities, especially those committed against the United States of America in the great cities of New York and Washington, have presented to Jews and Christians a very real enemy in militant Islam. This enemy despises Judaism and Christianity precisely because they both have accepted political secularity in the form of modern democracy and economic secularity in the form of capitalism.

We can, of course, find much commonality in our struggle against our common enemies. Yet this commonality could easily turn out to be one more ephemeral political alliance within modern political secularity itself. Enemies, after all, come and go, even as we remain. Current political anxiety often propels us into desperate political ventures, where we blindly embrace or are embraced by political ideologies that need no justification from Judaism or Christianity, even if they are not explicitly hostile to our traditions. When this happens, it is often impossible to discern just who is using whom. Jews and Christians should be wary of allowing Judaism or Christianity or even the commonality between them — what is best called "biblical religion" — to become the religious frosting on somebody else's ideological cake. If opposition to a common enemy is all we have in common politically, we risk slipping into all the usual political paranoia — that is, the *need* for a common enemy. Because of that temptation, we need to discover a commonality between us that is more positive and more enduring. For me, that commonality must come out of our concern with what Baruch Spinoza rightly called — even if he wrongly perceived it — the *theological-political* question, which is the third level of mutual discovery by Jews and Christians.

The theological-political question is not primarily the theological question of how we respectively affirm God, nor is it primarily the political question of how we prosecute the various wars we have to fight. Instead, it is the question of how faithful Jews and faithful Christians can enter into civil society together and survive there intact, let alone flourish there, without, however, either conquering civil society or being conquered by it. It is the question of how those who worship the Lord God of Israel, and who derive their law from this God's Torah, can in good faith join modern civil societies — which we have seen are inherently secular — and actively "seek the peace of the city" (Jer. 29:7). And it is the question of whether or not we need each other for that entrance into civil society.

The important thing to remember here is that although Jews and Christians participate in various societies, *as* Jews or Christians they are each members of one community above all others. The one is always prior to the many. These fundamental, constituting communities are even prior to political associations. There is, one might say, a profound difference between being a *participant in* something and being a *part of* something. Many Jews and many Christians are theologically and politically confused because they do not understand this essential difference and what follows from it. As Jews or Christians, we are parts of but one community — a true "body politic" — founded and sustained by God. As citizens of modern nation-states, by contrast, we are participants in civil societies and their institutions.

We Jews are part of the Jewish people, and that is our primary identity. Christians are part of the Church — the body of Christ — and that is their primary identity. Only subsequently do Jews and Christians participate in various associations, and we can only participate in these associations in good faith when we justify that participation by reference to the ends for which our own communities live and thrive. Furthermore, unlike totalitarian regimes that regard those under their political control to be *dispensable* and *disposable* parts, the Jewish people and the Church regard themselves as covenanted communities elected by God, both collectively and individually. Since God's election creates an everlasting covenant with all the members of His people, everyone of us is, therefore, *indispensable* and *nondisposable* — at least in this world. We are all elected in our communities and we are all promised ultimate redemption with them — if we remain faithful with them to our God. Covenantal election, either by birth or by conversion, means that we can never be fully excluded from the people of God — at least in this world. The most that can happen to us here is that we need to be subjected at times to communal disapproval, even to the point of social isolation. But that is never permanent expulsion. The promise of reacceptance makes repentance possible and desirable. That explains why we can be loyal to our primary communities in a way we can never be loyal to any other human association of the world.

For these reasons, Jews and Christians can never regard any civil society, even that of liberal nation-states where they have thrived, as a comprehensive whole of which they are parts. No matter how much we love our current political associations, no matter how patriotic we might become when our state promotes God's law of universal justice, no matter how much we might be willing to risk our lives for the liberty of our own society, no Jew and no Christian should ever regard any other human group in which he or she participates to be the Chosen People. Only Israel is chosen, whether defined by Jews or by Christians. I do not see how any Jew can say he is practicing Judaism — or how any Christian can say he is practicing Christianity — while thinking of himself as a part of something larger, more inclusive, and thus more important than the people of God. That is the case with any worldly society, no matter how beneficent it is to us, no matter how just it is to others, no matter how noble.

To be a Jew, essentially and not just accidentally, is to regard the Jewish people as one's sole primal community. Election by the unique God requires total and unconditional loyalty to one people. All other social bonds are partial, however long-standing, however just, however lovable. No human society in which we participate can ask us to subordinate our membership in God's people to that society's ultimacy. A person can have multiple temporal locations in this world, but he or she can only be part of one body forever. Whatever other societies a Jew is connected to, he or she is only *a participant therein, never a part thereof.* As Augustine has taught Christians (a teaching, incidentally, that Jews can recognize as prophetic in origin), there is always a tension between the city of God and the city of man, even when it is a tension that benefits both the city of God and the city of man.

No authentic Judaism or Christianity can look to a human society for its primary orientation in the world. This theological-political fact provides a broader and firmer foundation for Jewish and Christian dialogue than any theological fact or any political fact taken separately. That is because Judaism and Christianity are religions that originate in God's election, are constituted by God's covenant, and anticipate God's redemption. Thus, when Thomas More was willing to suffer death as a martyr at the hands of Henry VIII because he insisted on being "the king's good servant, but God's first," he did not mean that his service to God was that of the Englishman, Thomas More. Rather, he meant that his service to God was that of Thomas More the Catholic, who is a part of the Catholic Church, which, in turn, is linked directly to God. To reverse the priority of the Church to the State, as More judged King Henry to be doing, is to substitute a humanly ordained society for the divinely ordained "congregation of the Lord" (1 Chron. 28:8). But God's people and human authority can only coexist when human authority takes itself to be conditional, not absolute. As the Talmud puts it about abuses of human authority becoming absolute, "To whom do we listen, to the words of the master or to the words of the pupil?"

This great difference, this great ordering of our priorities as Jews and Christians, was brought home to me several years ago by an eloquent Christian woman at a conference held at the University of Toronto. This woman was born and raised in Barbados. Her ancestors were brought there as slaves from Africa. She had originally come to Canada as a domestic servant, and then became a high school teacher in Toronto. At this conference, one of the main speakers was an African-American political activist, and the main point of his remarks was to claim that the primary definition of who we are derives from race. Following these remarks, the

woman stood up and with consummate dignity made the following remarks. "Sir, I must differ with you. Of course, I am black, and being black
I have suffered the persecution and discrimination that has been the lot
of most blacks in Western societies. Nevertheless, I will not allow you to
define me as a person by the color of my skin. I am a Christian first and
foremost. I am a black *Christian* like I am a Canadian *Christian*. Both 'black'
and 'Canadian' modify the name 'Christian,' not vice-versa. What I ask of
society is the freedom to be a good Christian and that society enable all
people to be treated with just respect."

Following this statement there was a moment of stunned silence, during which I was quite jealous that this great soul wasn't a Jew speaking for
us Jews. But she did speak for at least this Jew. What she was saying is that
our identity does not come from definitions like race — definitions in
which, as Jean-Paul Sartre rightly noted about anti-Semitism, our persecutors are allowed to tell us and the world who we are. This woman was
saying that we must not allow our persecutors to define our primary community. Jews and Christians are defined by God's relationship with us, by
our election into the covenant, and how we respond to that covenantal
election. In hearing this authentically Christian voice, I heard an echo of
the voice of Jonah, who when asked who his god was, finally declared, "I
am a Hebrew and I fear the Lord, God of the heavens" (Jon. 1:9). Only after
this admission could he go to the pagan city of Nineveh and have anything at all to say there.

This moving story illustrates two important points about the
theological-political situation in which we Jews and Christians find ourselves at the moment. The first point involves something Christians can
learn from Jews, and the second point something Jews can learn from
Christians.

Christians can learn from Jews that to be a Christian — to be one of
the two peoples in the world who are covenanted by the Lord God of Israel — is also to be but one of many peoples in the as-yet-unredeemed
world. Although Christians are convinced — as are Jews about themselves
— that the Church is in the vanguard of the Kingdom of God on earth,
they also believe that the Kingdom of God on earth will not be brought
any nearer by assuming that the Church can or should claim to rule others in the world as it is presently constituted politically. The task of any
people of God is to survive in the world, and to work in the world to en-
sure that the political order allows for our survival and the flourishing of
our faith. That means working not only for a political order in which religious liberty is the most important right, but also one in which enhanc-

ing the dignity of human life in its various forms serves as the raison d'être of the society, especially the state created by that society.

Indeed, the protection of religious liberty, which is the political right to respond to or turn away from the God who elects us, is the right on which all other rights are grounded. In theological terms, it means that humans are made in the image of God, and that they are capable of a relationship with God. In political terms, it means that civil society must be seen as subsequent in authority to this supreme relationship. Civil society must respect the prior human freedom to either accept or reject any historical revelation that purports to realize the relationship between God and humans. And revelation is *in the world, not of it.* This recognition that we are not ultimately beholden to the political orders of the world, that they do not own our souls, is a Jewish point best appreciated by black Christians, who have suffered great persecution and see their redemption as Christians coming from God and not from any human power. That is why black Christians more than most other Christians have so identified with the initiation of God's redemption of His people Israel in the Exodus from Egypt.

What we Jews can learn from Christians is that (regardless of whatever else we might be) we are first and foremost a religion. Now, unfortunately, many Jews and many Christians have been deluded by Jewish secularists to think that Judaism — or "Jewishness" — is not a religion because even nonreligious Jews are considered to be part of the Jewish people. Therefore, it is argued that Jews are an "ethnic group" for whom Jewish religion is an arbitrary form of identification. But this is backward. Even nonreligious Jews, even atheistic Jews, are part of the Jewish people *because to be a Jew is to be a member of a community elected by God.* That is fundamentally different both from choosing one's own society and from the mere accident of birth. It is God who makes a Jew a Jew. It is not a human choice — neither our own, nor that of our ancestors, nor that of our enemies. Election is a fundamentally religious event initiated by God, not man. Thus those who repudiate their obligation to keep the commandments of the Torah — that is, Judaism — may have left Judaism in practice, but they are still part of Judaism by their very existence. Speaking figuratively, they have gone AWOL, but they may not be court-martialed. Of course, we practicing Jews hope and pray that these sons and daughters who have strayed from the covenantal home will return, but neither our souls nor theirs would be well served if we attempted to coerce them back into the fold.

For most Jews, election begins at birth; it thus precedes any choice on the part of the Jew. As for those who convert to Judaism, their decision must be conceived as a compulsion that originally comes from God alone. Their free consent is a necessary but not sufficient condition of their being accepted as Jews. The same is true for Christians. If baptism is indelible, and if most Christians are baptized as infants, then most Christians become Christians like most Jews become Jews. This is so even in the cases of Christians who are "born again" and who are baptized as adults. Birth is, after all, the most involuntary event possible. (Incidentally, the term "born again" appears in Greek in the New Testament and in Hebrew in the Talmud.) It is only a modern, voluntaristic view of the covenant as a social contract that supposes that being a Jew or being a Christian is an individual option that is initiated or terminated by human will.

Of course, some Jewish secularists have conceived of Jewish identity along racial, even racist, lines. In the end, though, this means that it is the persecutors of the Jews who define who we are. But election into the covenant must not be taken as a matter of blind fate, as an accident of birth. If Jewish identity is conceived along racial lines, then to be a Jew today means little more than to be someone who escaped Hitler's genocide. But victimhood is not election. In the end, victimhood can only be cursed. Election, conversely, is a blessing, even if it sometimes means being more vulnerable than others in the world.

For these reasons, everything that is associated with Jewish ethnicity, including our Jewish attachment to the land of Israel and support of the Jewish state, is seen in the proper light only when it is defined in essentially religious categories. That should be our Jewish sense of self-identity, both to ourselves, to Christians, and to the various secular polities in which we now live. Neither racist definitions of Jewishness, which require no free acceptance or rejection of one's fate, nor voluntaristic definitions of Jewishness, which are based on the illusion of self-creation, can represent a coherent picture of who is a Jew. Being a Jew is neither fatal nor autonomous. It is only covenantal. Christians who truly appreciate the covenantal character of Christianity are in the best position to understand who Jews essentially are because they understand who they themselves are.

Because some modern nation-states have demanded the total subordination of their citizens, with horrendous historical results, many thoughtful people in our society have re-embraced the idea of the social contract along liberal, Lockean lines. Like any contract, the Lockean social contract is conditional and therefore limited. Like any contract, it does not create its parties; rather, its parties create it for the sake of their own prior interests. We exist both before and after the agreement itself. We come from somewhere else, and we transcend the agreement by our insistence on a right to return whence we came.

But where is that "somewhere else"? Indeed, those secularists who think that the democratic polity itself is their true home often weaken democracy by denying the legitimacy of any place beyond it. They have "nowhere else" to return to at the end of the political day. As such, they cannot coherently limit the power of the state and the civil society it makes possible. They can only hope to capture that power in order to realize their own partisan interests. Unlike the philosophers of Plato's ideal republic, these doctrinaire secularists do not strive for a vision of a transpolitical good, one beyond all human procedures. For them, what you see now is all you ever get. No wonder they are so impatient with Jews and Christians, who do have such meta-political, even metaphysical, commitments.

Secularists, whether self-identified or not, can be either liberals or conservatives. Despite their apparent differences, most of those who now call themselves liberals and conservatives accept the idea of the social contract and its corollary of the moral necessity of a limited state. They differ only on what should limit the power of the state. Moreover, contemporary liberals and conservatives each accept the most basic liberal idea that individual persons are fundamentally possessive in nature. The specific difference between them seems to be that conservatives emphasize the possession of material property, whereas liberals emphasize self-possession — that is, the possession of their own bodies. As the Talmud once noted, some people prefer their property over their bodies; other people prefer their bodies over their property. (But the Talmud assumes that we are to love God more than either our property or our bodies.) Both liberals and conservatives seem to want to be able to look forward to long weekends away from their political world, when and where they can enjoy either their property or their bodies. So much for keeping the Sabbath holy.

Because the idea of bodily self-possession is used by most liberals to justify such biblically prohibited practices as abortion, euthanasia, and homosexual unions, many thoughtful Christians and Jews have been gravitating in a more conservative political direction of late. The conservative — or, perhaps, "libertarian" — idea of possession of material property is less likely to be used as a warrant for biblically prohibited practices than the liberal idea of self-possession. Only when it comes to a perceived indifference to or rejection of biblically mandated concern for the poor do some conservatives seem to be religiously objectionable. Furthermore, whereas most liberals today seem to explicitly derive their morality from their secular political commitments, more conservatives seem to explicitly derive their morality from such pre-political commitments as biblical religion. The drift of Jews and Christians toward conservatism is thus understandable.

Nevertheless, Jews and Christians, as distinct from either liberals or conservatives today, come to the social contract not as individuals but as fully communal beings. The covenant characterizes a divinely chartered human community which, although not perfect in itself, testifies to the perfect Kingdom of God. As such, we can make the promises any contract presupposes because we are already bound by the covenantal promise of God, the initial part of which has already been fulfilled. We live in the city of God, however weak it now appears. We are only passing through the city of man, however strong it now appears. We do not look to the city of man for our salvation, now or ever. Indeed, those who look to the city of man for their salvation are inevitably disappointed and thus often become tempted by a dangerous cynicism.

This is precisely how Jews in medieval Europe were able to live with integrity in Christian polities. It was because the Christian monarchs with whom they could contract did not require the ultimate existential commitment of the Jews. In other words, they offered the Jews a secular modus vivendi. In contrast, when the ultimate existential commitment of the Jews was required by Christian monarchs — as it was in 1492 by Ferdinand and Isabella of Spain in their demand for conversion or expulsion — faithful Jews had to remove themselves from such societies.

Jews and Christians must be wary of any social contract that has a beginning but no final limit. Being a human device, such a contract can only be a rival to the covenant made by God with His people, which also has a beginning but no final limit. Hence any contract Jews and Christians enter must be both humanly initiated and humanly terminable. Only then can the covenant truly transcend this political arrangement. Civil society must be our challenge, not our temptation. Fortunately for us, the type of democratic polity that has emerged in the West does not require the absolute commitment required by God and His covenanted community. Only secularist totalitarianisms have attempted to replace the covenant with their own absolute claims on our total existential commitments. That is why Jews and Christians have such a stake in the success of the democratic polity. And, indeed, because our entrance into the social contract comes out of our covenantal commitments, we Jews and Christians can enjoy a far greater personal attachment to our social contract with a democratic polity than we could to any private contract negotiated between merely individual parties.

The entrance of Jews and Christians into the social contract as communal beings, already socialized elsewhere, means that we bring forms of human community to civil society that need to be officially recognized by civil society and the state for the sake of our own communal interests. We also bring these forms of human community to civil society for the benefit of all its citizens, even those who are secularists. These two purposes function in tandem. It is in our communal interest to live in societies that affirm in law and public policy what we consider to be universally just. Only in such a political order can Jews and Christians live our own communal life in a way that does not make us, in the deepest sense, outlaws.

Moreover, the forms of human community we bring to civil society, such as marriage, are so socially beneficial that most of us would not object to their being appropriated even by those members of civil society who do not want to have any religious affiliation at all. Indeed, our desire should be to give more to civil society than we take from it. That too makes the social contract more like a biblical covenant, especially more like "the covenant between the king and the people" (2 Kings 11:17). Indeed, it can be shown historically that even Lockean notions of the social contract were very much influenced by the covenantal political theology of the English Puritans.

Now, of course, our common Jewish and Christian definition of marriage is currently under siege. It is very important that serious Jews and serious Christians stand up and take notice of what is happening and what is at stake. We are witnessing a concerted attack on the traditional idea that marriage is a heterosexual union. Many secularists now argue that marriage should be understood as a publicly sanctioned "relationship," and that the sex of the participants, even the number of participants, in that relationship is irrelevant. In other words, their view of marriage is essentially contractual. All that is required of the participants in such a relationship is that they be consenting adults.

That is quite different from the biblical idea of marriage in which man and woman "become one flesh" (Gen. 2:24). That is, in our idea of marriage, only "a man and a woman" can be *parts of* one flesh in the same sense that Jews are truly parts of the Jewish people, and Christians are truly parts of the Church. Only a man and a woman can work with God in the creation of *one flesh*. That is not only a point made in biblical revelation; it is a matter of natural justice. That is why we can argue for it in the context of civil society and the law of the state. It is not something that is confined to our religious preserve. Carefully thinking out the best rational defense of this now vulnerable social institution by Jews and Christians will bring about more theological-political unity than a more narrowly "political" strategy ever could.

Jewish and Christian interests are thus parallel in many matters. But do we have something more than just parallels going for us? Is there some point at which we truly intersect?

On the theological level, as we have seen, we do intersect in the sense that both Judaism and Christianity are the traditions of two separate communities who are still emerging out of the same Hebrew Bible and the same Second Temple Judaism. The recovery of that reality has been an exercise of fruitful commonality between Jews and Christians of late, especially among our scholars. And that scholarship has had an effect on our broader communities, too. Nevertheless, theological intersection is limited by the agreement of both sides in the Jewish-Christian dialogue to avoid proselytizing. That necessarily means that we cannot make our full truth claims to each other theologically and expect the other side to sit still and listen to what could only be perceived as conversionist rhetoric. As such, theological dialogue between Jews and Christians can only work when these ultimate claims are consciously bracketed. That is why many Jews and Christians have stayed away from the dialogue. But today, truth be happily told, many Jewish and Christian theologians have begun to speak to each other under this constraint in good faith and with good results. Yet, at this point, our lines are still more parallel than perpendicular. Our theological intersection is little more than the affirmation of our common beginning.

On the political level, however, we can intersect with each other in the present and do so with less caution and restraint. But as we have seen, political intersection commonly ends up taking the form of ephemeral political alliances in the secular world. Here, too, our present political lines are more parallel than perpendicular. It is thus on the theological-political level that a deeper and more enduring intersection can and should be found and nurtured.

One of the greatest Jewish political theologians is the third century (Christian era) Babylonian rabbi, Mar Samuel of Nehardea. One of his most important aphorisms reads: "The only difference between the days of the Messiah and this world is the rule of the earthly kingdoms." The Messiah is an essentially theological-political reality. On this messianic level, one can see the greatest Jewish-Christian difference. Christians think the Messiah has already come; we Jews think the Messiah is yet to come. Yet the contrast with the world of modern secularism is far more dramatic. For secularists, there is no Messiah. Only those who wait for the Messiah's arrival or return can hope for a truly transcendent future and steel themselves against the allure of a fantastic, and impossible, utopia. So our greatest commonality, our most lasting intersection in this world, takes place when we understand each other to be waiting for the Kingdom of God — the coming-world — and refuse to settle for anything in this world as a substitute.

It is on this matter that we perpetually intersect, as we continually pass by, one another. We appear to collide at various oases in the wilderness because we are both travelers who can only temporarily rest before the end of the journey. And that restlessness includes — or ought to include — our refusal to be satisfied with whatever power we have in this world. We must refuse to see the Kingdom of God as an imperious extension of our own, rather pitiful, earthly power. The intersection of our mutually hopeful anticipation of the end is more positive and more profound than our current, ephemeral political alliances against common enemies, and this intersection surpasses our various theological conflicts in this world. As T. S. Eliot put it, "What we call the beginning is often the end. And to make an end is to make a beginning. The end is where we start from."

It is when we better understand how and why we both need to carefully pass through the earthly kingdoms, whichever ones they might be, and when we refuse to take shortcuts around them into a global future or flee away from them into a sectarian past, that we have the most in common. It is this journey itself that is common to us both, even when at any fixed point it is traveled separately and alone. Recognizing that might well enable each of us and both of us to transverse this world, this vale of tears, with more hope, more compassion, more care, perhaps even with more joy. "Let them go from strength to strength; let each one of them appear before God in Zion" (Ps. 84:8).

When Jews Are Christians

By now it is obvious that in the past twenty-five years or so there has been considerable progress in the Jewish-Christian relationship. Overcoming centuries of mutual hostility and indifference, some Jews and Christians are now able to engage in honest and fruitful dialogue and, as religious communities struggling in a larger secular society and culture, they are now able to recognize a number of overlapping interests. For Christians, this progress has required overcoming triumphalist attempts to delegitimize post-biblical Judaism. For Jews, this progress has required overcoming the assumption that Christianity is incorrigibly anti-Jewish and that all Christians are ultimately, if not immediately, anti-Semites. Progress has grown out of a healthy balance between otherness and commonality. Some Jews and Christians are now able to recognize the otherness of the other community as something to be respected rather than feared. And they are now able to recognize enough commonality in terms of common past origins, common present concerns, and common hopes for the future to enable a genuinely mutual relationship to take root and grow.

Despite this progress, a problem lies just beneath the surface. It is a problem that must be discussed if the progress we have experienced in the Jewish-Christian relationship is not to regress. The problem concerns a new type of Jewish convert to Christianity, who has of late become more visible and more vocal.

This essay previously appeared in *First Things* 17 (November 1991): 42-46. It was subsequently reprinted in *The Chosen People in an Almost Chosen Nation: Jews and Judaism in America,* ed. Richard John Neuhaus (Grand Rapids: Eerdmans, 2002), pp. 92-102.

It has always been inevitable that, living as a small minority among a Christian majority, some Jews would convert to Christianity. At certain times of great persecution, like the Inquisition, some Jews feigned Christianity by becoming "secret Jews" (the so-called Marranos). Faced with the alternative of death or exile, they would adopt some kind of pseudo-Christianity, which might be abandoned at the first opportunity. By a grisly irony, the Inquisition correctly assumed that such Jewish converts were not really Christians and never had been. Other Jews converted to Christianity and remained in the Church because they saw it as socially or economically advantageous. Finally, still others converted to Christianity because they sincerely believed that Christianity is the true faith. Although by Christian standards Jews who convert to Christianity for opportunistic reasons are clearly "bad" Christians, and Jews who convert to Christianity for religious reasons are clearly "good" Christians, the one thing they had in common was that they both believed themselves to be Christians and no longer Jews. Both kinds of converts believed that they had made a decisive leap from one community to another.

As far as Christianity was concerned, they had, like any other converts, indeed become members of the Church. Following Paul's assertion that "there is no such thing as Jew and Greek . . . in Christ Jesus" (Gal. 3:28), the Church refused to recognize any special status for Christians of Jewish origin in its ranks. For their part, the Jewish authorities considered converts to Christianity to be apostates *(meshumadim)* whose return to Judaism was a hope never to be abandoned, however unlikely that return might in fact be. And the Jewish converts to Christianity themselves almost always accepted the Church's definition of their new status. They no longer regarded themselves as Jews and were often quite vehement in repudiating their former identity.

Now, however, there is a new kind of Jewish Christian, one who poses an altogether new problem for both the Jewish and the Christian communities. These Jewish converts to Christianity not only claim to be Jews, they also claim still to be practicing Judaism. Some of them insist that they are indeed practicing *the* true Judaism, implying that all other Jews are practicing a false Judaism. Others merely insist that they are practicing *a* true Judaism, thus implying if not actually demanding that their practice be accepted as a legitimate form of Judaism. The vast majority of Jews refuse to accept either what might be termed the maximalist claim or even the minimalist claim of the Jewish Christians.

In relation to the Christians, the new Jewish Christians claim a special role for themselves within the Church, offering themselves as a kind of personal link between the now gentile Church and its Jewish origins. This claim often includes a demand for recognition of their right, or even obligation, to perform the ritual commandments of the Torah, from which all other Christians have been exempted by Christ (see Matt. 12:8). Some of them go so far as to refuse the name "Christian" altogether, preferring to call themselves "Messianic Jews." For even though the Greek *Christos* is no more than a translation of the Hebrew *Mashiah*, the connotation of the word has come during the course of history to mean something quite different.

The various branches of the Church have reacted variously to this new type of Jewish Christian. Yet it would seem that any formal conferral of a unique status upon them would mark the acceptance of a permanent division of Christians *de jure* into a Jewish and a gentile branch. This would, theologically speaking, pose a far greater threat to Christian ecumenism than the present *de facto* divisions within the Church — divisions, after all, that can be seen as merely temporary obstacles for Christians to overcome.

Beyond posing a special kind of problem both to the Jewish community and the Christian community, these Jewish Christians also constitute a problem to the new Jewish-Christian relationship. For the acceptance of their unique status by some Christians strongly suggests to many Jews — very much including those most favorably disposed to the new Jewish-Christian relationship — that the Jewish Christians are being held up to the rest of the Jews as exemplars. In other words, Christian recognition of their unique status strongly suggests a new form of proselytizing, specifically directed at Jews, that is quite different from a general Christian proclamation of the Gospel to the entire world. Inasmuch as the Gospel is in essence similar to the Jewish proclamation that "it shall come to pass in the end of days . . . from Zion shall the Torah go forth and the word of the Lord from Jerusalem" (Mic. 4:1-2), most Jews can live with it. But proselytizing efforts that are specifically directed at Jews must be abandoned by Christians who wish to engage in any dialogical relationship with Jews. For we Jews cannot be expected to allow ourselves to be the objects of efforts designed specifically to lure us eventually, if not immediately, away from what we believe is our own true covenantal identity. In fact, those of us in the Jewish community who favor dialogue and cooperation with Christians have had to contend against certain of our fellow Jews who see the new Jewish-Christian relationship as a clever ruse designed by sophisticated Christians to take in gullible Jews. Thus Christian acceptance of the self-proclaimed Judaism of the new Jewish Christians, as opposed to accepting them simply as *any* converts are accepted, can only undermine the position of the pro-dialogue and cooperation party within the Jewish community.

Jewish rejection of the claim of the Jewish Christians that they remain part of the life and faith of the people of Israel has taken legal form in several important decisions of the State of Israel's Supreme Court. The most recent decision of the Court on that issue, in 1989, involved two Jewish Christians, Jerry and Shirley Beresford, who petitioned for Israeli citizenship as Jews under the Law of Return *(hoq ha-shevut)*, which guarantees immediate Israeli citizenship to every Jew. The Court rejected their petition on the grounds that the Law of Return specifically precludes from the right it confers any Jew who has affiliated with another, non-Jewish, religious community. In this decision, the Court essentially followed the precedent of the 1962 rejection of a similar petition by Oswald Rufeisen, a Jew who had become a Roman Catholic monk under the name of Brother Daniel. (The only basic difference between these two cases is that Rufeisen was clearly a member of a discernible non-Jewish community, the Roman Catholic Church, whereas it was somewhat unclear just what Christian community the Beresfords are members of.)

The Court's rejection of this petition, which is wholly consistent with the attitude of virtually all of world Jewry, has angered a number of Christians, even some who are otherwise favorably disposed to the new Jewish-Christian relationship. For does it not seem to single out Jewish Christians for rejection? Why, some of them have asked me and other Jewish friends, are Jewish Christians any less Jewish than Jewish atheists? These questions are quite understandable, and they must be addressed by thoughtful Jews, especially Jewish theologians who have been able to communicate with Christians on a theological level.

Being, on the whole, biblical literalists, the Jewish Christians assume that they can simply pick up where the Jewish Christians in the earliest Church left off. The Jewish Christians, especially when they designate themselves as "messianic," assume that they are that branch of the Jewish people who have accepted Jesus of Nazareth as the Messiah. In their opinion, it is merely that the rest of the Jewish people have not yet done so. Thus they see the messiahhood of Jesus as the sole point of difference between themselves and their fellow Jews. Like most biblical literalists, they choose to ignore the testimony of intervening history. But that intervening history also counts as an indispensable factor for the normative judgments of both Judaism and Christianity.

And it is intervening history that has made any simple division between messianic and non-messianic Jews inappropriate. The question of which Jews accept Jesus as the Messiah and which do not is no longer applicable. The fact is that neither Jews nor gentiles relate to Jesus as the Messiah now. Messiahhood is a political designation for a divinely restored (or, at least, divinely sanctioned) Jewish king in Jerusalem, who will gather in the exiles, establish a state governed by the Torah, and rebuild the Temple. For Christians, Jesus is different from, and a good deal more than, that; he is also believed to be divine. He is mainly acknowledged as the incarnate Son of God, the second person of the Trinity. His messiahhood, for Christians, has now been postponed to the Second Coming, when Christians believe he will rule on earth as Christ the King (see John 18:36). In Jewish belief, on the other hand, Jesus was not the Messiah precisely because he did not bring about the full restoration of the Jewish people to the Land of Israel and God's universal reign of peace.

The real issue that now separates Jews and Christians is not messiahhood but the Incarnation and the Trinity. Unlike the issue of messiahhood, which arose when Jews and Christians were members of the same religio-political community and spoke the same conceptual language, the issues of the Incarnation and the Trinity divide people who are no longer members of the same community and who no longer speak the same language. There is no longer any common criterion of truth available for debating, much less resolving, the fundamental differences between Judaism and Christianity.

Once the Church decided that gentile converts no longer had to undergo halakhic conversion to Judaism first (see Acts 15:8-11), it was inevitable that Jews and Christians would separate into two distinct communities. Eventually the Church condemned as "judaizing" any suggestion that Christians could practice Jewish rites in good faith, and contemporary Jewish authorities were equally disapproving of this type of syncretism. Although Christians, in their rejection of the Marcionite heresy (which attempted to sever Christianity from its roots in Judaism), still consider themselves part of the Jewish story *(aggadah),* they do not consider themselves to be subject to Jewish law *(halakhah).* In place of the Jewish commandments *(mitsvot)* came the sacraments, which are like the Jewish commandments in that they are structured by their own law (what became the canon law of the Church). This legal separation enabled the Church to evolve from a Jewish sect into a fully independent religious community. Gradually, many Jewish authorities came to look upon the now independent Christian Church as an essentially gentile community, but one uniquely related to Judaism because of its acceptance of Jewish Scripture as authoritative in some basic matters of faith and morals.

Today's Jewish Christians, then, are not a simple throwback to the first Jewish Christians. They can, rather, be more closely compared to the Jewish Christian syncretists of the second and third centuries. But neither normative Judaism nor normative Christianity has been willing to tolerate such syncretism. Both communities have seen it as a type of error that is inconsistent with the independence of each of them.

The important thing to remember when dealing with the issue of the Jewish Christians is that according to normative Judaism, they are still Jews. Jewish status is defined by the divine election of Israel and his descendants. One does not become a Jew by one's own volition. Even in the case of converts to Judaism (whose number is increasing today), they are not "Jews by choice," as some would erroneously call them. A gentile's choice to become a Jew is a necessary but not sufficient condition of conversion. No conversion is valid without the express consent of the convert, to be sure, but the convert's choice is not sufficient to make him or her a Jew: it only makes one a *candidate* for conversion. The actual conversion itself is the act of an authoritative Jewish tribunal who, in effect, *elect* the candidate before them, as God elects Israel and his descendants. Like God, the tribunal is under no compulsion to elect, which is to say convert, anyone.

Since Jews are elected by God, there is absolutely nothing any Jew can do to remove himself or herself from the Covenant. The rule concerning individual apostates is based on a talmudic judgment about the Jewish people as a whole: "Even when it has sinned, Israel is still Israel."[1] No one who accepts the authority of normative Judaism can rule that Jewish Christians are not Jews. What they can and do rule, however, is that the Christhood (incarnational/trinitarian status) of Jesus of Nazareth is not an option within God's everlasting Covenant with the people of Israel. Jewish Christians are still Jews, but they are no longer practicing a religion Jews regard as part of Judaism.

Why is Christianity not a legitimate covenantal option for Jews? There are two ways to answer the question.

One way might be termed exegetical. This had a complex development in ancient and medieval times, and it frequently reappears in modern times in encounters between Jewish fundamentalists and their Christian counterparts. Here Jews invoke Jewish Scripture because it is accepted as authoritative by Christians too as their "Old Testament." Through exegesis of commonly acknowledged Scripture, Jews have tried to show that the

---

1. *B. Talmud:* Sanhedrin 44a.

messiahhood of Jesus is invalid according to scriptural criteria, and that the Christian doctrines of the Incarnation and the Trinity have no true foundation in Scripture at all. Of course, through their own exegesis, Christians have tried to show that the contrary position is validated by Scripture. Frequently, the most intense exegetical disputations between Jews and Christians have involved the very same scriptural passages. Just think of how much ink has been spilled over the issue whether Isaiah 7:14 should be interpreted "behold the young woman [ha'almah] shall conceive and bear a son" (the Jewish version), or "behold the virgin [hē parthenos] shall conceive and bear a son" (the Christian version). Nevertheless, one can conclude from studying the long history of these Jewish-Christian exegetical disputations that they have largely been exercises in futility, convincing only the already convinced.

The reason for the inconclusiveness of this exegetical method of argumentation is not difficult to find. Modern Jewish and Christian scholars have alike come to the understanding that scriptural exegesis is much more a process whereby the teachings of the tradition of a religious community (what Jews call *Oral Torah* and Catholics call the *magisterium*) are *connected to* Scripture than it is one in which these teachings are simply *derived from* Scripture in some unproblematic fashion. Thus it is that Jews and Christians can read a common text so differently and therefore cannot resolve their differences by appealing to the authority of Scripture. The commonality between Judaism and Christianity can be affirmed and developed only in those areas where our respective traditions do indeed overlap. But on the whole question of who Jesus is, they do not overlap. All our divergences pale in comparison to this one fundamental difference. Many Jews — I among them — and many Christians now believe that this fundamental difference will remain until God's final redemption of the world at the end of history.

Since Jews and Christians are still *within* history rather than at its end, the best approach to the question as to why Christianity is not a legitimate covenantal option for Jews is historical rather than exegetical.

From the fact that the first generation of Christians were mostly Jewish ("according to the flesh," as Paul put it in Romans 4:1), one could argue that Christianity was *at that time* a form of Judaism, perhaps even a heterodox form of pharisaic Judaism. (There is a voluminous scholarly literature on this subject by both Christian and Jewish scholars.) However, it is clear from the historical record that in the succeeding generations, the Church became a predominantly gentile community. This was because gentile converts to Christianity were no longer required to convert to Judaism by following the halakhic prescriptions of circumcision and acceptance of all the commandments of the Torah *and Jewish tradition.* (The halakhic requirement of immersion was adapted by the Church into the requirement of Baptism.) The descendants of the original Jewish Christians quickly became gentiles themselves through intermarriage with gentile Christians in the Church.

Had the Church decided otherwise, that is, had it chosen what might be called the "halakhic" Christianity of the "pharisaic Christians" mentioned in Acts 15:5, it is conceivable that the whole Jewish-Christian relationship might well have developed altogether differently than it did. However, history cannot be erased (not, at least, by human creatures). The choice of the Church has been to be a gentile community according to the flesh — even though it sincerely claims to be grafted onto Israel according to the spirit (Rom. 11:21), a point with which many Jews could basically agree. This historical choice led Jews subsequently to identify the different doctrines and practices of this now gentile community as doctrines and practices prohibited to Jews.

The refusal of the Supreme Court of the State of Israel in 1989 to grant Jerry and Shirley Beresford Israeli citizenship *as Jews,* and its insistence that they could become Israeli citizens only *as Christians* (who are eligible for Israeli citizenship, too), is the decision of a secular court in a secular state. Nevertheless, there were two opinions in the case. In practice, both opinions ruled against the petition of the Beresfords as the Court had ruled against the petition of Brother Daniel in 1962. But in theory, the two opinions are quite distinct. This distinction has important theological implications.

The minority opinion based its conclusion on what might be called "ordinary language" criteria, that is, the theory that says that the meaning of terms is determined by the way they are currently used in ordinary conversation, not by the way they are defined in learned texts. By this criterion, the minority opinion based itself on the fact that in ordinary language Jews and Christians are considered to be two separate groups, that one cannot simultaneously be a member of both communities. If one were to ask the proverbial "man in the street" if a Christian could also be a Jew, or a Jew also a Christian, the answer would surely be a simple "no."

The Court's majority opinion, on the other hand, did base itself on Jewish tradition, "following the language of the Torah, not the ordinary language of humans," as the Talmud puts it. The exclusion of the Beresfords from Jewish status in the State of Israel is based on the tradi-

tional power of the authorities of the Jewish community to exclude those
considered apostates from many of the privileges of the community.
Thus, for example, apostates are to be excluded from the privilege of being called to the reading of the Torah in the synagogue, or even to be
counted in the quorum of ten *(minyan)* required for a full synagogue service to be conducted. The apostate is still a Jew; no human court can
change that fact. But the apostate is excluded from communion with the
normative Jewish community *(keneset yisrael)*.

I purposely use the term "communion" because Christians, especially
Catholic Christians, can recognize the same process in "excommunication." Since Catholics regard baptism to be indelible, no one is ever totally
removed from the body of the Church. Excommunication means that because of serious mortal sin — such as apostasy — someone is not allowed
the privilege of receiving communion, that is, participating in the Eucha-
rist. Proper repentance can lead to the removal of the ban of excommunication. No doubt a Catholic who converted to Judaism would be subject
to such excommunication. This does not mean that the Church is denying its roots in Judaism. It simply means that it does not regard Judaism
to be a legitimate type of Christianity, a point with which very few Jews
would disagree. Similarly, by regarding the Jewish convert to Christianity
as an apostate does not mean that Judaism is denying that Christianity is
uniquely connected to it. It simply means that it does not regard Christianity to be a legitimate type of Judaism, but rather regards it as an independent religious community in its own right, a point with which very
few Christians would disagree.

The question of why Jewish authorities are harder on Jewish Christians than on Jewish atheists is one that Jewish theologians must answer.
Christian anger about what might appear to be a double standard would
otherwise be entirely understandable.

In a purely religious context, such as a synagogue service, for example,
a professed Jewish atheist has no more right to be a participant than a
professed Christian. By "participant" I mean one capable of being
counted in the quorum of ten and being called to the reading of the Torah. Anyone, of course, may attend a synagogue service. Anyone may attend a church service, but not everyone may receive communion. Practically speaking, there is little likelihood that a professed Jewish atheist of
any moral integrity would want to participate in a *religious* service. Until
quite recently, there was equally little likelihood that a professed Christian, of whatever origins, would want to participate in a *Jewish* religious
service. At present, however, there are certain Jewish Christians who re-

gard themselves as Jews — even religious Jews — who do want to participate in Jewish religious services. Whereas Jewish atheists do not regard
their atheism as a Jewish *religious* option, some Jewish Christians do regard their Christianity as such an option. Since there is a greater possibility for confusion regarding Jewish Christians than Jewish atheists, Jewish
authorities have to be harder on Jewish Christians. Considering the claim
of many Christians throughout history to be the "true Israel" *(verus Israel)*
— a claim made by no other religious community — strong Jewish reaction
to Jewish Christians who seem to be repeating that claim, one so offensive
to Jews, should come as no real surprise.

Another reason why Jewish Christians are to be treated more severely
than Jewish atheists is that, despite all their protestations to the contrary,
Jewish Christians have joined *another,* non-Jewish, community, and Jewish
atheists have not. (A distinction has to be made here between doctrinaire
Jewish atheists and the many secularized Jews who may not act on, but
nevertheless have not explicitly renounced, Jewish religious belief and
practice.) This basic point was an integral part of the Israeli Supreme
Court's decision to deny the Beresfords citizenship as Jews. Here again,
historical experience as much as theological-legal definition played a key
role. For non-fundamentalists, moreover, history and theology and law
are integrally related.

Jewish Christians, then, pose unique problems of one kind for Judaism and unique problems of another for the Church. In addition, they
pose problems for the cause of a new, improved Jewish-Christian relationship. I am not asking Christians to reject them, or even to question
the sincerity of their belief that their form of Jewish Christianity is not a
figment of their imaginations. (For this reason, I did not see it to be my
business as a Jew to join some other Jews who protested Pope John
Paul II's beatification of the Jewish Christian Edith Stein. When the
Church accepted Edith Stein as a convert, she became a member of its religious community. I mourn her death along with the deaths of all the
victims of Nazi idolatry, Jewish or gentile.) But as one who has worked
long and hard for the progress of this new, improved relationship — especially on the theological level — I do ask Christians to regard the Jewish
Christians who claim to be practicing Judaism as an exception rather
than the rule. To see them as a unique link between the Jewish people
and the Church, and to expect faithful Jews to concur in that judgment,
asks too much of us.

In our open society, there are going to be Jews who become Christians
for religious reasons just as there are going to be Christians who become

Jews for religious reasons. But these great existential decisions are not meant to be cost-free. In any religious conversion, something is gained and something lost.[2] I believe at the end of time God will show each one of us whether the gain or the loss is greater in the ways we chose to listen to His voice.

2. B. *Talmud:* Yevamot 47a-b; Matt. 10:34-39.

Theology and Philosophy:
An Exchange with Robert Jenson

My friendship with Robert Jenson over the past twelve years or so has been a blessing in my life and a benefit to my own work as a Jewish theologian. The blessing and the benefit are inextricably mixed in that Jenson's theology is very much the work of "Jens" the man, and that "Jens" is the man he is in large part because of the theology of Jenson the Christian theologian. This has been acutely brought to mind in reading volume one of his *Systematic Theology: The Triune God.* It is truly a systematic presentation of many insights his friends have been hearing over the years in conversations both official and spontaneous. Accordingly, reading the book is not so much déjà vu as it is a chance once more to pick up a conversation with Jens that has never really ended since it deals with those matters which, in traditional Jewish parlance, "stand at the height of the very cosmos."

From my perspective, the conversation with Jens has been so good not only because of Jens's great intelligence and deeply engaging personality but much more so because the conversation has been essentially theological, even when we are only engaging in "small talk." What could be of greater importance to theologians than theology? Perhaps more than any other discipline, theology calls for the passion of its practitioners. Theology has provided our conversation enough commonality to make it possible. Furthermore, that theological commonality is not just about any

Parts of this essay were first presented at the Dulles Colloquium, an ongoing forum of the Institute of Religion and Public Life in New York, which includes Catholic, evangelical, and Jewish theologians, and in which Robert Jenson and I have been colleagues from its inception. This essay appeared subsequently in *Trinity, Time, and Church: A Response to the Theology of Robert W. Jenson,* ed. Colin E. Gunton (Grand Rapids: Eerdmans, 2000), pp. 42-61.

"god" (the *theos* in "theology") — a point we would have in common with "theists" outside Judaism or Christianity — it is about the Lord (YHWH), who has named himself as "the God of Abraham, the God of Isaac, and the God of Jacob" (Exod. 3:15).

Theology also provides enough of a difference to make our conversation a genuine dialogue and not an antiphonal monologue. The theological difference is that as a Christian and a Jew, Jens and I are existentially dedicated to faith assertions (i.e., willing to die for them if need be) about the truest relationship with God available in this world, which are undeniably not just distinctive but mutually exclusive head-on. Which is the best way to and from the Lord God of Israel: the Torah or Christ? (Conversely, Jews, Christians, and Muslims commonly worship the God of Abraham, but that commonality is not nearly as specific and concrete as the common Jewish-Christian worship of the Lord God of Israel since it is not made over the proper interpretation of the same Scripture and does not involve a dispute over the nature of the community covenanted with this God.)[1]

A further commonality between Jens and myself is that we are both theologians in regular touch with philosophy; indeed, we could not do our work without that contact. This point of contact, both with each other and with the philosophers, is where I would like to conduct this exchange with Jens. Yet instead of directly commenting on Jens's thoughts on the relation of theology and philosophy, I would like to present some of my own thoughts on the subject and intersperse them with some of Jens's thoughts. My thoughts will have a necessarily Jewish cast to them. As Jens's great teacher Karl Barth said somewhere, "I cannot see with eyes other than my own." Hopefully, this exchange will give readers of this volume a sense of the flavor of our ongoing conversation that, God willing, will continue for many years to come. If nothing else, it might give readers a sense of what I have learned from Jens and with Jens over the years. (In this paper, when his written work is being formally cited, he is called "Jenson.")

Of late, some Jewish thinkers have attempted to designate themselves "Jewish philosophers" who are engaged in a discipline called "Jewish philosophy." It is even suggested that Jews "do Jewish philosophy" whereas

---

1. For the view that Judaism has more in common with Islam than with Christianity because of monotheism, see L. E. Goodman, *God of Abraham* (New York: Oxford University Press, 1996), pp. 34-35. This is a question that has been debated ever since the early Middle Ages.

Christians "do Christian theology." As I shall argue here, however, there is no discipline of "Jewish philosophy," that is, one that can be cogently defined, even though it is used now more than ever. I do believe, however, that there is a discipline of "Jewish theology," which has enough concerns in common with Christian theology for them both to be called "theology." There is also a discipline of "philosophy," which functions independently of theology. As such, I think the term "Jewish philosophy" only makes sense when it speaks of the relation of Judaism *and* philosophy in much the same way "Christian philosophy" speaks of the relation of Christianity *and* philosophy. The question is whether this relation is a positive correlation or a negative dissonance.

Most modern philosophers, having a decided prejudice against any theology, especially when it is Jewish or Christian, would accordingly ask: Aren't philosophy and theology antithetical? Isn't philosophy the product of reason, which can be universally validated? Isn't theology the product of faith, whose validation comes from a revelation to a particular historical community, and which is preserved by their tradition?

Since it is assumed by most philosophers, following Plato, that the universal should fully include the particular, whereas the particular cannot include the universal, it would seem that any interrelation of philosophy and theology would have to be on philosophy's terms.[2] That is how, most impressively, Hegel interrelated the two in his "philosophy of religion," which in effect was his "philosophical religion."[3] This is where philosophy has presented itself as metaphysics, whereby it attempts to subsume theology into its own operations by denying theology its own foundations in revelation and thereby substituting its own, supposedly more universal, foundations for them. Of course, no self-respecting theologian could possibly accept that since no faithful Jew or Christian could accept such theological surrender. The Lord God of Israel does not tolerate a pantheon, let alone a pantheon in which He is subordinate to a larger "divine" order, even if it is a pantheon where He is the first person. He is very much a jealous God, before whom no other gods may be acknowledged, even secondarily.[4]

The way to counter this type of philosophical capture of revelation

2. Nevertheless, Plato had to admit the universal never does include all particulars; see *Timaeus,* 49D-E.

3. See G. W. F. Hegel, *Lectures on the Philosophy of Religion,* trans. R. F. Brown, P. C. Hodgson, and J. M. Stewart (Berkeley: University of California Press, 1988), pp. 401-2.

4. See *Mekilta de-Rabbi Ishmael,* de-ba-Hodesh, chap. 8 on Exod. 20:3, vol. 2, trans. J. Z. Lauterbach (Philadelphia: Jewish Publication Society of America, 1934), pp. 262-63.

(about which theology speaks) is to deny the universal claims of philosophy as metaphysics. As Robert Jenson writes, "The West's Mediterranean-pagan religious heritage — truly no more anchored in universal humanity than any other — was elevated to be the judge of its biblical heritage."[5] Soon thereafter, he notes that "Greek philosophy was simply the theology of the historically particular Olympian-Parmenidean religion, later shared with the wider Mediterranean cultic world" (*ST* I, 10). Thus, he makes the point, "what must not continue is only the Enlightenment's elevation of the Greek element of our thinking to be the unilateral judge of the whole" (*ST* I, 9). What I learn from this is that the question between philosophy and theology is not which is more universal and which is more particular. At the ontological level, both philosophy and theology are universal inasmuch as they both make assertions about the entire cosmos. Both are also particular inasmuch as they both stem from the constructions of cosmic reality by particular cultures, cultures that locate their origins in a revelation given to them. Each, then, is universal in principle, but particular in fact.[6]

At this level, it would seem that theology, which is more explicit about its roots in a revelation than is philosophy, has a decided edge. That is because a devotion to the truth that characterizes metaphysics can hardly be separated from the sociality that is essential to human nature. The religions of revelation — Judaism, Christianity, and Islam — have ontologically constituted coherent communities, which have locations in space and duration in time (traditions). Greek religion's enunciation as philosophy can now claim only scattered individual adherents. That might well explain why in the West it has been easier for theologians to incorporate philosophy into their work than it has been for philosophers to incorporate theology into their work. This itself is an aspect of the way the religions of revelation all accept converts, who themselves were previously pagan. Even though, for Jews and Christians, conversion is being "born again," these former pagans are encouraged to bring the best of their former culture with them into the new religion.[7] Indeed, some theologians see the best of the pagan culture as the basis for seeking the revelation of the (for them) new God of Israel. The search for the unknown God there can lead to the God who begins to make Himself known here and now.

5. Jenson, *Systematic Theology*, vol. I: *The Triune God* (Oxford: Oxford University Press, 1997), p. 8. Hereafter abbreviated *ST*, by volume and page. Italics in quotations are Jenson's.

6. Along these lines, see Alasdair MacIntyre, *Whose Justice? Which Rationality?* (Notre Dame: University of Notre Dame Press, 1987), chap. 1.

7. See *Babylonian Talmud* (hereafter "B."): Yevamot, 22a. Cf. John 3:3-7.

My assumption that there is such a discipline as "Jewish theology" has hardly gone unchallenged, however. There are many who would question its possibility, let alone its cogent presence. For them, following Baruch Spinoza, Moses Mendelssohn, and, especially, Immanuel Kant, Judaism is essentially law.[8] However, despite all its obviously legal content, doesn't Judaism claim that its law is the law of God? Isn't the very assertion of a "law of God" a theological assertion? Certainly, the legal claims of Judaism *(halakhah)* rest squarely on theological foundations. Furthermore, these theological foundations not only undergird the Jewish legal system, they permeate it as well, especially in discussions of the "reasons of the commandments" *(ta'amei ha-mitsvot)*. As for the nonlegal aspects of Judaism known as *aggadah* (literally, "narrative"), a good part of it consists of "God-talk," which is the literal definition of *theo-logy*. Thus the separation of law and theology in Judaism is formal not substantial. One could look upon *halakhah* as the practical pole of Judaism, *aggadah* as the theoretical pole, and the Jewish life of the commandments *(mitsvot)* as being conducted within these two poles. Sometimes that life is closer to one, sometimes it is closer to the other, but never is it so close to one that the other can be totally ignored.[9] In the area of esoteric Jewish thought known as Kabbalah, God-talk is ubiquitous; there is nothing else there.

Jewish theology is possible for any kind of Jewish thought that is not legalistic per se, that is, Jewish thought concerned with the ontological origins of Judaism. Jewish theology can engage philosophy when it can recognize the phenomenological independence of the world, since philosophy comes from the world. Revelation, conversely, comes to the world.[10] As we have also seen, however, especially as taught to us by Jenson, theology cannot be systematically connected, with integrity, to any metaphysics a priori. The most it can do ontologically is to selectively incorporate some insights of philosophically constituted metaphysics that help explicate points already found in the theological tradition itself. That is inevitable since, as Jenson notes, "Theologians of Western Christianity [one could just as easily say "Western Judaism"] must indeed converse with the philosophers because and insofar as both are engaged in the same sort of exercise" (*ST* I, 10). Thus Jenson speaks of

---

8. For a critique of this view, whether held by non-Jews or by Jews themselves, see Abraham Joshua Heschel, *God in Search of Man* (New York: Farrar, Straus & Cudahy, 1955), pp. 320-35.

9. See David Novak, *Law and Theology in Judaism*, vol. 1 (New York: KTAV, 1974), chap. 1.

10. That is why the denial of the dogma "the Torah is from God" has been designated the first Jewish heresy. See *Mishnah: Sanhedrin* 10.1.

the theological error of "finding the 'right' metaphysics among those offered by officially designated philosophers" (*ST* I, 21). He notes in this regard that, contrary to the usual designation of Thomas Aquinas as an "Aristotelian," this is "exactly what Thomas did not do. He *conversed* with Aristotle, and in the conversations was stimulated and helped to his own metaphysical positions" (*ST* I, 21). Among Jewish theologians, one could say the same about Philo in relation to Plato, or Maimonides in relation to Aristotle, or Franz Rosenzweig in relation to Hegel, or Abraham Joshua Heschel in relation to Max Scheler.

It would seem, then, that the best a Jewish or Christian theologian can do with religious integrity is to *use* philosophical methods to better understand Judaism or Christianity. However, it must always be explicit that Judaism or Christianity is the irreducible datum present (best named by the German *das Urphaenomen*). This is, of course, the function of philosophy when taken to be the "handmaiden of theology" *(ancilla theologiae),* a concept that was a staple of medieval theology.[11] One can see this use of philosophical method when Jewish theology is called "a philosophy of Judaism." Indeed, this was how one of the greatest Jewish theologians of the twentieth century, my late revered teacher Abraham Joshua Heschel, subtitled his central work, *God in Search of Man.* Heschel seemed rather unconcerned with there being any real distinction between a philosophy *of* Judaism and Jewish theology per se. In fact, he also called his own philosophy of Judaism presented in this same book "depth theology."[12] In using the word "depth," Heschel wanted to distinguish his foundational approach from a kind of dogmatism that takes the theological statements of the past and treats them as if they were legally mandated norms simply to be clarified and applied rather than to be critically examined in the light of the entire phenomenon of revelation and the subsequent tradition that preserves its content.

This seeming reduction of Jewish philosophy to philosophy of Judaism and hence to Jewish theology does raise an important question for philosophers. Just why does any philosopher choose to direct his or her own attention and interest (what is called *Sorge* in German) to one phenomenon rather than to another? The notion of a philosophy *of* anything presupposes that philosophy itself does not provide its own object for itself but,

11. For the history of this concept, see H. A. Wolfson, *Philo,* vol. 1 (Cambridge, Mass.: Harvard University Press, 1947), pp. 145-47.

12. Heschel, *God in Search of Man,* pp. 7-8.

rather, that philosophy is a method for understanding the phenomenon already there before one. Philosophers will quickly recognize such a presupposition as that of phenomenology.

As Plato had Parmenides point out to Socrates, and as his critics pointed out to Edmund Husserl, just *any* phenomenon will not do.[13] For a philosopher to be able to truly, that is, philosophically, sustain his or her attention and interest in the object before him or her, that object has to be supremely worthy of such profound attention and interest. Yet if a philosopher accepts this great challenge, then isn't he or she veering very close to theology? Theologians explicitly deal with an object whose very name must minimally mean "that than which nothing greater can be conceived."[14] If the philosophical quest for the highest truth intends an object of *ultimate concern,* to use the term employed most famously by Paul Tillich, doesn't that object immediately mean the object theologians designate "God"?[15] Could anyone be ultimately concerned with anything else?

This applies to the God of Abraham, Isaac, and Jacob as well as it applies to the God of Aristotle (the "God of the philosophers" par excellence, to borrow from Blaise Pascal). Weren't Aristotle and Hegel, to cite two God-centered philosophers, in effect functioning as theologians? Isn't Aristotle's metaphysics a type of Greek theology, and isn't Hegel's metaphysics modeled after Aristotle's, albeit with a large detour through a certain type of scholastic theology?[16] Could either thinker have discovered the "God" of whom they respectively speak if they had not uttered a name they had already heard and which their hearers and readers had already heard? Wasn't René Descartes right when he insisted that the very notion of God as absolute had to have been presented to the mind rather

13. See Plato, *Parmenides,* 130B-D; Martin Heidegger, *Being and Time,* trans. J. Stambaugh (Albany, N.Y.: SUNY Press, 1996), pp. 32-34 (sec. 7).

14. See Karl Barth, *Anselm: Fides Quaerens Intellectum,* trans. I. W. Robertson (London: SCM Press, 1960), pp. 74-75.

15. See Tillich, *Systematic Theology,* vol. 1 (Chicago: University of Chicago Press, 1951), pp. 12-14; also, Thomas Aquinas, *Summa Theologiae* 1, q. 2, a. 3.

16. See G. W. F. Hegel, *Phenomenology of Spirit,* trans. A. V. Miller (Oxford: Oxford University Press, 1977), p. 12 (preface). Let it not be forgotten how Aristotle begins his discussion about God as the supreme cosmic *telos,* "thought thinking thought," namely, "A tradition has been handed down *[paradidotai]* by the ancient thinkers of very early times, and bequeathed to posterity in the form of a myth, . . . that the heavenly bodies are gods and that the Divine *[to theion]* pervades the whole of nature" (*Metaphysics,* 1074b1-3, trans. H. Tredennick [Cambridge, Mass.: Harvard University Press, 1935], pp. 162-63. See also Plato, *Laws,* 966E-967A.

than be taken as something constructed by it, even if he wrongly assumed that this notion need not be mediated by a specific historical tradition?[17] Could Aristotle and Hegel have truly invented the God each constituted philosophically? Didn't they differ from the theologians of their own *polis,* Aristotle from those in Athens and Hegel from those in Berlin, only by virtue of the fact that their respective theologies are more coherent and more comprehensive than those of their fellow theologians, those having less intelligence and imagination than they? (In this sense, Kant to my mind was more radical theologically than either Aristotle or Hegel since he constituted a God who is clearly not the absolute.[18] With Kant as with Alfred North Whitehead, we are back to a demiurge like that of Plato, that is, a god who mediates between the ultimate and what lies below it.)[19] When metaphysics forgets its theological origins, does it not in effect assume all the pitfalls Ludwig Wittgenstein saw in any "private language," which is a language in which the current speaker presents himself or herself as the first speaker, the founder of his or her own speech acts?[20]

Ontology (of which "metaphysics" is but one kind) always veers so close to theology that it becomes in the end a more articulate form of some theology or other. The challenge, then, to philosophers unwilling to make such ontological commitments is just what is distinctive about what they are doing. Thus, for example, what distinguishes a philosopher of law from a methodologically reflective jurist, or a philosopher of science from a methodologically reflective scientist, or a biomedical ethicist (most of whom now see themselves as philosophers) from a methodologically reflective physician, or a philosopher of language from a methodologically reflective linguist? In other words, what distinguishes philosophy from *Weltanschauung,* as Hegel asked?[21] The very refusal to deal with

17. Descartes, *Meditations* 3, trans. A. Wollaston (Baltimore: Penguin Books, 1960), p. 127.

18. For the attempt to overcome Kant's inadequate notion of God by a Jewish philosopher most heavily influenced by Kant, see Hermann Cohen, *Ethik des reinen Willens,* 4th ed. (Berlin: Bruno Cassirer, 1923), pp. 455-70; also, David Novak, *The Election of Israel: The Idea of the Chosen People* (Cambridge: Cambridge University Press, 1995), pp. 54-64.

19. See A. N. Whitehead, *Process and Reality* (New York: Macmillan, 1929), p. 112. Cf. Plato, *Timaeus,* 29E-30D. For an attempt to constitute *Transzendenz* as what is beyond God, which also represents a Platonic-like theology, see Karl Jaspers, *Philosophy,* vol. 1, trans. E. B. Ashton (Chicago: University of Chicago Press, 1969), pp. 87-89.

20. See Ludwig Wittgenstein, *Philosophical Investigations,* 2d ed., trans. G. E. M. Anscombe (New York: Macmillan, 1958), pp. 88-89 (1.240-46).

21. See Hegel, *Phenomenology of Spirit,* pp. 41-42 (preface); also, Emil L. Fackenheim, *The Religious Dimension in Hegel's Thought* (London and Bloomington: Indiana University Press, 1967), pp. 16-17.

this question, it seems to me, constitutes the very positivism that Plato so well saw as the death knell of philosophy itself.[22] (Let it be remembered that Plato sought to reform Greek theology from within, not to eliminate it altogether.)[23] This is also a challenge made to philosophy by Pope John Paul II in his recent encyclical, *Fides et Ratio,* where he warns how trivial, even insipid, philosophy becomes when it loses its historical contact with theology.[24] Here again, Jenson's point about the earliest philosophers having been theologians themselves is most apt.[25]

So, is there a relation between philosophy and theology? The question assumes that there is enough that distinguishes the two for such a relation to be possible. However, is there a relation that does not reduce theology to philosophy or philosophy to theology? Haven't both reductions failed?

Let me suggest that there is a third model, which can be presented as preferable to the two that I have been examining above. I would call this model "philosophical theology," or more accurately, "philosophically informed theology." One can well think of Robert Jenson as a model practitioner of this kind of philosophically informed theology in his own work.

To assume that there can be a *philosophical* theology also assumes that the word "philosophical" functions as an adjective modifying the noun "theology." This also implies that there are other forms of theology that are minimally nonphilosophical, and maximally antiphilosophical. What, then, distinguishes philosophical theology from nonphilosophical theology? I propose that the difference between philosophical and nonphilosophical theology lies in the theological constitution of the world. By "the world" I mean that which appears outside the realm of revelation.

---

22. See Plato, *Republic,* 511B-C.

23. See Plato, *Republic,* 379A-E.

24. See *Fides et Ratio* (London: SCM Press, 2002), chap. 5.

25. The late Leo Strauss (d. 1973) made much of the chasm between philosophy and theology, insisting that philosophers do not accept arguments from traditional authority as theologians do. However, Strauss cites as his main sources Plato and Aristotle, both of whom were theologians. See Strauss, *Natural Right and History* (Chicago: University of Chicago Press, 1953), chap. 3. For a critique of Strauss's attempt to make philosophy ahistorical, see Hans-Georg Gadamer, *Truth and Method,* trans. G. Barden and J. Cumming (New York: Crossroad, 1982), pp. 482-90. Perhaps, contra Strauss, one can say that just as Augustine and Anselm could propose *credo ut intelligam* as a way of directly apprehending revealed truth *after* having indirectly received it through tradition and its authority, so Plato and Aristotle were attempting to do the same with what had been revealed to Greek culture by their gods. See Plato, *Republic,* 499B; *Laws,* 747E. Cf. Augustine, *De Libero Arbitrio,* 2.2.5-6 re Isa. 7:9; also, Novak, *Law and Theology in Judaism,* chap. 15.

In Judaism, this difference has most often been located in the question of creation. Creation both precedes revelation in time (it happened first) and exceeds revelation in space (it happens to everything). Jenson explains this quite clearly when he writes, "Israel knew that her beginning had a date within history, and thus Israel acknowledged a history of humankind and of her God before there was an Israel. Therefore Israel had . . . to acknowledge a Creation not identical with her own origin" (*ST* I, 48). (Hence creation and revelation are only finally reconciled in redemption, a point most insightfully made and theologically developed among Jewish thinkers by Franz Rosenzweig.)[26]

To follow this line of thought, it might be well to infer the positive from the negative, that is, to begin by looking at what could be considered *the* most antiphilosophical Jewish theology possible: Kabbalah. I say that Kabbalah is not just nonphilosophical but antiphilosophical because, as Gershom Scholem suggested in many of his great historical studies, Kabbalah very much involves the rejection of the philosophical theology of earlier Jewish theologians like Saadiah and Maimonides.[27] A main point that distinguishes this new theology from the older theology is the prominence of the doctrine of creation in the older theology and its near absence in the newer theology. In Kabbalah, God's relation to the world is not through creation *(beri'ah)* but, rather, through *atsilut* (literally, "approximation"), what we usually call "emanation."[28] The reality and meaning of the world lies totally in its being some aspect or other of the Godhead *(elohut)*. The world is not externally related to the creator God; it is, rather, a mediated participation in the larger substantial reality. Even the most mundane aspects of the world are taken to be symbolic manifestations *(sefirot)* of the one and only reality, which is divine. Such a radically panentheistic theology becomes just as radically acosmic.

Whereas in pantheism God and the world are interchangeable, namely, *deus sive natura,* in kabbalistic theology, unlike Spinoza, there is only *natura naturans* (that is, nature as person); there is no *natura naturata* (that is, nature as a system of distinct entities).[29] True *science* here can only be revealed and received, that is, it must be *kabbalah* (literally, "what has been

---

26. See Rosenzweig, *The Star of Redemption,* trans. W. W. Hallo (New York: Holt, Rinehart & Winston, 1970), pp. 380-92.

27. See Scholem, *Major Trends in Jewish Mysticism* (New York: Schocken Books, 1946), pp. 23-25.

28. See Scholem, *On the Kabbalah and Its Symbolism,* trans. R. Manheim (New York: Schocken Books, 1969), pp. 66-77.

29. Cf. Spinoza, *Ethics* I, prop. 29.

received" and "how it has been received"); hence no truth can be derived from any nonrevealed source. Anything taken to be substantially separate from God, what the kabbalists call "the other side" *(sitra ahra)*, is by definition unintelligible, indeed, demonic.[30] In short, our experience of the world, outside of revelation, in truth has nothing in common with revelation at all. This world is but an illusion.

Both the kabbalists and the philosophical theologians like Saadiah and Maimonides attempted to avoid the type of dualism that characterizes much of what could be called nonphilosophical Jewish theology. Historically speaking, this type of theology is usually prephilosophical, that is, it has been conducted by thinkers who have never been confronted with systematically impressive philosophy. (This turns out to be what the Rabbis called *hokhmah yevanit,* "Greek wisdom.")[31] In this type of theology, the Torah and the world become separate realms, at least as regards the methods formulated to understand each realm. Here, theology simply speaks about its own particular tradition much like the discourse of positive law. Such theology is ontologically naïve. However, such a methodological dualism seems to entail a type of ontological dualism that is ultimately foreign to the Pharisaic project (from which all subsequent Judaisms stem) of bringing the Torah to bear on everything experienced in the world. As the Mishnah states about the Torah, "everything is in it."[32] Thus to avoid this dualism, both epistemological and ontological, the kabbalists see the method for knowing everything and anything, all of which is real only within the life of the Godhead, as being innate within the Torah itself. The Torah for them is not "from God" *(min ha-shamayim)* but is itself the various permutations of the divine name per se.[33] The Torah itself is uncreated since it is essentially divine. There is no external world since there is nothing else to talk about. All relations are inner relations, which makes creation a lesser form of emanation at best.

For the philosophical theologians, conversely, for whom creation is an extradivine event, a transitive, effective act of God, the world that is independent of but related to God must provide its own intelligibility, at least prima facie. Since creation precedes revelation, the method for under-

---

30. See Gershom Scholem, *The Messianic Idea in Judaism* (New York: Schocken Books, 1971), p. 187.

31. For the origin of this term, see B. Baba Kama 83a; also, Saul Lieberman, *Hellenism in Jewish Palestine,* 2d ed. (New York: Jewish Theological Seminary of America, 1962), pp. 100-114.

32. *Mishnah:* Avot 5.22.

33. See Scholem, *On the Kabbalah and Its Symbolism,* pp. 36-45.

standing the Torah itself must come from the world itself. This is so, as Maimonides insisted, because the Torah, like the world, is a creation *by* God.[34] The Torah itself, though, is not divine. Because the Torah is a more specific creation by God than is the world as a whole, the methodology for understanding the more general created entity, the world, must be applied to the understanding of the more specific created entity, the Torah, even if the Torah is taken to be the ultimate form of all creation.[35] As Maimonides (who is inevitably *the* methodological model — even when he is not the ontological model — for every subsequent Jewish philosophical theologian) well put it, "although the Torah itself is not natural [that is, from the world], it enters into nature."[36] One might say, it is *in* the world not *of* it, that is, not *from* it.

In a legal responsum, when he is asked about the liturgical appropriateness of praising God as "the teacher of the Torah *(ha-melamed torah)* to his people Israel," Maimonides rules against it for explicitly theological reasons. (A Jewish version, no doubt, of *lex orandi est lex credendi.)* Although God is the giver of the Torah *(noten ha-torah),* expressed liturgically in a way Maimonides can endorse, it is humans, not God, who teach the Torah to themselves — as they similarly teach themselves about the world that God gives them as the created order.[37] That is why Maimonides and others like him are so fond of the rabbinic dictum "The Torah speaks in human language" *(dibrah torah ke-lashon benei 'adam).*[38] That is, the Torah is given to humans in the world of which they are already part and from which they have already derived their powers of speech and understanding.

This approach, which attempts to learn from philosophy how there is an opening for revelation in the created world, is quite consistent with the whole covenantal thrust of the Jewish tradition. This is especially so with what theologians can learn from political philosophy, which might well be seen as the social construction of reality.

Both the record of Scripture itself and the findings of modern historical-critical scholarship indicate that the primary Jewish polity, the

---

34. See Maimonides, *Guide of the Perplexed,* 1.65.

35. See *Genesis Rabbah* 1.1.

36. Maimonides, *Guide of the Perplexed,* 2.40.

37. Maimonides, *Teshuvot ha-Rambam,* ed. Y. Y. Blau (Jerusalem: Miqitsei Nirdamim, 1960), p. 333 (2, no. 182).

38. See Maimonides, *Guide of the Perplexed,* 1.26. For the much different earlier meaning of this term in rabbinic literature, see J. M. Harris, *How Do We Know This?* (Albany, N.Y.: SUNY Press, 1995), pp. 71-72.

covenant *(berit)*, of which the Torah (biblical and traditional) is the constitution (what in German would be called its *Rechtsordnung*), is not something the Torah itself introduced into the world. It was already present in the world as a form of relationship between a sovereign and his subordinates. These subordinates were given a certain amount of self-rule, which was more for the sake of the relationship *with* the sovereign than it was simply an application of law *from* him. The covenant derives its initial form from what scholars call the "suzerainty treaty."[39] What the Torah introduced to the world socially constructed is a direct relationship in history (hence temporally and spatially finite), one that is located between the creator God and a singular human community. Since the Torah addresses itself to created human nature per se, and since it anticipates God's redemption of the whole world, which is the ultimate reconciliation of God and creation, the covenantal Torah is of cosmic significance.[40] The point of contact with the world and its worldly wisdom — philosophy — is located in the quest for the truth that law per se teaches. Indeed, it is no accident that the translation of the Torah into another language, Greek, rendered the Hebrew *torah* as *nomos.*

Contrary to much misunderstanding, this emphasis of law is not where a Jewish theologian and a Christian theologian like Jenson — especially a Lutheran Christian theologian — have to part theological company and end the discussion as a draw. The question of law is not an antinomy forming an impasse between Jewish theology and Christian theology. The question is not whether or not law is central to the God-human relationship *(quod sit lex?)* but, rather, where is the exact locus of the law of God here and now for the covenant *(quid est lex?)*. Christianity is no more antinomian (that is, without law) than Judaism is legalistic (that is, nothing but law). When Paul saw Christ as superseding "the law" *(ho nomos)*, he meant that Christ himself had superseded the Mosaic law (and its Pharisaic-rabbinic tradition) as the covenantal norm per se.[41] It is to this question, not to a Christian rejection of law per se, that Jews have said no. Moreover, only the parts of that law historically contingent on pre-Christian events have been superseded; the more general theological and moral norms remain authoritative. To assert otherwise would be to succumb to Marcionism, the first heresy the Church had to repudiate.

---

39. See D. R. Hillers, *Covenant* (Baltimore: Johns Hopkins University Press, 1969).

40. See B. Pesaḥim 68b re Jer. 33:25.

41. See Rom. 10:2-4; also, E. P. Sanders, *Paul and Palestinian Judaism* (Philadelphia: Westminster Press, 1977), pp. 550-51.

This point, it seems to me, comes out in Jenson's dispute with his fellow Lutheran theologian, George Lindbeck. Heavily influenced by Ludwig Wittgenstein's later philosophy of language, Lindbeck has proposed that theology is the grammar of the language-form religion.[42] Although accepting the lawlike character of grammar for theology, Jenson criticizes Lindbeck's grammatical definition of theology for two reasons. First, it seems to reduce theology to a descriptive role: tracing what is already there rather than prescribing what is to be. He writes, "If Christian theology is grammar, then it is prescriptive grammar. . . . Secular modernity has supposed that grammar cannot prescribe usage but can only describe it, because secular modernity could acknowledge no one to give the prescriptions. . . . Speakers of Christianese need not share this privation, not having lost their king" (*ST* I, 20). Second, Lindbeck seems to be willing to leave theological grammar at the level of semiotics, that is, internal references within a linguistic field. Yet Jenson insists that "theological propositions seem, however, never actually to appear as pure grammatical rules . . . [they] say something not just about language but also about an extralinguistic entity . . . and the drafters and promulgators of the doctrine would certainly have denied that it could accomplish its grammatical task except just as it has this descriptive force."[43]

These two departures from Lindbeck are very much connected since prescription and "extralinguistic entity" can be correlated. This can be done, I think, by enlisting the help of philosophy, in this case Kant's philosophical notion of the-thing-in-itself *(Ding an sich)*.

Despite the fact that Kant confines all of our knowledge of the world to the conceptualization of our perception of phenomena, he nevertheless posits that behind these phenomena, as it were, there lies an entity that is more than just the subject matter of our phenomenal experience. He posits its existence *(an sit)* but not its essence *(quid est)*. He, moreover, calls this entity *noumenon*, namely, an entity having an intelligibility known to a mind that knows it far more intimately than we humans can with our limited phenomenal equipment.[44] In the realm of theoretical or speculative reason, Kant simply leaves the matter at that existential level. (Thus it is no wonder that post-Kantian philosophers, such as Hegel and Hermann Cohen, who moved in an idealistic direction, sought to eliminate

---

42. Lindbeck, *The Nature of Doctrine* (Philadelphia: Westminster Press, 1984), pp. 79-84.

43. *ST* I, 18. See *ST* I, 19n.45 for his sharpest criticism of Lindbeck, where he says that "Lindbeck may not have shaken off positivist prejudgments."

44. See Kant, *Critique of Pure Reason*, B306-8.

this surd altogether from philosophical consideration.)[45] However, at the level of practical or moral reason, Kant sees the *noumenon* in the self-consciousness of the acting being, the being who can command itself and others by analogy to do the good.[46] Such a being is *autonomous:* it can make law for itself and any other rational being in similar circumstances. Thus unlike theoretical reason, the knower here is a creator, not just a spectator. Really and not just retroactively, this knower knows a priori and not just a posteriori: before the fact and not after it. In this real sense, only a maker can know his own work in advance, that is, when he intends its being.

If one sees Kant's notion of the autonomous moral being as being a colossal deconstruction of the biblical God, namely, the transfer of unique divine attributes to human reason, then it is theologically quite useful to deconstruct his deconstruction and set the world right again.[47] That is, we can restore to talk about God what Kant misplaced in his talk about man. In the case of Jenson's critique of Lindbeck, we can learn from this deconstruction of Kant's deconstruction of traditional Jewish and Christian creation theology and revelation theology. What we can learn is that whereas descriptive grammar cannot carry us to a point where a truly extra-linguistic entity appears, prescriptive grammar can carry us to such a point. How? Prescription itself requires a person behind the commanding voice, *someone* whose will is being enunciated, and someone who cannot be reduced to an internal function of the prescription itself in the way that a cause can be reduced to an internal function of a phenomenal field for Kant.[48] As such, the extralinguistic entity that theological grammar intends is not the being lying *beyond* it as an object like the self-knowing *telos* in Aristotle's metaphysics.[49] Instead, God is the subject who stands *behind* us, whose commandment is addressed to us: the voice from heaven *who* reaches *down* to us on earth. What we know of God is from the command-

---

45. See Hegel, *The Encyclopedia Logic*, trans. T. F. Geraets, W. A. Suchting, and H. S. Harris (Indianapolis and Cambridge: Hackett, 1991), p. 194 (sec. 125); H. Cohen, *Logik der reinen Erkenntnis*, 3rd ed. (Berlin: Bruno Cassirer, 1922), pp. 271, 376-77. This rejection seems to be followed by Edmund Husserl in his notion of "bracketing" *(epochē)* of the question of being; see *Ideas*, trans. W. R. Boyce Gibson (New York and London: Collier, 1962), pp. 99-100 (sec. 32).

46. See Kant, *Groundwork of the Metaphysic of Morals*, trans. H. J. Paton (New York: Harper & Row, 1964), pp. 104-15.

47. See Kant, *Religion within the Limits of Reason Alone*, trans. T. M. Greene and H. H. Hudson (New York: Harper & Brothers, 1960), p. 157 and note.

48. See Kant, *Critique of Pure Reason*, B280.

49. See Aristotle, *Metaphysics*, 1074b1-35.

ments he as prime Subject addresses to us as privileged objects. We do not know God as the supreme Object whom our own subjective consciousness intends and who transcends our own projections because it is more than an ideal. For biblically based Judaism and Christianity, God is the "I" and we are the "thou," not vice versa.[50] Speaking to God about God is possible only because God has spoken to us about Himself first; indeed, it is not only possible, it is necessary for those who listen to God (see *ST* I, 80). As I have heard Jens say on several occasions, "We are involved in a conversation in which God is the first speaker." Any speaker, and certainly the first speaker, by the very act of speaking to us makes a demand that we listen to him. The task of such direct address is to persuade the listeners that what is being proposed is for our own good, that it gives us the objects of our deepest strivings. To acknowledge the extralinguistic character of the commanding voice, a voice that can choose to speak or be silent, is necessary and not arbitrary for us.

The ontological relation of the Torah and the world, which the methodological relation of theology and philosophy enunciates, can be seen on two levels. The one level is the attempt to apply the teaching of the Torah *to* the world in which it is to function. The second level is the attempt to see how the world allows the Torah to enter *into* it, even before it actually transforms it.

At the level of application, the more general the phenomenon being addressed by the Torah, the more appropriate a philosophical perspective becomes in and for that application. Thus in the area of civil and criminal law, for example, where the subject matter is not uniquely Jewish at all, philosophical questions concerning political rights and duties come to the forefront. Because of greater interaction between Jewish and non-Jewish thinkers today, especially when political-ethical questions are at hand, even the normative study of Jewish law is becoming more and more philosophically oriented. Even the discussion of more intimately Jewish matters such as marriage and divorce is involving more and more philosophical reflection on such general issues as embodiment, gender, and reproduction.[51]

Indeed, those Jewish thinkers, especially those Jewish legal scholars

---

50. See Abraham Joshua Heschel, *Man Is Not Alone* (Philadelphia: Jewish Publication Society of America, 1951), pp. 125-29.

51. See, e.g., David Novak, *Jewish Social Ethics* (New York: Oxford University Press, 1992), chap. 4.

who are either nonphilosophical or antiphilosophical, when having to deal with questions of principle over and above questions of specific norms per se, inevitably introduce what can only be designated unexamined prejudices in place of the rigorous examination philosophical reflection entails. Such prejudices almost always boil down to rather crude arguments from personal authority. These prejudices can be faulted on legal grounds, especially that aspect of the law that deals with judicial procedures. Yet it is that aspect of the law that throws one rather quickly into both theological and philosophical questions. The greater worldly involvement of even very traditional Jewish legal scholars (who are now called by the neologism "halakists") inevitably requires that a more philosophical perspective be employed in dealing with many questions of law, which are themselves informed and transformed by this growing worldliness.

At the level of what might be termed presuppositions of theology, the question of the relation of the Torah and the world becomes the question of how the world's self-limitation can make entry of the Torah into it possible — but not necessary. (If it were necessary, then the Torah could be derived from the world itself instead of being brought to it.)[52] This requires what I would call a Kantian-critical move, one conducted methodologically but not one that accepts Kant's ontology.

Kant's project required him to constitute and limit the range of speculative reason in order to make room for the authentic exercise of practical reason, where alone the rational person can be noumenally constituted.[53] Similarly, Jewish and Christian philosophical theology must make close alliances with those philosophies that allow a transcendent horizon for the world and which do not present any rationally constructed totalizing structure in and for the world. In my view, those close alliances, which are always partial and never surrenders, are best formed now with phenomenology and those types of analytic philosophy closest to the concerns of the later Ludwig Wittgenstein.[54]

At the ethical level, the presuppositional status of the world constituted by philosophy takes on great significance. Here the highest ethical

52. See David Novak, *Natural Law in Judaism* (Cambridge: Cambridge University Press, 1998), pp. 142-48.

53. See Kant, *Critique of Pure Reason*, B823-24. This is quite similar to what Heidegger called *Seinlassen*; see *Being and Time*, pp. 78-79 (sec. 18); also, *Kant and the Problem of Metaphysics*, trans. J. S. Churchill (London and Bloomington: Indiana University Press, 1962), pp. 30-31.

54. For this selective use of philosophy, both positively and negatively, see *ST* I, 19, 120-21.

standard philosophy can propose in the world, which is the standard of justice, becomes the *conditio sine qua non* for the proper interpretation of the Torah's norms governing interhuman relationships. This function is best expressed by the talmudic principle "Nothing prohibited to humans in general is permitted to Jews specifically."[55] This principle and its corollaries have provided a powerful critical limit on all sorts of fanatical and chauvinistic interpretations of Jewish law. That has been the case essentially when it has been assumed that what is prohibited to humans in general is determined by human reason's discovery of natural law in the world, namely, the adequacy of *inclinatio rationalis* to *inclinatio naturalis*.

Here is where philosophy is most important to theology, for the discovery of standards of justice in the world involves us in the simultaneous discovery of the worthiness of human nature for justice, however unworthy most human action really is. Only a prior appreciation of the worthiness of human nature, which even human sin cannot destroy, enables us to see why God's address to humankind and God's redemption of humankind are possible for and desirable by human persons. Philosophy at its best helps us to appreciate what our nature is capable of. I hope this is a role for philosophy that is consistent with the great theological project of Robert Jenson.

---

55. B. Sanhedrin 59a.

Are Philosophical Proofs of the Existence of God Theologically Meaningful?

Proofs of the existence of God have comprised the border area between philosophy and theology. They combine philosophy's concern for certainty with theology's concern for God. However, this border status of the proofs has made them troublesome for both philosophers and theologians. Many philosophers have regarded these proofs as asserting too much, as drawing conclusions unsupported by the premises whence they have been drawn. Many theologians have regarded these proofs as asserting too little, as being inadequate to the richness of God who presents Himself in revelation. Yet despite the efforts of some philosophers to deny the philosophical relevance of this question by making it an issue for dogmatic theology, it has, nevertheless, reappeared in contemporary philosophical discussion.[1] On the other hand, despite the efforts of some theologians to deny the theological relevance of this question by making it an issue for scholastic philosophy, it has, nevertheless, reappeared in contemporary theological discourse.[2]

As a theologian, I shall attempt to show in this paper how the three proofs of the existence of God (ontological, teleological, cosmological), outlined by Immanuel Kant in the *Critique of Pure Reason*,[3] are theologi-

1. See, e.g., Norman Malcolm, "Anselm's Ontological Arguments," in *The Existence of God*, ed. John Hick (New York: Macmillan, 1964), pp. 48ff.

2. See, e.g., Hick, *The Existence of God*, pp. 253ff.; Germain Grisez, *Beyond the New Theism: A Philosophy of Religion* (Notre Dame: University of Notre Dame Press, 1975), pp. 36ff.

3. Kant, *Critique of Pure Reason*, B612ff; trans. Norman Kemp Smith (New York: St. Martin's Press, 1929).

This essay previously appeared in *Conservative Judaism* 34 (1980): 12-22 (© the Rabbinical Assembly; reprinted here with permission). It was subsequently reprinted in *God in the Teachings of Conservative Judaism*, ed. Seymour Siegel and Elliot Gertel (New York: Rabbinical Assembly, 1985).

cally meaningful statements if one reinterprets them within the context of theology and abandons the hope that they are or can ever be philosophically convincing. In other words, rejection of the philosophical claims made by some of their proponents does not make these statements about God themselves theologically meaningless.

I have purposely chosen Kant's outline of these three proofs for two reasons. First, his outline has become so commonplace that it is quickly recognizable, even though I use it differently than he did. Second, by using his outline of the proofs, I attempt to answer his charge that they have no necessary connection with our understanding of experience. I shall attempt to show that if one takes revelation to be a distinct type of experience, then the three proofs can be constituted as having a necessary connection with that experience: the ontological proof as a condition and the teleological and cosmological proofs as postulates. To borrow from the Psalmist, "The stone which the builders have rejected has become the cornerstone" (Ps. 118:22).

The Ontological Argument

In order to understand the meaning of a proof of the existence of God, theologically or otherwise, one has to understand what happens when something is "proven."

It would seem that "proof" is either logical or ontological. Logical proof is essentially formal, that is, it does not refer to real referents but, rather, makes such reference possible. Thus Ludwig Wittgenstein noted, "A proposition that has sense states something [*Der sinnvolle Satz sagt etwas aus*], which is shown by its proof [*Beweis*] to be so. In Logic every proposition is the form of a proof."[4] Since proofs of the existence of God all intend a real referent, one cannot classify them as essentially logical.

Ontologically, proof is a type of presentation or re-presentation; that is, a method designed to make an entity which is now absent present. It thus constitutes a relation between a knowing subject and a knowable object. The object should determine the method of presentation. As Martin Heidegger well noted, "Every inquiry is a seeking *[Suchen]*. Every seeking gets guided beforehand by what is sought. Inquiry is a cognizant seeking for an entity both with regard to the fact that it is and with regard to its Being as it is [*in seinem Dass-und Sosein*]."[5]

4. Wittgenstein, *Tractatus Logico-Philosophicus*, 6.1264, trans. D. F. Pears and B. F. McGuinness (London: Routledge, 1961), pp. 130-31 (italics mine). See 2.221, 2.222, 3.142.

5. Heidegger, *Being and Time, Introduction*, 1.2, trans. John Macquarrie and Edward Rob-

Discovery

There are three types of such ontological presentation. The most familiar type of such ontological presentation is empirical discovery. Here an inquiring subject, motivated by curiosity, seeks to discover an object, that is, seeks to make it appear to his senses. Experimentation is the device whereby this discovery is described, that is, made repeatable in public; in a word, *proven*. It should be clear that this type of presentation is meaningless when applied to the presence of God in revelation.

Now some medieval theologians rejected such an empirical approach because it presupposes the corporeality of God, a point they regard as blasphemous.[6] However, this is not where elimination of this empirical model of presentation should begin, because the incorporeality of God is an inference from revelation, not a datum of it. Although in the Torah God makes many statements about Himself — for example, "I am the Lord your God" (Exod. 20:2); "I am the first and I am the last" (Isa. 44:6) — nowhere does He declare "I am incorporeal."[7]

There is a more convincing theological rejection of this type of presentation, namely, it contradicts the dynamism of the relationship between God and man which is *the* datum of revelation. It is a contradiction because it makes God the passive object of discovery and man the active discoverer. In the Torah it is God who seeks man, and it is man who either responds or hides. "And the Lord God called to man and He said, 'Where are you?'" (Gen. 3:9).[8] God is thus the seeking subject, man the responding subject, and neither of them is at all passive. Moreover, the moments of the God/man encounter are unpredictable and do not admit of experimental representation. "Do not hide Your presence from me" (Ps. 27:9). Because of this, one should drop the specific term "proof" when speaking of the religious quest for God. As a mode of ontological presentation it only has meaning in the context of empirical confirmability. The relationship of God and man cannot be constituted in this context. The primary reason for this elimination, then, is not the metaphysical inference that God is incorporeal but, rather, the

---

inson (New York: Harper & Row, 1962), p. 24 = *sein und Zeit*, 15th ed. (Tübingen: Max Niemeyer Verlag, 1979), p. 5.

6. See Maimonides, *Guide of the Perplexed*, 1.55.

7. For this reason Maimonides' chief theological critic, Abraham ben David Posquières, refused to accept his designation of anyone who believed in the incorporeality of God as a heretic. See gloss to *Mishneh Torah*: Repentance 3.7.

8. See Abraham Joshua Heschel, *Man Is Not Alone: A Philosophy of Religion* (New York: Jewish Publication Society, 1951), pp. 125ff.

phenomenological insight that objective passivity cannot be constituted as an essential component of this relationship. Also, both the freedom of God and the freedom of man make the moments of mutual encounter unpredictable events.[9] One relates differently to God than one does to the world. The purely aesthetic appreciation of nature, which is the beginning of scientific observation, is not the beginning of man's response to the revelation of God.

Invention

The Torah itself explicitly rejects from the God/man relationship the second type of ontological presentation, namely, invention. In this type of presentation man *qua homo faber* invents a thing for his own use. The criterion of invention is pragmatic. However, not only can man not invent God, he cannot even invent the method whereby God's presence can be controlled or conjured up. Thus the same logic which is used to reject idolatry, as the substitution of something else for God, is used to reject any attempts to make God's presence controllable by human *technē*. "Behold, the very heavens do not contain You; can this house which I have built?" (1 Kings 8:27).

Personal Communion

It is in the context of the third type of ontological presentation, namely, personal communion, that talk of the God/man relationship is meaningful. In this type of presentation the primary data are persons rather than objects or things, as in the first and second types of presentation respectively. The inappropriate features of the first two types of presentation, namely, passivity, predictability, and manipulation, are absent from this type. Neither God nor man is passive. Their encounters are surprises to man, and although God commands man, that very commandment carries with it a recognition of human freedom and responsibility. In the context of the covenant and the commandments it entails, God does not manipulate man as a thing.[10] Furthermore, although the direct confrontations between God and man are unpredictable events, they are not amorphous. They have

9. My late revered teacher, Prof. Abraham Joshua Heschel, wrote, "An event is a happening that cannot be reduced to a part of a process. It is something we can neither predict nor fully explain. . . . The belief in revelation claims explicitly . . . that a voice of God *enters the world* which pleads with man to do His will." *God in Search of Man: A Philosophy of Judaism* (New York: Farrar, Straus & Cudahy, 1955), p. 210.

10. Maimonides, *Mishneh Torah:* Repentance 5.4.

a structure, and that structure is normative. God's revelation to man makes demands. "I am the Lord your God who brought you out of the land of Egypt . . . you shall have no other gods in My pre.,ence" (Exod. 20:2-3).[11] Moreover, man is given the right to insist that God's authority not function in a capricious, unjust way. "Shall the judge of the whole earth not do justice?" (Gen. 18:25). Now, this being the case, the type of certainty sought in the philosophical proofs of the existence of God is to be found in a satisfactory constitution of God's commanding presence rather than in the constitution of His intelligibility or His accommodation to human *technē*.[12]

At this point we can see how the so-called ontological argument is the necessary condition for the constitution of the authority of God. This argument — if it can be called that anymore than a "proof" — was presented most famously by Anselm, Archbishop of Canterbury, in the form of a prayer. That fact in and of itself should force us to abandon once and for all the designation "proof" or even "argument" for Anselm's quest. Any proof or argument that presupposes what it is trying to prove is nonsense.

Note what Anselm states, "And so, Lord, may You who give understanding to faith, give me, so far as You know it to be profitable, to understand that You are as we believe. . . . And, indeed we believe that You are a being than which nothing greater can be conceived *(aliquid quo maius nihil cogitari non potest)*."[13] Thus we see that the ultimate greatness of God is already accepted by faith's positive response to God's revelation. Understanding then is insight into the necessary conditions of faith. The most necessary condition of faith is that there is no authority beyond God. This ontological condition can only be seen in the direct relationship between God and man in which faith is man's participation. Therefore, at this direct level it would be inappropriate to refer to any other relationship in which either God or man is involved, for reference to any other relationship would bring mediation into that relationship between God and man which is unmediated. Thus, both the teleological argument, which sees God's presence *through* the value of the world, and the cosmological argument, which sees God's presence *through* the structure of the world, must constitute the world before constituting the relationship between God and man.[14] That is why

11. See David Novak, *Law and Theology in Judaism,* vol. 1 (New York: KTAV, 1974), pp. 136ff.

12. See Emil Fackenheim, *God's Presence in History* (New York: New York University Press, 1970), pp. 14-19.

13. *Proslogion,* chap. 2, trans. S. N. Deane, in *The Ontological Argument,* ed. Alvin Plantinga (Garden City, N.Y.: Anchor Books, 1965), pp. 3-4 = *Opera Omnia* I (Seccovi: n.p., 1938), p. 101.

14. "In arguments for the existence of God the world is given and God is sought. Some characteristics of the world make the conclusion 'God' necessary. God is derived from the

Anselm cannot formulate an approach to God which simply reiterates what philosophers have stated before outside the context of revelation and faith. The methodological rigor of his approach might well be philosophical, but the formulation itself must be theological to be authentic.

As a theologian, I can appreciate Anselm's insight better when comparing it with the too easy identification of the philosophical and theological quests made by Thomas Aquinas. Thomas Aquinas, at the beginning of his *Summa Theologiae*, presented five proofs of the existence of God, all based on inferences from our experience of the world. After each of these proofs, he added a remark like, "And this is what we say is God . . . ."[15] However, are any of the five proofs that Aquinas brings truly descriptive of the God to whom the faithful respond? Is not this relationship with God direct because of revelation? In all five proofs, conversely, all of which have philosophical antecedents, the apprehension of God's presence is necessarily subsequent to the constitution of the world. Thus the world mediates between God and man. But revelation, as God's direct presentation to man, must be constituted before God's relationship with man through the world, or His relation to the world itself. If this is not the case, then man's relation to the world will compete with revelation. Either revelation will become an act of knowing in the world, that is, a form of worldly wisdom, or the world will disappear in the face of some sort of *unio mystica* of God and man. Neither alternative, although having its respective adherents in the history of theology (Jewish, Christian, and Islamic), is based on the Torah. Concerning the uniqueness of man's apprehension of God in revelation we read, "Has a people ever heard the voice of God speaking from the midst of fire as you have heard and lived?" (Deut. 4:33). Concerning the reality of the world we read, "Thus says the Lord: the heaven is My throne and the earth My footstool . . . all of these things My hand has made and all of these things have come to be . . ." (Isa. 66:1-2). Anselm's approach, unlike that of Aquinas, avoids these inevitable theological dilemmas.

The theological meaning of Anselm's ontological presentation was best brought out by Karl Barth: "All that the formula says about this object is, as far as I can see, this one thing, this one negative: *nothing greater than it can be imagined that in any respect whatsoever could or would outdo it* . . . It remains to be said: We are dealing with a concept of strict noetic content which Anselm describes here as a concept of God."[16] In other words, Anselm is

---

world." Paul Tillich, *Systematic Theology*, vol. 1 (Chicago: University of Chicago Press, 1951), p. 205.

15. *Summa Theologiae* I, q. 2, a. 3. Cf. *Summa Contra Gentiles*, 1.13.

16. *Anselm: Fides Quaerens Intellectum*, trans. I. W. Robertson (London: SCM Press, 1960),

saying that *given* the revealed God who is affirmed by faith, such an affirmation, involving as it does man's total commitment, is inconceivable if man does not immediately deny the possibility that anything greater than He can be conceived. Thus the ontological interpretation of God's revealed presence is essentially a *via negativa,* that is, it negates anything that could be presented as a competitor with God's greatness.

It would seem that the religious doctrine of *creatio ex nihilo* begins to become intelligible in the context of the theological statement of the ontological argument. The doctrine of *creatio ex nihilo* should not be confused with the cosmological argument. This latter argument (as we shall soon see) infers a Supreme Orderer from the structure of the world. The doctrine of *creatio ex nihilo,* however, is much more radical. Whereas a Supreme Orderer can be immanent in the world, a *Creator ex nihilo* transcends the world. Thus, if man attempts to religiously constitute the world *before* his relationship with God, the world becomes nothing; it has no real independence *(ex nihilo nihil fit).*[17] Thus the world can in no way compete with the greatness of God, which is the exact point made by the theological statement of the ontological argument.[18]

Anselm is not altogether explicit about what he means by the greatness of God. However, if I am correct about revelation providing the only meaningful context for such statements, then we can only understand God's greatness normatively, namely, no authority surpasses (or equals) or is able to surpass (or equal) the authority of God. Talk of God's greatness as the Maker of the natural order or the value of the world is certainly to be found in the Torah. "The heavens declare the glory of God, and the firmament tells of the work of His hands" (Ps. 19:2). "He opens His hand, satisfying every living being with favor" (Ps. 145:16). Nevertheless, God's existence is not inferred from these observations but is, rather, presupposed by them. It is the prior normative relationship with God

---

p. 117n.24. For the Augustinian background of this approach, see David Novak, "The Origin and Meaning of *Credere ut Intelligam* in Augustinian Theology," *Journal of Religious Studies,* 6.2–7.1 (Fall 1978/Spring 1979): 43-45.

17. For precisely this reason, viz., the denial of the "Selbstaendigkeit" of the world. Jean-Paul Sartre rejects this doctrine. See *Being and Nothingness,* trans. Hazel Barnes (New York: Philosophical Library, 1965), p. lxiv.

18. In his "Notes on Proofs of the Existence of God" (*Hebrew Union College Annual,* vol. 1 [1924]: 185-86), the late Prof. H. A. Wolfson viewed the cosmological argument as a philosophical version of Gen. 1:1. However, the doctrine of *creatio ex nihilo,* which subsequent theology saw in Gen. 1:1, seems to be a theological version of the ontological argument because it states more about God than the mere cosmological assertion that He *made* the world. See also L. Gilkey, *Maker of Heaven and Earth* (Garden City, N.Y.: Doubleday, 1959), pp. 41ff.

that makes these observations possible. "Who is for me in heaven besides You? I have none upon earth . . . the nearness of God is my good" (Ps. 73:25, 28). Man might admire God *through* vision of His handiwork, he might appreciate God *through* use of His bounty, but his direct relationship with God is first and foremost his obedience to His commandments, which are authoritative because of God's most intimate and concerned knowledge of man and his needs.[19] "And God saw the children of Israel and God knew" (Exod. 2:25). Understanding God's causality is secondary to understanding His revealed authority. The covenant, not nature, is the context of this relationship. And, whereas in theologies not based on revelation nature *includes* both God and man and is thus prior to them, in theologies based on revelation the covenant is what comprises the relationship *between* God and man and gives it duration.[20] The covenant is thus subsequent to them both.

The use of the "ontological interpretation," as I now prefer to call it, is the initial part of theology's critical function, an area where philosophical method is still the most important *ancilla theologiae*. Theological inquiry must deepen its understanding of the meaning of faith's assertions about the God/man relationship. On the *a priori* level it must understand what conditions are required for these assertions to have meaning. On this level philosophy functions methodologically, offering no independent religious assertions of its own, because it has no realm of independent experience. It would seem, then, that both the analytical and the phenomenological philosophical approaches offer the theologian invaluable critical tools he or she should neither neglect nor overestimate.

The Teleological Argument

In reinterpreting the ontological argument, we have seen that the constitution of the direct God/man relationship must not be subsequent to the constitution of either God's relation to the world or man's relation to the world. However, these relations are themselves components in revelation, as we have just seen, and must, therefore, be adequately constituted by philosophically critical theology. Understanding their apodictic sequence enables this constitution to be successful.

Man relates to the world as either a realm of things (culture) or a realm

19. See David Novak, *Law and Theology in Judaism*, vol. 2 (New York: KTAV, 1976), pp. 20-22.

20. See, e.g., A. N. Whitehead, *Process and Reality* (New York: Free Press, 1969), pp. 286, 410. Cf. Aristotle, *Metaphysics*, 1015a15.

of objects (nature). The former realm is constituted technologically, the latter scientifically. If interpersonal relationships are primary in the development of human consciousness, or, theologically speaking, if man's covenantal status is primary, then it would seem that man's consciousness first extends into the world of things before it extends into the world of objects. Things are defined in terms of their *personal* value.[21]

Man *qua homo faber* relates to the world as a realm of things either in his use or as something potentially ready for such use. The philosophical version of the teleological argument infers from man's experience of the *usefulness* of the world the conclusion that the world has been so ordered by a supernatural benevolent Intelligence. It is not the crude anthropocentric notion that the world is made for man but, rather, that man can fulfill his values because he exists in a *valuable* world.[22] Teleology provides the ontological context for the concept of value.[23]

The theologian cannot accept this argument as primarily descriptive of the God/man relationship because it constitutes a fundamental mediator between man and God. However, once the direct God/man relationship in revelation is adequately constituted, this teleological assertion becomes an important postulate of that relationship. For we can now reinterpret this assertion to state that God's relation to the world and man's relation to the world must complement the covenant and not mitigate against it.

If man's technological relation to the world is not for the sake of the covenant, then his dominion over the world will inevitably lead to disobedience of God. "And you will say in your heart: my strength and the might of my hand have made for me all this wealth" (Deut. 8:17). Therefore, man must include all the results of his labor in the relationship with God. This would explain the importance of sacrifice in the act of worship. This emphasis requires that man look upon his technological success as caused by God for the sake of the covenant: "And you shall remember the Lord your God, that it is He who gives you strength to make wealth in order to uphold His covenant" (Deut. 8:18).

This recognition is a postulate of the primary relationship we have

21. A philosophical parallel to this scheme might be found in Heidegger's discussion of "Zuhanden" and "Vorhanden" in *Being and Time*, 1.3.16, pp. 102-6.

22. See Maimonides, *Guide of the Perplexed*, 3.13. Cf. Saadiah Gaon, *The Book of Beliefs and Opinions*, chap. 4.

23. "The chief points of the physico-theological proof are as follows: (1) In the world we everywhere find dear signs of an order in accordance with a determinate purpose . . ." Kant, *Critique of Pure Reason*, B654, trans. Smith, p. 521.

been discussing all along. As Kant noted, "Postulates are not theoretical dogmas but presuppositions of necessarily practical import."[24] In our case here we are required to affirm God's benevolent causality because without such an affirmation man's practical relation to the world of things would continually conflict with his obedience to God's commandments. The world on the practical level must be viewed as the product of God's providence. This affirmation enables us to see biblical promises of tangible values not as *quid pro quo* rewards but, rather, as the necessary certitude that God will allow the things of the world to be included in the covenant by being useful for man's obedience to God. Thus the twelfth-century Jewish theologian Maimonides wrote, "We have been assured in the Torah that if we observe it in joy . . . that He will remove from us all those things which prevent us from observing it, such as sickness, war, famine and the like."[25] In other words, the Torah is not viewed as the means to the end of technological success with the world but, rather, the world is now looked upon as the means for man to observe the Torah with full physical, mental, and emotional attention. The Torah is not for the sake of the world, but the world is for the sake of the Torah.

The teleological argument is helpful in formulating this postulate of revelation because it is the result of viewing the world as *valuable*. The reformulation of this argument constitutes God's relation to this valuable world in a way that permits an ontological foundation for man's practical use of the world in his covenantal response to God. This is exactly how the postulates of pure practical reason functioned for Kant. The logic is the same, but the fundamental practical reality is essentially different, for covenantal man is essentially different from morally autonomous man.[26] However, in both systems human *praxis* requires the cooperation of the non-human world. The cooperation is first required so that man *qua* covenantal participant and man *qua homo faber* do not mutually exclude each other, thus making for a paralyzing human tension.

---

24. Kant, *Critique of Practical Reason*, 1.2.6, trans. Lewis White Beck (New York: Liberal Arts Press, 1956), p. 137.

25. *Mishneh Torah:* Repentance 9.1.

26. For the use of postulates in theology à la Kant, see David Novak, *Suicide and Morality: The Theories of Plato, Aquinas, and Kant and Their Relevance for Suicidology* (New York: Scholars Studies Press, 1975), pp. 126-27.

The Cosmological Argument

The cosmological argument states that the world requires a first cause. Kant saw it as the ontological argument in inverse order.[27] In other words, whereas the ontological argument moves from the concept of a Supreme Being *(ens realissimum)* to absolute existence in relation to contingent existence, the cosmological argument moves from the experience of the contingent existence of the world *(a contingentia mundi)* to the concept of a Supreme Being and His absolute existence. However, what Kant failed to realize is that the cosmological argument as presented by such philosophers as Aristotle and Aquinas presupposes that we are already experiencing the world as ordered in some sort of linear hierarchy.[28] Without this presupposition the search for a *first* cause makes no sense because causality, as opposed to creation, is constituted *serially,* that is, as a process rather than an event. For the theologian *creatio ex nihilo* is an event rather than a process. Now, if, as we have seen earlier, the ontological argument really expresses God's radical transcendence of the world, which is the meaning of the doctrine of *creatio ex nihilo,* then the cosmological argument is not reducible to the ontological argument. A Creator is essentially different from a First Cause.[29] This observation does not, however, make the cosmological argument any more convincing philosophically because one can argue whether our experience of a structured world in and of itself requires such a remote first cause, or, indeed, a concept of linear causality at all.[30]

Theological interest in the cosmological argument is motivated by an opposite concern than that which motivated its interest in the teleological argument. Interest in the teleological argument was motivated by a concern to constitute the world of things as immanent in the God/man relationship. This is where teleology is crucial. For if the end of human life is to be obedient to God, then the end of the world under man's actual

27. "The procedure of the cosmological proofs is artfully designed to enable us to escape having to prove the existence of a necessary being *a priori* through mere concepts. . . . Accordingly, we take as the starting-point of our inference an actual existence (an experience in general), and advance, in such manner as we can, to some absolutely necessary condition of this existence." *Critique of Pure Reason,* B638, p. 512.

28. Aquinas, *Summa Theologiae,* 1, q. 2, a. 3. Cf. *Summa Contra Gentiles,* 1.13. See also Aristotle, *Physics,* 241b24ff.; *Metaphysics,* 1072a25ff.

29. See Maimonides, *Guide of the Perplexed,* 1.69.

30. See Bertrand Russell, *Mysticism and Logic* (Garden City, N.Y.: Doubleday, 1957), p. 201.

or potential control is to function as the physical means which intends a state of active being included in that end; that is, it is immanent.[31]

The cosmological argument, on the other hand, constitutes the world as transcendent to man. It views the causal structure of the world as essentially independent of actual or potential human use. It does not assign any purpose to the causal structure of the world. That structure simply depends on a process of efficient causality of which God is the first member. Man's presence in that world is wholly irrelevant. Man's relation to the world of objects, motivated by his curiosity, is impersonal. He attempts to view it as it is, making his own subjective viewing as inconspicuous as possible. This interest follows from man's recognition of his finitude, for his recognition of the world of objects, which essentially transcends the interpersonal realm, saves him from the dangerous illusion of anthropocentricity. The natural world of objects reminds man of his essential limitation by showing an order far more complex and impressive than the world of man's own making. Nature transcends culture. For theology such a recognition of the transcendence of nature is expressed by the constant reminder to man that God's presence is not limited to His covenant with man. The relationship between them is not a symbiosis. As such man sees nature as a realm subject to a divine authority in which he is not a participant but only a spectator. Both man and nature are subject to God's authority, but they are subject to it in radically different ways. Thus nature is not in essence simply a potential field waiting for man's technological control. On the other hand, because man is covenantally related to God, nature is not the medium of that relationship. Man is a participant in the covenant before he can admire God through viewing nature. Nevertheless, this very respect for the inner structure of nature reminds man that he cannot reduce God's presence to his own limited experience of it. "Then the Lord answered Job out of the whirlwind, saying . . . I will question you and you may inform Me. Where were you when I laid the foundations of the earth? Tell me if you have any understanding" (Job 38:1, 3). This theological use of the cosmological interpretation saves man's relation to the created order of nature from becoming either anthropocentric or cosmocentric. As such it performs a necessary philosophical service for theology.

---

31. See Aristotle, *Nicomachean Ethics*, 1098b10-15.

Conclusion

The classical proofs of the existence of God are theologically meaningful if they are understood as statements of the ontological conditions and postulates of revelation. By not having their meaning constituted outside the realm of revelation, the "proofs," now regarded as *modes of presentation,* strengthen theology's critical function with philosophical tools.

At the beginning of this paper I delineated three types of ontological presentation: personal communion, invention, and discovery. We can now see how the three quests which motivated these three respective types of presentation reappear in the modes of divine presentation. The quest for personal communion is the motivation for the ontological mode; the quest for value (invention) is the motivation for the teleological mode; the quest for structure (discovery) is the motivation for the cosmological mode. A philosophically critical theology can constitute these respective modes of presentation in an apodictic order within the context of revelation.

We can thus see a working relation between theology and philosophy which, at least from the vantage point of theology, is most fruitful. It would seem that the type of philosophy which lends itself to such a relation is either of the analytical or the phenomenological variety. Philosophers of these schools, even if not interested in theological inquiry into revelation, should nevertheless be pleased at the widening range of applicability of their methods. Theologians should be grateful for methods of intelligent inquiry which enable them to be more precise and lucid in their understanding of the Word of God: of what it presupposes and what it implies.[32]

---

32. A similarly motivated approach can be seen in the following excerpt from the 1965 essay *The Lonely Man of Faith* (New York: Doubleday, 1992) by the contemporary Jewish theologian Dr. Joseph B. Soloveitchik: "While one may speak of the cosmic confrontation of man and God as an experiential reality, it is hard to speak of a cosmological experience. When God is apprehended *in* reality it is an experience; when God is comprehended *through* reality it is just an intellectual performance. . . . The trouble with all rational demonstrations of the existence of God, with which the history of philosophy abounds, consists in their being exactly what they were meant to be by those who formulated them: abstract logical demonstrations divorced from the living primal experiences in which these demonstrations are rooted. For instance, the cosmic experience was transformed into a cosmological proof, the ontic experience into an ontological proof. . . . The most elementary existential awareness as a subjective 'I exist' and an objective 'the world around me exists' awareness is unattainable as long as the ultimate reality of God is not part of this awareness" (pp. 51-52n.1).

Acknowledgments

The author and publisher gratefully acknowledge permission to reprint the following essays from the following sources:

"Are Philosophical Proofs of the Existence of God Theologically Meaningful?" *Conservative Judaism* 34 (1980): 12-22. Reprinted with permission of Jewish Theological Seminary Publications.

"Avoiding Charges of Legalism and Antinomianism in Jewish-Christian Dialogue," *Modern Theology* 16, no. 3 (July 2000): 275-91. Reprinted with permission.

"Before Revelation: The Rabbis, Paul, and Karl Barth," *Journal of Religion* 71, no. 1 (1991): 50-66. Reprinted with permission.

"Buber and Tillich," *Journal of Ecumenical Studies* 29, no. 2 (Spring 1992): 159-74. Reprinted with permission.

"Jewish-Christian Relations in a Secular Age," *First Things* 89 (January 1999): 20-25. Reprinted with permission.

"Jews, Christians, and Civil Society," *First Things* 120 (February 2002): 26-33. Reprinted with permission.

"Karl Barth on Divine Command: A Jewish Response," *Scottish Journal of Theology* 54, no. 4 (2001): 463-83. Reprinted with permission.

"Maimonides and Aquinas on Natural Law," in *St. Thomas Aquinas and the Natural Law Tradition: Contemporary Perspectives,* edited by John Goyette (Washington: Catholic University Press, 2004). Reprinted with permission of the Catholic University of America Press, Washington, D.C.

"The Moral Crisis of the West: The Judeo-Christian Response," *Scottish Journal of Theology* 53 (2000): 1-21. Reprinted with permission.

"What Does Edith Stein Mean for Jews?" *First Things* 96 (1999): 15-17. Reprinted with permission.

"What to Seek and What to Avoid in Jewish-Christian Dialogue," in *Christianity in Jewish Terms,* edited by Tikva Frymer-Kensky, Peter Ochs, David Novak, Michael Signer, and David Sandmel. Copyright © 2000 by Westview Press, a member of Perseus Books Group. Reprinted with permission of Westview Press, a member of Perseus Books, L.L.C.

"When Jews Are Christians," *First Things* 17 (November 1991): 42-46. Reprinted with permission.

Index of Subjects and Names

Index of Ancient Sources